Technician Unit 15

CASH MANAGEMENT AND CREDIT CONTROL

For assessments in 2004 and 2005

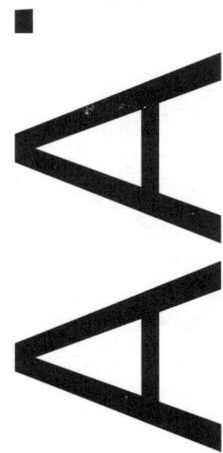

Interactive Text

In this May 2004 new edition

- For assessments under the **new standards**
- Layout designed to be easy on the eye – and easy to use
- Clear language and presentation
- Lots of diagrams and flowcharts
- Activities checklist to tie in each activity to specific knowledge and understanding, performance criteria and/or range statement
- Thorough reliable updating of material to 1 April 2004

FOR 2004 AND 2005 SKILLS BASED ASSESSMENTS

First edition May 2003s
Second edition May 2004

ISBN 0 7517 1604 9 (Previous edition 0 7517 1135 7)

British Library Cataloguing-in-Publication Data
A catalogue record for this book
is available from the British Library

Published by

BPP Professional Education
Aldine House, Aldine Place
London W12 8AW

www.bpp.com

Printed in Great Britain by Ashford Colour Press

All our rights reserved. No part of this publication may be reproduced, stored in a retrieval system or transmitted, in any form or by any means, electronic, mechanical, photocopying, recording or otherwise, without the prior written permission of BPP Professional Education.

We are grateful to the Lead Body for Accounting for permission to reproduce extracts from the Standards of Competence for Accounting, and to the AAT for permission to reproduce extracts from the mapping and Guidance Notes.

©
BPP Professional Education
2004

Contents

Introduction

How to use this Interactive Text – Technician qualification structure –
Unit 15 Standards of competence – Assessment strategy – Building your portfolio

		Page	Answers to activities

PART A Cash management

1	Cash and cash flows	3	263
2	Forecasting cash flows	27	265
3	Cash budgeting techniques	57	268
4	Banks and economic policy	83	271
5	Dealing with banks	97	273
6	Raising finance	111	274
7	Investing money	131	277

PART B Credit control

8	Credit control: policies and procedures	159	280
9	Assessing creditworthiness	185	283
10	Managing debtors	213	290
11	Remedies for bad debts	239	293

CONTENTS

	Page	Answers to activities
Answers to activities		263
Index		299

Order form

Review form & free prize draw

Introduction

How to use this Interactive Text

Aims of this Interactive Text

> To provide the knowledge and practice to help you succeed in the assessment for Technician Unit 15 *Operating a cash management and credit control system*.

To pass the assessment successfully you need a thorough understanding in all areas covered by the standards of competence.

> To tie in with the other components of the BPP Effective Study Package to ensure you have the best possible chance of success.

Interactive Text

This covers all you need to know for the skills based assessment for Unit 15. Numerous activities throughout the text help you practise what you have just learnt.

Assessment Kit

When you have understood and practised the material in the Interactive Text, you will have the knowledge and experience to tackle the Assessment Kit for Unit 15. This aims to get you through the assessment, whether in the form of the AAT simulation or in the workplace.

Passcards

These short memorable notes are focused on key topics for the xTechnician Units, designed to remind you of what the Interactive Text has taught you.

INTRODUCTION

Recommended approach to this Interactive Text

(a) To achieve competence in Unit 15 (and all the other units), you need to be able to do **everything** specified by the standards. Study the Interactive Text carefully and do not skip any of it.

(b) Learning is an **active** process. Do **all** the activities as you work through the Interactive Text so you can be sure you really understand what you have read. There is a checklist at the end of each chapter to show which knowledge and understanding, performance criteria and/or range statements are covered by each activity.

(c) After you have covered the material in the Interactive Text, work through the **Assessment Kit**.

(d) Before you take the assessment, check that you still remember the material using the following quick revision plan for each chapter.

  (i) Read and learn the **key learning points**, which are a summary of the chapter. This includes key terms and shows the sort of things likely to come up in an assessment. Are there any gaps in your knowledge? If so, study the section again.

  (ii) Do the **quick quiz** again. If you know what you're doing, it shouldn't take long.

  (iii) Go through the **Passcards** as often as you can in the weeks leading up to your assessment.

This approach is only a suggestion. Your college may well adapt it to suit your needs.

Quick quizzes

> These include multiple choice questions, true/false and other formats not used by the AAT. However, these types of questions are usually very familiar to students and are used to help students adjust to otherwise unfamiliar material.

Remember this is a **practical** course.

(a) Try to relate the material to your experience in the workplace or any other work experience you may have had.

(b) Try to make as many links as you can to your study of the other Units at Technician level.

(c) Keep this text, (hopefully) you will find it invaluable in your everyday work too!

Technician qualification structure

The competence-based Education and Training Scheme of the Association of Accounting Technicians is based on an analysis of the work of accounting staff in a wide range of industries and types of organisation. The Standards of Competence for Accounting which students are expected to meet are based on this analysis.

New standards of competence were issued in 2002, which took effect from 1 July 2003.

The Standards identify the key purpose of the accounting occupation, which is to operate, maintain and improve systems to record, plan, monitor and report on the financial activities of an organisation, and a number of key roles of the occupation. Each key role is subdivided into units of competence, which are further divided into elements of competences. By successfully completing assessments in specified units of competence, students can gain qualifications at NVQ/SVQ levels 2, 3 and 4, which correspond to the AAT Foundation, Intermediate and Technician stages of competence respectively.

Whether you are competent in a Unit is demonstrated by means of:

- *Either* an Exam Based Assessment (set and marked by AAT assessors)
- *Or* a Skills Based Assessment (where competence is judged by an Approved Assessment Centre to whom responsibility for this is devolved)
- Or *both* Exam *and* Skills Based Assessment

Below we set out the overall structure of the Technician (NVQ/SVQ Level 4) stage, indicating how competence in each Unit is assessed. In the next section there is more detail about the Skills Based Assessments for Unit 15.

Units 10, 15, 17 and 22 are assessed by Skills Based Assessment. Units 8, 9, 11–14, 18 and 19 are assessed by Exam Based Assessment.

INTRODUCTION

NVQ/SVQ Level 4

Group 1 Core Units – All units are mandatory.

Unit 8 Contributing to the Management of Performance and the Enhancement of Value	Element 8.1	Collect, analyse and disseminate information about costs
	Element 8.2	Monitor performance and make recommendations to enhance value

Unit 9 Contributing to the Planning and Control of Resources	Element 9.1	Prepare forecasts of income and expenditure
	Element 9.2	Produce draft budget proposals
	Element 9.3	Monitor the performance of responsibility centres against budgets

Unit 10 Managing Systems and People in the Accounting Environment	Element 10.1	Manage people within the accounting environment
	Element 10.2	Identify opportunities for improving the effectiveness of an accounting system

Unit 22 Contribute to the Maintenance of a Healthy, Safe and Productive Working Environment	Element 22.1	Contribute to the maintenance of a healthy, safe and productive working environment
	Element 22.2	Monitor and maintain an effective and efficient working environment

NVQ/SVQ Level 4, continued

Group 2 Optional Units – Choose **one** of the following **four** units.

Unit 11 Drafting Financial Statements (Accounting Practice, Industry and Commerce)	Element 11.1 Draft limited company financial statements
	Element 11.2 Interpret limited company financial statements

Unit 12 Drafting Financial Statements (Central Government)	Element 12.1 Draft Central Government financial statements
	Element 12.2 Interpret Central Government financial statements

Unit 13 Drafting Financial Statements (Local Government)	Element 13.1 Draft Local Authority financial statements
	Element 13.2 Interpret Local Authority financial statements

Unit 14 Drafting Financial Statements (National Health Service)	Element 14.1 Draft NHS accounting statements and returns
	Element 14.2 Interpret NHS accounting statements and returns

INTRODUCTION

NVQ/SVQ Level 4, continued

Group 3 Optional Units – Choose **two** of the following **four** units.

Unit 15 Operating a Cash Management and Credit Control System	Element 15.1	Monitor and control cash receipts and payments
	Element 15.2	Manage cash balances
	Element 15.3	Grant credit
	Element 15.4	Monitor and control the collection of debts

Unit 17 Implementing Auditing Procedures	Element 17.1	Contribute to the planning of an audit assignment
	Element 17.2	Contribute to the conduct of an audit assignment
	Element 17.3	Prepare related draft reports

Unit 18 Preparing Business Taxation Computations	Element 18.1	Prepare capital allowances computations
	Element 18.2	Compute assessable business income
	Element 18.3	Prepare capital gains computations
	Element 18.4	Prepare Corporation Tax computations

Unit 19 Preparing Personal Taxation Computations	Element 19.1	Calculate income from employment
	Element 19.2	Calculate property and investment income
	Element 19.3	Prepare Income Tax computations
	Element 19.4	Prepare Capital Gains Tax computations

Unit 15 Standards of competence

The structure of the Standards for Unit 15

The Unit commences with a statement of the **knowledge and understanding** which underpin competence in the Unit's elements.

The Unit of Competence is then divided into **elements of competence** describing activities which the individual should be able to perform.

Each element includes:

(a) A set of **performance criteria.** This defines what constitutes competent performance.

(b) A **range statement.** This defines the situations, contexts, methods etc in which competence should be displayed.

(c) **Evidence requirements.** These state that competence must be demonstrated consistently, over an appropriate time scale with evidence of performance being provided from the appropriate sources.

(d) **Sources of evidence.** These are suggestions of ways in which you can find evidence to demonstrate that competence. These fall under the headings: 'observed performance; work produced by the candidate; authenticated testimonies from relevant witnesses; personal account of competence; other sources of evidence.' They are reproduced in full in our Assessment Kit for Unit 15.

Knowledge and understanding required for the unit as a whole are listed first, followed by the performance criteria and range statements for each element. Performance criteria are cross-referenced below to chapters in this Unit 15 Interactive Text.

Unit 15: Operating a Cash Management and Credit Control System

What is the unit about?

This unit consists of four elements. Element 15.1 is concerned with the monitoring and forecasting of cash receipts and payments, the consultation with appropriate staff and the appropriate corrective action in accordance with organisational policy. The second element, Element 15.2, focuses on the management of cash balances. Element 15.3 considers the granting of credit, using valid internal and external sources of information. The final element, Element 15.4, addresses the management and control of the debt-collection process.

Although they are presented as four separate elements, there are significant interrelationships between the four. In particular, Elements 15.1 and 15.2 consider cash management and 15.3 and 15.4 address the credit control function. Significantly, Unit 15 requires students to have an understanding of legal, organisational and banking issues as well as the ability to apply accounting techniques to cash management and credit control activities for a wide range of organisations.

Guidance by element

Element 15.1 Monitor and control cash receipts and payments

Guidance

The first criterion is concerned with the basic business of regularly monitoring (daily, weekly, monthly) cash receipts and payments against a cash budget. The fifth criterion requires students to identify cash shortfalls or surpluses and to identify the most appropriate means to manage the situation. Therefore, students require a clear knowledge of the main types of cash receipts and payments.

- regular receipts and payments, such as cash and credit sales

INTRODUCTION

- payroll and operating costs
- capital costs, such as the purchase of new equipment or premises
- drawings
- dividends
- financial payments
- instances of exceptional receipts and payments

Students also need to be able to distinguish between cash and non-cash elements (such as depreciation and provisions).

The second and third criteria require students to appreciate how cash forecasts are put together using a synthesis of information from accounting, sales and technical staff. The fourth criterion requires students to be aware of the two different forms of cash budgets – ie modifying profit and loss account and balance sheet data to calculate cash flow, and also using a simple cashier's forecast of receipts and payments.

Alongside developing a cash forecast, students need to be able to apply basic statistical techniques for estimating future trends, including moving averages and the ability to apply different inflation factors to a forecast. Students should also be able to understand the appropriateness of computer models, such as spreadsheets, to assess the sensitivity of the forecast to changes in individual elements.

Element 15.2 Manage cash balances

Guidance

The first, second, fourth and fifth criteria are concerned with relating the cash forecast to the action required to manage the cash deficit or surplus predicted. In the case of a cash deficit, students are required to be aware of the different ways of funding such a deficit, including bank overdrafts, medium and long-term loans, and leasing or asset-based financing. This will also require an understanding of the structure of the UK banking system and the relationships between different types of financial institutions.

Students also need to be aware of different alternatives for investing surplus cash. These might include bank deposits and investment in marketable securities such as bills of exchange, certificates of deposit, government securities and local authority short loans. Although management of a portfolio of securities is beyond the scope of the Standards of Competence required at this level, students should have an understanding of the terms and conditions attached to each of these investments and their specific risks.

All of this is set in the context of an organisation's structure, systems and procedures and the nature of its business transactions.

Element 15.3 Grant credit

Guidance

The first three criteria are concerned with establishing a customer's credit status and the credit-granting decision. In making this decision, students are expected to be able to make use of both internal and external sources of information. These might include analysing accounting information, or informal information from sales staff or trade contacts. External information would include information from credit reference agencies, banks and official publications. In making the credit-granting decision, students are expected to be able to manage the paradox of conflicting information and make a suitable credit decision. The fourth criterion concerns how the credit-granting decision is communicated to the customer – in all instances in a courteous and tactful manner.

The element has a significant legal element and students are expected to be aware of the terms and conditions relating to the granting of credit and the effect of the Data Protection Act 1998 on credit control information. Students are also required to be able to calculate the cost of discounts for prompt payment and understand why such discounts are offered to credit customers.

Element 15.4 Monitor and control the collection of debts

Guidance

Criteria A–C are concerned with the monitoring and communication to other individuals of the status of debtors' accounts. Such an analysis might make use of an age analysis of debtors, the calculation of average periods of credit given and received and of the incidence of bad and doubtful debts.

Criterion D focuses on communication with debtors, emphasising the need for courtesy but also with due regard for the need to recover amounts due. As with Element 15.3, there is an important legal component to Element 15.4. In this respect, students are required to understand the legal remedies for breach of contract and the legal and administrative procedures for the collection of debts. In addition, an elementary understanding of the effect of bankruptcy and insolvency is required.

The fifth criterion addresses the need to identify the most appropriate debt-recovery method. In this regard, students are expected to have an understanding of the costs and benefits of other (external) means of debt collection, including factoring arrangements and debt insurance.

Knowledge and understanding

The Business Environment

1. The main types of cash receipts and payments: regular revenue receipts and payments; capital receipts and payments; drawings/dividends and disbursements; exceptional receipts and payments (Element 15.1)
2. The basic structure of the banking system and the money market in the UK and the relationships between financial institutions (Element 15.2)
3. Bank overdrafts and loans; terms and conditions; legal relationship between bank and customer (Element 15.2)
4. Types of marketable security (Bills of exchange, certificates of deposit, government securities, local authority short term loans); terms and conditions; risks (Element 15.2)
5. Government monetary policies (Element 15.2)
6. Legal issues: basic contract; terms and conditions of contracts relating to the granting of credit; Data Protection Legislation and credit control information (Element 15.3)
7. Sources of credit status information (Element 15.3)
8. External sources of information: banks, credit agencies and official publications (Element 15.3)
9. Legal issues: remedies for breach of contract (Element 15.4)
10. Legal and administrative procedures for the collection of debts (Element 15.4)
11. The effect of bankruptcy and insolvency on organisations (Element 15.4)

Accounting Techniques

12. Form and structure of cash budgets (Element 15.1)
13. Lagged receipts and payments (Element 15.1)
14. Basic statistical techniques for estimating future trends: moving averages, allowance for inflation (Element 15.1)
15. Computer models to assess the sensitivity of elements in the cash budget to change (eg price, wage rate changes) (Element 15.1)
16. Managing risk and exposure (Element 15.2)
17. Discounts for prompt payment (Element 15.3)
18. Interpretation and use of credit control information (Element 15.3 & 15.4)
19. Methods of collection (Element 15.4)
20. Factoring arrangements (Element 15.4)
21. Debt insurance (Element 15.4)
22. Methods of analysing information on debtors: age analysis of debtors; average periods of credit given and received; incidence of bad and doubtful debts (Element 15.4)
23. Evaluation of different collection methods (Element 15.4)

Accounting principles and theory

24. Cash flow accounting and its relationship to accounting for income and expenditure (Element 15.1)
25. Liquidity management (Elements 15.2, 15.3 & 15.4)

INTRODUCTION

The organisation

26 Understanding that the accounting systems of an organisation are affected by its organisational structure, its administrative systems and procedures and the nature of its business transactions (Elements 15.1, 15.2, 15.3 & 15.4)

27 Understanding that recording and accounting practices may vary in different parts of the organisation (Elements 15.1 & 15.4)

28 An understanding that practice in this area will be determined by an organisation's specific financial regulations, guidelines and security procedures (Element 15.2)

29 An understanding that in public sector organisations there are statutory and other regulations relating to the management of cash balances (Element 15.2)

30 Understanding that practice in this area will be determined by an organisation's credit control policies and procedures (Element 15.3)

31 An understanding of the organisation's relevant policies and procedures (Elements 15.1, 15.3 and 15.4).

Element 15.1 Monitor and control cash receipts and payments

	Performance criteria	Chapters in this Text
A	Monitor and control cash receipts and payments against budgeted cash flow	1
B	Consult appropriate staff to determine the likely pattern of cash flows over the accounting period and to anticipate any exceptional receipts or payments	2
C	Ensure forecasts of future cash payments and receipts are in accord with known income and expenditure trends	2, 3
D	Prepare cash budgets in the approved format and clearly indicate net cash requirements	2
E	Identify significant deviations from the cash budget and take corrective action within defined organisational policies	2, 3

Range statement

Cash flows to be monitored: regular revenue receipts and payments; capital receipts and payments; drawings or dividends and disbursements; exceptional receipts and payments 1, 2, 3

Element 15.2 Manage cash balances

	Performance criteria	Chapters in this Text
A	Arrange overdraft and loan facilities in anticipation of requirements and on the most favourable terms available	4, 5, 6
B	Invest surplus funds in marketable securities within defined financial authorisation limits	7
C	Ensure the organisation's financial regulations and security procedures are observed	7
D	Ensure account is taken of trends in the economic and financial environment in managing cash balances	4, 7
E	Maintain an adequate level of liquidity in line with cash forecasts	6, 7

Range statement

Maintain liquidity through the management of: cash, overdrafts and loans 5, 6, 7

INTRODUCTION

Element 15.3 Grant credit

Performance criteria		Chapters in this Text
A	Agree credit terms with customers in accordance with the organisation's policies	8, 9
B	Identify and use internal and external sources of information to evaluate the current credit status of customers and potential customers	8, 9
C	Open new accounts for those customers with an established credit status	9
D	Ensure the reasons for refusing credit are discussed with customers in a tactful manner	9
Range statement		
1	Internal information derived from: analysis of the accounts; colleagues in regular contact with current or potential customers or clients	8, 9
2	External information derived from: credit rating agencies; supplier references; bank references	8, 9

Element 15.4 Monitor and control the collection of debts

Performance criteria		Chapters in this Text
A	Monitor information relating to the current state of debtors' accounts regularly and take appropriate action	10, 11
B	Send information regarding significant outstanding accounts and potential bad debts promptly to relevant individuals within the organisation	11
C	Ensure discussions and negotiations with debtors are conducted courteously and achieve the desired outcome	10, 11
D	Use debt recovery methods appropriate to the circumstances of individual cases and in accordance with the organisation's procedures	10, 11
E	Base recommendations to write off bad and doubtful debts on a realistic analysis of all known factors	11
Range statement		
1	Information on debtors: age analysis of debtors; average periods of credit given and received; incidence of bad and doubtful debts	10, 11
2	Appropriate action: information and recommendations for action passed to appropriate individual within own organisation; debtor contacted and arrangements made for the recovery of the debt	10, 11

Assessment strategy

Unit 15 is assessed by **skills based assessment**.

Skills based assessment is a means of collecting evidence of your ability to carry out practical activities and to **operate effectively in the conditions of the workplace** to the standards required. Evidence may be collected at your place of work or at an Approved Assessment Centre by means of simulations of workplace activity, or by a combination of these methods.

If the Approved Assessment Centre is a **workplace** you may be observed carrying out accounting activities as part of your normal work routine. You should collect documentary evidence of the work you have done, or contributed, in an **accounting portfolio**. Evidence collected in a portfolio can be assessed in addition to observed performance or where it is not possible to assess by observation.

Where the Approved Assessment Centre is a **college or training organisation**, skills based assessment will be by means of a combination of the following.

(a) Documentary evidence of activities carried out at the workplace, collected by you in an **accounting portfolio**

(b) Realistic **simulations** of workplace activities; these simulations may take the form of case studies and in-tray exercises and involve the use of primary documents and reference sources

(c) **Projects and assignments** designed to assess the Standards of Competence

If you are unable to provide workplace evidence, you will be able to complete the assessment requirements by the alternative methods listed above.

Building your portfolio

What is a portfolio?

A portfolio is a collection of work that demonstrates what the owner can do. In AAT language the portfolio demonstrates **competence**.

A painter will have a collection of his paintings to exhibit in a gallery, an advertising executive will have a range of advertisements and ideas that she has produced to show to a prospective client. Both the collection of paintings and the advertisements form the portfolio of that artist or advertising executive.

Your portfolio will be unique to you just as the portfolio of the artist will be unique because no one will paint the same range of pictures in the same way. It is a very personal collection of your work and should be treated as a **confidential** record.

What evidence should a portfolio include?

No two portfolios will be the same but by following some simple guidelines you can decide which of the following suggestions will be appropriate in your case.

(a) **Your current CV**

This should be at the front. It will give your personal details as well as brief descriptions of posts you have held with the most recent one shown first.

(b) **References and testimonials**

References from previous employers may be included especially those of which you are particularly proud.

(c) **Your current job description**

You should emphasise financial **responsibilities and duties**.

(d) **Your student record sheets**

These should be supplied by AAT when you begin your studies, and your training provider should also have some if necessary.

(e) **Evidence from your current workplace**

This could take many forms including **letters, memos, reports** you have written, **copies of accounts** or **reconciliations** you have prepared, **discrepancies** you have investigated etc. Remember to obtain permission to include the evidence from your line manager because some records may be sensitive. Discuss the performance criteria that are listed in your Student Record Sheets with your training provider and employer, and think of other evidence that could be appropriate to you.

(f) **Evidence from your social activities**

For example you may be the treasurer of a club in which case examples of your cash and banking records could be appropriate.

(g) **Evidence from your studies**

Few students are able to satisfy all the requirements of competence by workplace evidence alone. They therefore rely on simulations to provide the remaining evidence to complete a unit. If you are not working or not working in a relevant post, then you may need to rely more heavily on simulations as a source of evidence.

(h) **Additional work**

Your training provider may give you work that specifically targets one or a group of performance criteria in order to complete a unit. It could take the form of questions, presentations or demonstrations. Each training provider will approach this in a different way.

(i) **Evidence from a previous workplace**

This evidence may be difficult to obtain and should be used with caution because it must satisfy the 'rules' of evidence, that is it must be current. Only rely on this as evidence if you have changed jobs recently.

(j) **Prior achievements**

For example you may have already completed the health and safety unit during a previous course of study, and therefore there is no need to repeat this work. Advise your training provider who will check to ensure that it is the same unit and record it as complete if appropriate.

How should it be presented?

As you assemble the evidence remember to **make a note** of it on your Student Record Sheet in the space provided and **cross reference** it. In this way it is easy to check to see if your evidence is **appropriate**. Remember one piece of evidence may satisfy a number of performance criteria so remember to check this thoroughly and discuss it with your training provider if in doubt.

To keep all your evidence together a ring binder or lever arch file is a good means of storage.

When should evidence be assembled?

You should begin to assemble evidence **as soon as you have registered as a student**. **Don't leave it all** until the last few weeks of your studies, because you may miss vital deadlines and your resulting certificate sent by the AAT may not include all the units you have completed. Give yourself and your training provider time to examine your portfolio and report your results to AAT at regular intervals. In this way the task of assembling the portfolio will be spread out over a longer period of time and will be presented in a more professional manner.

What are the key criteria that the portfolio must fulfil?

As you assemble your evidence bear in mind that it must be:

- **Valid**. It must relate to the Standards.
- **Authentic**. It must be your own work.
- **Current**. It must refer to your current or most recent job.
- **Sufficient**. It must meet all the performance criteria by the time you have completed your portfolio.

What are the most important elements in a portfolio that covers Unit 15

You should remember that the unit is about **management** and **control**. Therefore you need to produce evidence not only demonstrating that you can carry out certain tasks, but also you must show that you can exercise control.

For Element 15.1 *Monitor and control cash receipts and payments* you not only need to show that you can prepare a cash budget, you also need to demonstrate that you have used the information given by the cash budget to monitor whether cash levels will be satisfactory. Reports or memos can provide the necessary evidence of monitoring of cash flows.

INTRODUCTION

The main evidence that you need for Element 15.2 *Manage cash balances* is detail of recommendations you have made about how to invest surplus funds and remedy shortfalls, and also any general guidance you have produced on how cash should be managed.

To fulfil the requirements of Element 15.3 *Grant credit* you need to demonstrate that you have used various sources of evidence to assess the creditworthiness of customers. You also need to provide evidence of active involvement in communication with customers by letter, telephone call, meeting etc.

For Element 15.4 *Monitor and control the collection of debts* you need evidence of active involvement in monitoring, such as written recommendations you have made for improvements in the system. You also must demonstrate involvement in the debt recovery process, for example recommendation of the best method to use to collect debts and notes of discussions with debtors who have overdue balances.

Finally

Remember that the portfolio is **your property** and **your responsibility**. Not only could it be presented to the external verifier before your award can be confirmed; it could be used when you are seeking **promotion** or applying for a more senior and better paid post elsewhere. How your portfolio is presented can say as much about you as the evidence inside.

> For further information on portfolio building, see the BPP Text *Building Your Portfolio*. This can be ordered using the form at the back of this Text or via the Internet: www.bpp.com/aat

PART A

Cash management

chapter 1

Cash and cash flows

Contents

1. Introduction
2. The cash flow cycle
3. Types of cash transaction
4. Profits and cash flow
5. Cash accounting and accruals accounting
6. The focus of cash and credit management
7. Treasury management

Performance criteria

15.1.A   Monitor and control cash receipts and payments against budgeted cash flow

Range statement

15.1.1   Cash flows to be monitored: regular revenue receipts and payments; capital receipts and payments; drawings or dividends and disbursements; exceptional receipts and payments

Knowledge and understanding

- The main types of cash receipts and payments: regular revenue receipts and payments; capital receipts and payments; drawings/dividends and disbursements; exceptional receipts and payments
- Lagged receipts and payments
- Understanding that the accounting systems of an organisation are affected by its organisational structure, its administrative systems and procedures and the nature of its business transactions
- Understanding that recording and accounting practices may vary in different parts of the organisation
- An understanding of the organisation's relevant policies and procedures

PART A   CASH MANAGEMENT

1 Introduction

This chapter provides an introduction to cash and credit management. You should appreciate the links between these and other elements of working capital (stock, debtors, creditors). The key objectives **liquidity, profitability** and **security** are particularly important.

We shall revise the major types of receipts and payments. You need to be aware of how significant they are and also how different types of cash flows have **different patterns**. Some cashflows will be **regular**, but others will be less frequent, or **unpredictable**, and these can have a major influence on an organisation's cash position.

You will have encountered the difference between **cash** and **accruals** accounting in your studies for the financial accounting units of AAT, but the distinction is important in this unit as well.

In this chapter we also describe how cash flows are **monitored** by management. Monitoring of activities is an important theme throughout this Interactive Text.

2 The cash flow cycle

2.1 The need for cash

A business which fails to make profits will go under in the long term. However, a business which runs out of cash, even for a couple of months, will fail, despite the fact that it is basically profitable. Why?

Example: Cash shortages

Minor Ltd has won a contract worth £1m from Mega plc, which will be paid in equal annual instalments of £200,000 over five years at the end of each year. Minor Ltd has a maximum bank overdraft of £200,000. The company finishes the work on the contract at the end of year 2: it incurs a total of £750,000 on expenses, £200,000 in year 1 and £550,000 in year 2.

	Year 1 £	Year 2 £	Year 3 £	Year 4 £	Year 5 £
Brought forward – surplus/(overdraft)	–	–	(200,000)	(150,000)	50,000
Received from Mega	200,000	200,000	200,000	200,000	200,000
Payments to creditors	(200,000)	(400,000)	(150,000)	–	–
Cash surplus/(overdraft)	–	(200,000)	(150,000)	50,000	250,000
Creditors outstanding		150,000			

Task

Comment on the implications of this forecast for Minor's relationship with its bank and with its creditors.

Solution

We can see that at the end of year 2, Minor Ltd is in trouble.

Minor Ltd has run up the maximum overdraft, but some creditors must wait over a year – until the end of year 3 – in order to get paid. Many will be unwilling to wait that long. Creditors can sue for the business to be wound up and may anyway refuse to supply goods until they are paid for previous supplies. This will prevent the business functioning at all.

The bank may take a similar view, although the overdraft will have been paid off by the end of year 4. The bank may worry about the length of its exposure.

Minor could have avoided this demise if it had planned things differently. Although the contract is profitable, **cash outflows** and **inflows occur** at **different times**.

2.2 Working capital cycle

The management of cash, debtors and creditors is essentially a **cycle**, a flow of funds in and out of the business, known as the **working capital cycle**. **Working capital** is the net difference between **current assets** (mainly stocks, debtors and cash) and **current liabilities** (such as trade creditors and a bank overdraft).

Current assets are items which are either cash already, or which will soon lead to the receipt of cash. Stocks will be sold to customers and create debtors; debtors will soon pay in cash for their purchases. Surplus cash can be invested in short-term investments.

Current liabilities are items which will soon have to be paid for with cash. Trade creditors will have to be paid. A bank overdraft is usually regarded as a short-term borrowing which may need to be repaid fairly quickly (technically on demand, i.e. immediately).

2.3 Operating cycle

The **operating cycle** (also known as the **cash cycle**) describes the connection between working capital and cash movements in and out. The cycle is usually in days or months.

The operating cycle measures the **period of time** between:

- **cash paid out** for raw materials
- **cash received** from debtors for goods sold

This cycle of repeating events may be shown diagrammatically.

PART A CASH MANAGEMENT

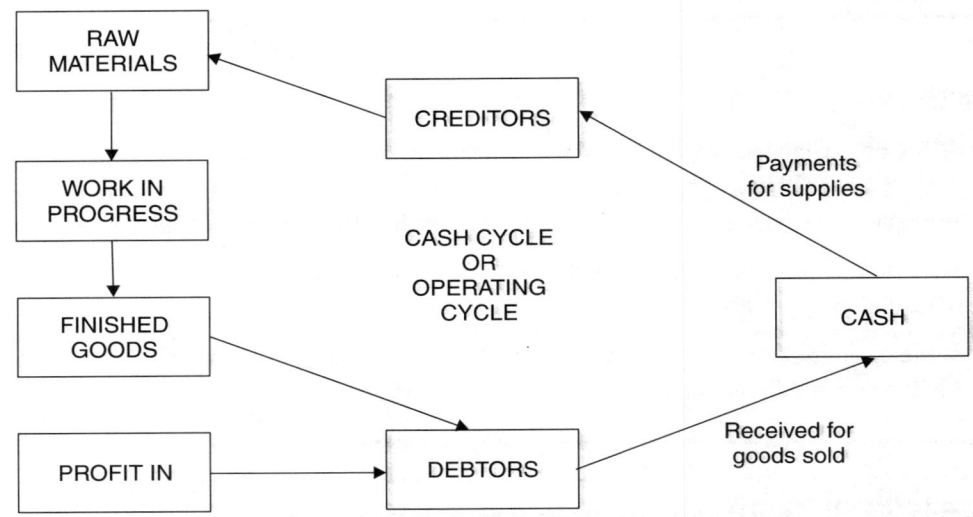

Suppose that a firm buys raw materials on 1½ months' credit, holds them in store for 1 month and then issues them to the production department. The production cycle is very short, but finished goods are held for 1 month before they are sold. Debtors take 2 months' credit. The operating cycle would be as follows.

	Months
Raw material stock turnover period	1.0
Less: Credit taken from suppliers	(1.5)
Finished goods stock turnover period	1.0
Debtors' payment period	2.0
	2.5

Suppose the firm purchases its raw materials on 1 January. The sequence of events would then be as follows:

	Date
Purchase of raw materials	1 Jan
Issue of materials to production (one month after purchase)	1 Feb
Payment made to suppliers (1½ months after purchase)	15 Feb
Sale of finished goods (one month after production begins)	1 Mar
Receipt of cash from debtors (two months after sale)	1 May

The operating cycle is the period of 2½ months from 15 February, when payment is made to suppliers, until 1 May, when cash is received from debtors.

Activity 1.1

Farmer Giles has just bought a tractor for use on the farm. The tractor will last many years. 'It's just what I need, a little capital expenditure to help me work. And I didn't have to borrow, either. I saved up the subsidy I get from the European Union every month. I suppose you accountants would call this working capital?'

Is he right?

2.4 Operating cycles of different types of business

Different types of business have their own operating cycle characteristics.

(a) In a **retailing business**, most sales are for cash or by credit and debit card, and the company receives most of its income at the time of sale. Supermarket chains selling goods within a few days of purchase might not pay their suppliers until *after* the goods are sold and cash received.

(b) In a **manufacturing business**, many sales will be on credit, as will many purchases. The operating cycle will therefore be more conventional, with payments preceding receipts.

Activity 1.2

(a) What are the three main elements in the cash cycle?
(b) Why do you think retailers (such as a supermarket) have a short cash cycle time?
(c) Lengthening the cash cycle will improve the cash balance for most companies. True or false?

Activity 1.3

A business purchases raw materials on 1 May, issues the raw materials to production on 16 June and sells the finished goods on 16 August. It pays its suppliers of raw materials on 1 June and receives money from its debtors on 16 November.

Task

Calculate the business's operating cycle.

3 Types of cash transaction

3.1 Cash transactions

There are many types of cash transaction. They differ in their purpose, their form, and their frequency.

Capital items	Revenue items
Relate to long-term functioning of business, eg raising money from shareholders, purchasing fixed assets	Relate to day-to-day operations eg operating cycle items or overdraft interest
Exceptional items	**Unexceptional items**
Unusual items eg costs of closing down a business.	Everything else
Regular items	**Irregular items**
Occur at predictable intervals eg salaries paid every month, telephone paid once a quarter, dividends paid twice a year	One-off items eg major repairs

3.2 Cash outflows

There are a large number of examples of cash outflows.

Types of expenditure	
Revenue expenditure	Payments to suppliers for goods purchased and employees for wages
Payments to government for taxes	Quarterly payments for corporation tax or VAT, PAYE
Payments to suppliers for finance	Dividends to shareholders, interest to bank, interest to debentureholders, drawings (money taken out of the business by sole traders or partners)
Capital payments	Payments for fixed assets, also instalments on leases
Payments to acquire investments	New businesses or short-term financial interests
Purchases of foreign currency for trading overseas	Businesses trading abroad may have to purchase goods from overseas suppliers in the suppliers' currencies

3.3 Cash inflows

There are also various examples of cash inflows.

Cash inflows	
Cash received from sales	Immediately from customers or from debtors for sales made on credit
Long-term grants	From the British government or EU
Cash received from providers of finance	Equity share capital or long-term loans
Cash received from asset sales	Fixed assets sold after their useful life has ended or short-term investments

3.4 Categorisation of cash flows

Another method of categorisation gives four groupings: operational, priority, discretionary and financial.

Types of cash flow	
Operational cash flows	Derive from normal trading operations eg cash receipts from sales, payments to suppliers
Priority cash flows	Payments made to keep company afloat, and which have priority over other non-operational payments eg interest and tax charges
Discretionary cash flows	Discretionary inflows include the sale of fixed assets, subsidiaries and financial investments, outflows include capital expenditure, payment for acquisitions and financial investments and dividends
Financial cash flows	Financial inflows include proceeds from issue of shares or new loans, outflows include loan repayments

3.5 Operational cash flows: the cash tank and the cascade effect

Priority cash flows have to be **met by cash inflows** from at least one of the other three sources.

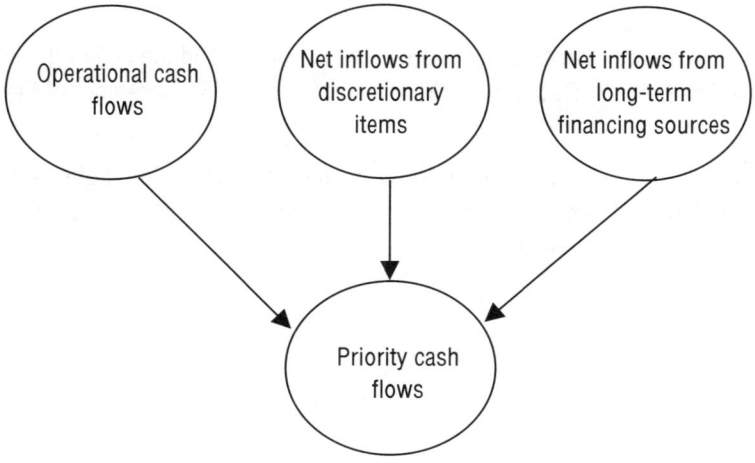

PART A   CASH MANAGEMENT

Operational cash flows will often be the **source of cash** from which all or most other cash payments can be made. You can think of operational cash flows as water going into and out of a water tank, representing the company's operations. There is a cascade effect, with the surplus cash outflows at one level and moving down to the next level for cash outflows.

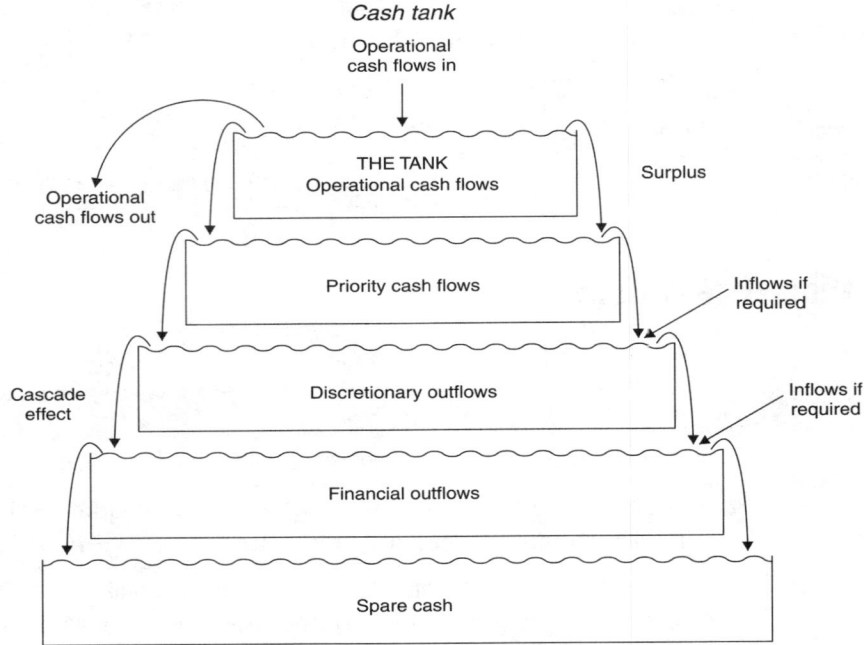

When operational cash flows are insufficient, the business will need a **'top-up'** of cash from **discretionary** or long-term **financing sources** (or by **using existing cash in hand**). A top-up may well be required when a company is **expanding its operations** rapidly, when it wishes to finance a large acquisition, or when it must repay a large debt.

Operational cash flow problems are more likely to occur when the company is making only **small profits**, or trading at a loss. Problems can also occur when the company is growing too fast and is **overtrading** (see later).

3.6 Net cash flow

Net cash flow is the net change in the cash position between the beginning and the end of the period. For example, if Janbruno Ltd holds cash of £5,000 at 31 December of Year 1 and £3,300 at 31 December of Year 2, there has been a negative net cash flow of £1,700.

Net cash flow is of little information value, however, unless you analyse its **component elements**. A **categorised cash flow** sets out the entire cash flows of the business, not just cash flows from trading operations. The categories will reflect the requirements for analysis. They might include:

	£
Cash flow from sales	17,000
Cash paid for purchases	(10,300)
Cash paid for wages, etc	(4,000)
Interest payments	(400)
Fixed asset expenditure	(10,000)
Bank loan	4,000
Issue of shares	2,000
Net cash flow	(1,700)

A categorised cash flow gives the component elements of net cash flow.

Activity 1.4

Cash flows can be classified between regular revenue receipts and payments and infrequent or irregular receipts and disbursements.

Give an example of each of the following.

(a) A regular revenue receipt
(b) An exceptional payment
(c) A capital payment
(d) An annual disbursement

3.7 Monitoring of cash flows

Accounts and treasury staff monitor cash flows:

(a) They should **assess the operating cycle,** and find out how near cash receipts are to coinciding with payments.

(b) They should plan for **exceptional items**, such as proceeds from share issues, in advance. There should be a short-term plan for investing the money.

(c) They should **monitor** the **cash account** to ensure that any **unexpected receipts** are **properly accounted** for, and any **unexpected outflows** are **investigated** and, if appropriate, corrected.

Monitoring should be a **continuous task**, conducted by **high level management.** The whole purpose of monitoring is to **know in advance when cash surpluses** and **deficiencies** are **likely to arise**, so that action to invest or borrow can be taken. We discuss borrowing and investment further in Chapters 6 and 7.

Activity 1.5

Why is a cash flow statement an important part of a company's accounts?

4 Profits and cash flow

4.1 Differences between profits and cash flows

A company can make losses but still have a net cash income from trading. Conversely a company can also make profits but have a net cash deficit on its trading operations. **Trading profits** and **cash flows** are different for a number of reasons.

(a) The profits and losses are calculated on the **accruals basis**. This means that sales in the profit and loss account will not be the same as cash received from customers, and purchases in the profit and loss account will not be the same as cash paid to suppliers. We shall look at the accruals basis further in the next section.

(b) Trading profits **include items** which are **not cash movements**, for example **depreciation** or **increases in provisions.**

(c) A business may obtain cash from a transaction which has **nothing to do** with **profit or loss**. For example, an issue of shares for cash has no effect on profit.

(d) Cash may be paid for the **purchase** of **fixed assets**, but the charge in the profit and loss account is **depreciation**, which is only a part of an asset's cost.

(e) When a fixed asset is sold there is a **profit** or **loss** on **sale** equal to the difference between the sale proceeds and the 'net book value' of the asset in the balance sheet. Cash, however, will increase by the amount of the **sale proceeds**.

4.2 Implications of differences between profits and cash flows

If a company is profitable but short of cash, one reason could be an **increase** in the **other elements** of **working capital**. If a company were to seek credit from a bank to finance the growth in working capital, the bank might ask the management whether it can **improve cash flows** by squeezing working capital.

DEBTORS ⟶ DEBTORS

STOCK ⟶ STOCK

CREDITORS ⟶ **CREDITORS**

If a company is making losses, it could try to maintain a positive operational cash flow by taking **more credit** (i.e. by increasing its creditors and so reducing working capital).

4.3 Negative operational cash flows

A company that trades profitably should earn **cash surpluses**, at least in the longer term. However, a profitable company can also suffer from negative cash flows in the short term.

- It might spend cash on fixed asset purchases and extra working capital.
- It might use cash to pay for business acquisitions.
- High inflation rates might force a company to increase its funding of business assets in money terms, even when there is no real growth in the business.
- Dividends might exceed cash surpluses for the year. In recession, for example, cash surpluses fall but there will be pressure from shareholders to maintain dividends.

Negative cash flows from operations would normally be an indicator of **financial distress**, unless the company is growing rapidly and profitably, and is having to invest heavily in additional working capital (stocks and debtors).

Activity 1.6

Why does the reported profit figure of a business for a period not normally represent the amount of cash generated in that period?

5 Cash accounting and accruals accounting

5.1 The accruals concept

The distinction between profits and cash flow has been a theme of this chapter so far. You must understand the principle, which is applied in nearly all businesses' accounts, that **accounts** are prepared on an **accruals (or earnings) basis**, **not** on a **cash basis**. That is, a sale or purchase is dealt with in the year in which it is made, even if cash changes hands in a later year.

PART A CASH MANAGEMENT

Example: Accruals concept (1)

The Koala Social Club has the following receipts and payments for the year ended 31 October 20X1, its first year of existence.

	£
Subscriptions	1,100
Refreshment sales	150
Refreshment purchases	125
Social event ticket sales	1,000
Social event expenses	950
Hall rent	400
Hall maintenance	75
Water	60
Electricity	140
Insurance	120
Telephone	110
Postage, printing and stationery	80
Miscellaneous expenses	25
Bank interest received	90

In addition the following information is available about assets and liabilities at 31 October 20X1.

	£
Subscriptions prepaid	420
Subscriptions owed	60
Insurance prepaid	30
Accruals: Water	15
Electricity	35

Task

Prepare the receipts and payments and income and expenditure accounts for the club for the year ended 31 October 20X1, and prepare a reconciliation between the income and expenditure account and net cash flows.

Solution

KOALA SOCIAL CLUB
RECEIPTS AND PAYMENTS ACCOUNT
FOR THE YEAR ENDED 31 OCTOBER 20X1

	£	£
Receipts		
Subscriptions		1,100
Refreshment sales		150
Social event ticket sales		1,000
Bank interest		90
		2,340
Payments		
Refreshment purchases	125	
Social event expenses	950	
Hall rent	400	
Hall maintenance	75	
Water	60	
Electricity	140	
Insurance	120	
Telephone	110	
Postage, printing and stationery	80	
Miscellaneous expenses	25	
		2,085
Surplus of receipts over payments		255

KOALA SOCIAL CLUB
INCOME AND EXPENDITURE ACCOUNT
FOR THE YEAR ENDED 31 OCTOBER 20X1

		£	£
Income			
Subscriptions (1,100 – 420 + 60)			740
Refreshments:	Sales	150	
	Purchases	(125)	
			25
Social events:	Receipts	1,000	
	Expenses	(950)	
			50
Bank interest			90
			905
Expenditure			
Hall rent		400	
Hall maintenance		75	
Water (60 + 15)		75	
Electricity (140 + 35)		175	
Insurance (120 – 30)		90	
Telephone		110	
Postage, printing and stationery		80	
Miscellaneous expenses		25	
			(1,030)
Excess of expenditure over income			(125)

PART A CASH MANAGEMENT

KOALA SOCIAL CLUB
RECONCILIATION OF INCOME AND EXPENDITURE ACCOUNT
TO NET CASH FLOWS FOR THE YEAR ENDED 31 OCTOBER 20X1

	£
Excess of expenditure over income	(125)
Subscriptions prepaid	420
Subscriptions owed	(60)
Insurance prepaid	(30)
Water charges owed	15
Electricity charges owed	35
Net cash flow	255

Because of the **subscriptions received in advance** and not paid promptly, and also because of the **prepaid and accrued expenses**, the receipts and payments account and the income and expenditure account give different 'bottom-line' figures.

Example: Accruals concept (2)

Katy has a business importing and selling cuddly toy cats. In May 20X7 she makes the following purchases and sales.

Invoice date	Numbers bought/sold	Amount £	Date paid
Purchases			
7.5.X7	20	100	1.6.X7
Sales			
8.5.X7	4	40	1.6.X7
12.5.X7	6	60	1.6.X7
23.5.X7	10	100	1.7.X7

Task

Calculate Katy's profit for May.

Solution

	£
Cash basis	
Sales	0
Purchases	0
Profit/loss	0
Accruals basis	
Sales (£40 + £60 + £100)	200
Purchases	(100)
Profit	100

Obviously, the accruals basis gives a 'truer' picture than the cash basis. Katy has no cash to show for her efforts until June. However her customers are legally bound to pay her and she is legally bound to pay for her purchases.

5.2 Matching

The accruals concept states that, in **computing profit**, **revenue earned** must be **matched** against the expenditure incurred in earning it. Katy's example illustrates this; profit of £100 was computed by matching the revenue (£200) earned from the sale of 20 cats against the cost (£100) of acquiring them.

If, however, Katy had only sold 18 cats, her profit and loss account would not be charged with the cost of 20 cats, as she would still have 2 cats in stock. If she intends to sell them in June she is likely to make a profit on the sale. Only the **purchase cost** of **18 cats** (£90) should be **matched** with her **sales revenue**, leaving her with a profit of £90.

Her balance sheet would therefore look like this.

	£
Assets	
Stock (at cost, ie 2 × £5)	10
Debtors (18 × £10)	180
	190
Liabilities	
Creditors	(100)
Net assets	90
Proprietor's capital (profit for the period)	90

In this example, the concepts of **going concern** and **accruals** are linked. Because the business is assumed to be a going concern it is possible to carry forward the cost of the unsold toy cats as a charge against profits of the next period.

5.3 Sales and purchases, debtors and creditors

The table below sets out the links between the **sales reported** in the **profit and loss account**, the debtor balances at the beginning and end of year, and the cash received from debtors.

	£
Debtors owing money at the start of the year	X
Sales during the year	X
Total money due from customers	X
Less debtors owing money at the end of the year	(X)
Cash receipts from debtors during the year	X

Similarly, the **profit and loss account reports the cost of goods sold** during the year, but some goods are purchased on credit, and some remain in stock over the year end. Therefore these are two separate reconciliations.

The relationship between the **cost of materials** in the materials cost of sales and **cash payments** for materials purchased is as follows:

	£
Cost of sales	X
Add: Closing stocks at the end of the year	X
	X
Less: Opening stocks at the start of the year	(X)
Purchases during the year	X

	£
Payments owing to creditors at the start of the year	X
Add: Purchases during the year	X
	X
Less: Payments owing to creditors at the end of the year	(X)
Equals cash payments to creditors during the year	X

Activity 1.7

Assume that Sarhall Ltd achieved sales turnover in a particular year of £200,000 and the cost of sales was £170,000. Stocks were £12,000, creditors £11,000 and debtors £15,000 at the start of the year. At the end of the year, stocks were £21,000, creditors were £14,000 and debtors £24,000.

Task

Find out the profits and the operational cash flow resulting from the year's trading.

5.4 Usefulness of accruals and cash flow information

The accruals basis of accounting is a way of letting investors know how much profit a business has made by matching income and expenditure. It has **no relevance whatsoever** to day-to-day cash management. Survival in business depends on the ability to generate cash, and businesses therefore need to focus on what cash they are generating.

The introduction of FRS 1, requiring larger companies to produce cash flow information as part of their accounts, highlighted the importance of cash flow information in financial reporting.

- Creditors (long and short-term) will be more interested in an entity's **ability** to **repay** them than in its profitability.
- Cash flow reporting satisfies the needs of other **financial report users** better.
- For management, it provides the sort of information on which **decisions** should be taken (in management accounting, 'relevant costs' to a decision are future cash flows).
- For shareholders and auditors, cash flow accounting can provide a satisfactory basis for **stewardship accounting**, demonstrating how well managers have used the business's resources under their control.

6 The focus of cash and credit management

6.1 Profitability, liquidity and security

In general terms, cash and credit management is concerned with **profitability**, **liquidity** and **safety** (or **security**). We introduce these topics here and discuss them further in Chapter 7 when we consider how cash should be invested.

6.2 Profitability

In the context of cash management, profitability relates to how the firm manages its cash in order to minimise costs and maintain a return.

Example: Profitability

At the end of month 1, Chrisbone Ltd finds it has cash balances surplus to requirements of £1,000, for which it has no conceivable use at the moment.

(a) It can leave it in the bank current account, where it will earn no interest.

(b) It can invest it in a deposit account where it will earn interest of £20 in month 2, provided the bank is given a *week's* notice should Chrisbone require the money.

(c) It can buy shares in Listhomas Ltd. At the beginning of the month they are worth £1,000: at the end, they are worth £1,040. Transaction costs are £10.

(d) It can go to the stock market and buy some shares in Elgrey plc for a month. The value of a share can go down as well as up. It costs £10 in total to buy and sell the shares. At the beginning of the month the shares are worth £1,000: at the end they are worth £995.

Task

Identify what the best use of funds is.

Solution

	Current account (a) £	Deposit account (b) £	Listhomas (c) £	Elgrey (d) £
Cash invested	(1,000)	(1,000)	(1,000)	(1,000)
Interest		20		
Principal/sale proceeds	1,000	1,000	1,040	995
Transaction costs	–	–	(10)	(10)
Profit/(loss)	None	20	30	(15)

Listhomas is the most profitable, but shares are more risky than the current or deposit accounts, as the example of Elgrey demonstrated.

Chrisbone would be foolish simply to let the cash pile up and earn no money, even if investing is not the company's main business. At the same time, it must balance the risk of a course of action, such as investing in shares, with the profit. Although (a) earns nothing, the cash will be on hand **immediately** if needed.

6.3 Liquidity

Liquidity is the ability of a company to pay its creditors on time.

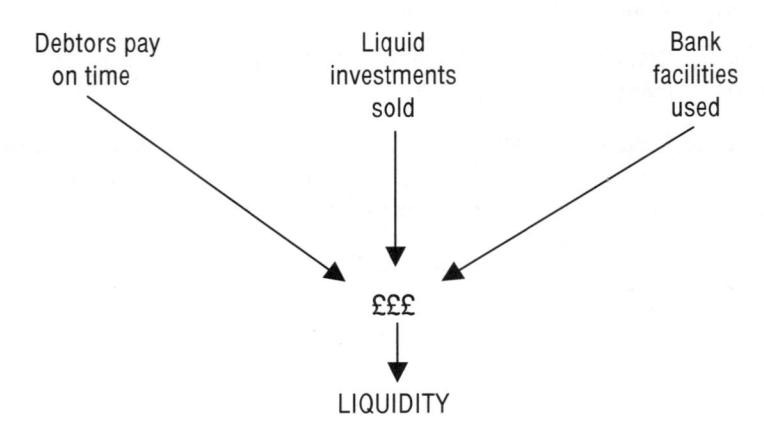

Debtors pay on time → £££ ← Liquid investments sold ← Bank facilities used

£££ → LIQUIDITY

Liquidity also refers to the **ease** with which something can be **converted into cash** for use. Cash is the most 'liquid' asset of all. A short-term investment can be sold. Some deposit accounts require notice. Buildings and property might be very illiquid, in that they are difficult to sell and convert into cash.

6.4 Security

Security refers to the **controls** over **cash and credit management** or the safekeeping of cash and other monetary assets.

Cash and credit transactions should not involve the company in any undue risk.

- Notes and coin should be **secure from theft**.

- Cheques etc and electronic systems should be **secure from fraud**.
- Short-term investments should be such that the firm does not risk **heavy losses** through falls in value. Shares can fall in price and are risky as a short-term investment.

6.5 Risk and return

There is a relationship between **risk** and **return**. Generally speaking safer investments offer lower rewards.

- The risk needs to be spread.
- The loss of the amount invested (the principal) can be a severe problem.

In general, the issues of **cash** and **credit** risk cannot be considered apart. Credit is 'near-cash'. Offering credit to a customer is more risky than asking for cash up front.

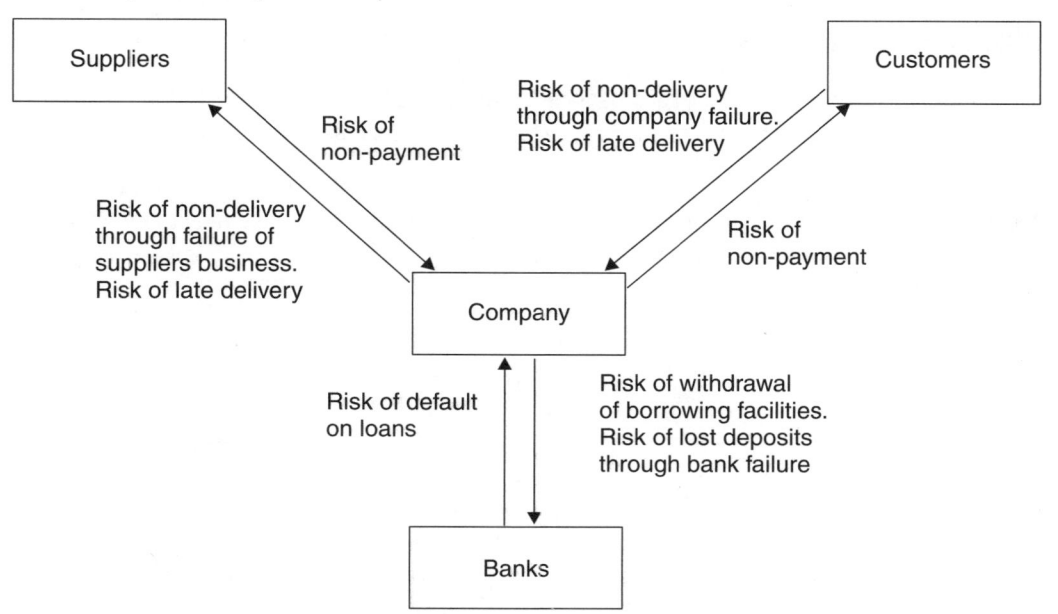

```
       Suppliers                                    Customers
           ↖                                           ↗
            ↖    Risk of         Risk of non-delivery
             ↖   non-payment     through company failure.
              ↘                  Risk of late delivery
   Risk of non-delivery                          Risk of
   through failure of                            non-payment
   suppliers business.
   Risk of late delivery
                      Company
                         ↕
            Risk of default    Risk of withdrawal
            on loans           of borrowing facilities.
                               Risk of lost deposits
                               through bank failure
                       Banks
```

Credit control is a way of controlling the risk of debts going bad. (Bear in mind that a bad debt is equivalent to a firm giving away the goods to the customer for free.)

We consider risk and return further in Chapter 7.

Activity 1.8

What are the three main issues underlying the management of cash and the control of credit? Would you say that one of them was always more important than the others?

7 Treasury management

7.1 Responsibility for treasury management

Treasury management can be defined as

> 'the corporate handling of all financial matters, the generation of external and internal funds for business, the management of currencies and cash flows, and the complex strategies, policies and procedures of corporate finance' (*Association of Corporate Treasurers*).

In small companies, the **financial director** or **chief accountant** will be responsible for all the various accounting and financial activities of the business.

7.2 Specialist treasury department

As companies increase in size however, specialist personnel are employed to deal with financial and budgetary issues. Different firms have different ways of organising the finance function, but a suggestion is provided in the **diagram below**.

To manage cash (funds) and foreign currency efficiently, many large companies have set up a separate **treasury department**. Cash forecasting and budgeting is likely to be a **joint exercise** between the **management accounting department** and **treasury department**. Clearly, the various departments must co-operate in the exchange and co-ordination of information and in financial planning.

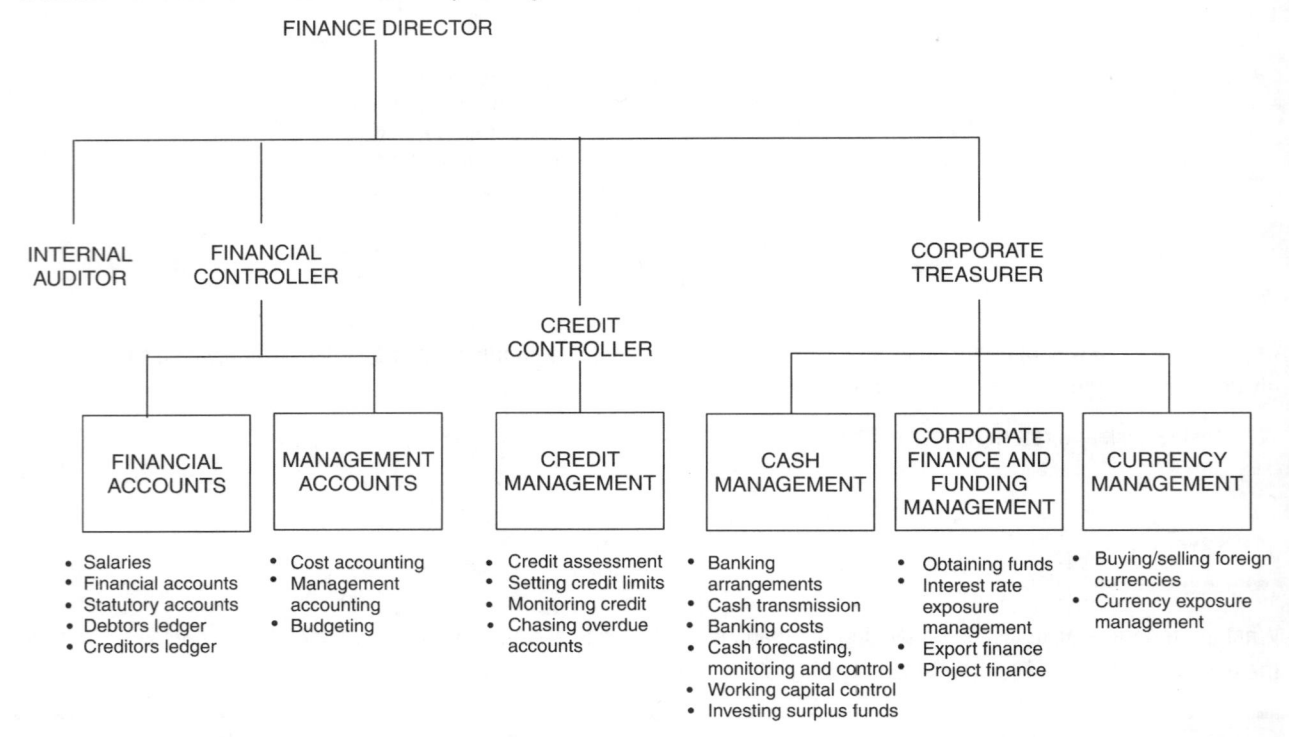

```
                            FINANCE DIRECTOR
        ┌──────────────┬──────────────────┬──────────────────┐
    INTERNAL        FINANCIAL                            CORPORATE
    AUDITOR        CONTROLLER                            TREASURER
                  ┌────┴────┐      CREDIT          ┌────────┼────────┐
                  │         │    CONTROLLER        │        │        │
             FINANCIAL  MANAGEMENT   CREDIT       CASH   CORPORATE  CURRENCY
             ACCOUNTS   ACCOUNTS  MANAGEMENT   MANAGEMENT FINANCE AND MANAGEMENT
                                                          FUNDING
                                                         MANAGEMENT
```

FINANCIAL ACCOUNTS	MANAGEMENT ACCOUNTS	CREDIT MANAGEMENT	CASH MANAGEMENT	CORPORATE FINANCE AND FUNDING MANAGEMENT	CURRENCY MANAGEMENT
• Salaries • Financial accounts • Statutory accounts • Debtors ledger • Creditors ledger	• Cost accounting • Management accounting • Budgeting	• Credit assessment • Setting credit limits • Monitoring credit • Chasing overdue accounts	• Banking arrangements • Cash transmission • Banking costs • Cash forecasting, monitoring and control • Working capital control • Investing surplus funds	• Obtaining funds • Interest rate exposure management • Export finance • Project finance	• Buying/selling foreign currencies • Currency exposure management

Key learning points

- ☑ **Cash** and **credit** are interrelated. A firm with poor cash flow is likely to be a high credit risk.
- ☑ Cash and credit management are concerned with **profitability, liquidity** and **safety** (or **security**).
- ☑ **Net cash flow** is the **total change** in a company's cash balances over a period of time.
- ☑ **Operational cash flow** is the net cash flow arising over a period from trading operations.
- ☑ **Operational flows** can be improved by better management of stocks, debtors and creditors (eg fewer stocks, collecting money earlier, paying it later).
- ☑ **Priority cash flows** do not relate to trade, but are vital to keep the company afloat.
- ☑ The **operating cycle** measures the period of time between cash outflows for materials etc, and cash inflows from sales or debtors.
- ☑ **Working capital** is the difference between a firm's current assets and current liabilities. These are assets or liabilities which are, or can be turned into, cash.
- ☑ Accounts showing **trading profits** – calculated on an **earnings (accruals)** basis – are not the same as statements of **cash flow.**
- ☑ **Cash budgets** are not prepared according to the accruals concept, which tries to ensure income and expenditure are matched. Instead they are prepared on a cash (receipts and payments) basis.
- ☑ **Cash flow monitoring** should mean that businesses know in advance when surpluses or deficiencies are likely to arise, so that early action to invest or borrow can be taken.
- ☑ **Treasury management** in a modern enterprise covers various areas.

PART A   CASH MANAGEMENT

Quick quiz

1. Working capital equals .... less ....

2. What period of time is measured by the operating cycle?

    A   The time between receipt of raw materials and selling the completed products to customers
    B   The time between receipt of raw materials and receipt of cash from debtors
    C   The time between payment of cash for raw materials and selling the completed products to debtors
    D   The time between payment of cash for raw materials and receipt of cash from debtors.

3. The difference between capital and revenue flows is that capital flows relate to the long-term functioning of the business; revenue flows relate to day-to-day operations.

    ☐ True

    ☐ False

4. Why are profits and cash flows different?

5. Dividends are an example of what sort of cash flow?

    A   Operational cash flow
    B   Priority cash flow
    C   Discretionary cash flow
    D   Financial cash flow

6. Name the three main focuses of cash and credit management.

7. The .... is the matching of revenues and costs to the period to which they relate.

8. Under what headings do the functions of a treasurer fall?

    - Cash management
    - Credit management
    - Corporate finance
    - Financial accounts
    - Funding management
    - Currency management
    - Management accounts

Answers to quick quiz

1. Working capital equals **Current assets (stocks, debtors, cash)** less **Current liabilities (creditors, overdraft)**.

2. D   The time between payment of cash for raw materials and receipt of cash from debtors.

3. True.

4. Profits are calculated using various non-cash items, whereas cash flows include receipts and payments and relate to activities that happened in other periods.

1: CASH AND CASH FLOWS

5   C   Discretionary cash flow.

6   Profitability, liquidity and security/safety.

7   The **accruals concept** is the matching of revenues and costs to the period to which they relate.

8   Cash management; corporate finance; funding management; currency management.

Activity checklist

This checklist shows which performance criteria, range statement or knowledge and understanding point is covered by each activity in this chapter. Tick off each activity as you complete it.

Activity		
1.1	☐	This activity deals with Knowledge and Understanding 1: the main types of cash receipts and payments: regular revenue receipts and payments; capital receipts and payments; drawings or dividends and disbursements; exceptional receipts and payments
1.2	☐	This activity deals with Performance Criterion 15.1.A: monitor and control cash receipts and payments against budgeted cash flow
1.3	☐	This activity deals with Performance Criterion 15.1.A: monitor and control cash receipts and payments against budgeted cash flow
1.4	☐	This activity deals with Knowledge and Understanding 1: the main types of cash receipts and payments: regular revenue receipts and payments; capital receipts and payments; drawings or dividends and disbursements; exceptional receipts and payments
1.5	☐	This activity deals with Knowledge and Understanding 31: an understanding of the organisation's relevant policies and procedures
1.6	☐	This activity deals with Knowledge and Understanding 13: lagged receipts and payments
1.7	☐	This activity deals with Knowledge and Understanding 13: lagged receipts and payments
1.8	☐	This activity deals with Knowledge and Understanding 31: an understanding of the organisation's relevant policies and procedures

PART A CASH MANAGEMENT

chapter 2

Forecasting cash flows

Contents

1. Introduction
2. Types of forecasts
3. Cash budgets in receipts and payments format
4. Cleared funds cash forecasts
5. Cash forecasts based on financial statements
6. Control and corrective action

Performance criteria

- 15.1.B Consult appropriate staff to determine the likely pattern of cash flows over the accounting period and to anticipate any exceptional receipts or payments
- 15.1.C Ensure forecasts of future cash payments and receipts are in accord with known income and expenditure trends
- 15.1.D Prepare cash budgets in the approved format and clearly indicate net cash requirements
- 15.1.E Identify significant deviations from the cash budget and take corrective action within defined organisational policies

Range statement

- 15.1.1 Cash flows to be monitored: regular revenue receipts and payments; capital receipts and payments; drawings or dividends and disbursements; exceptional receipts and payments

Knowledge and understanding

- The main types of cash receipts and payments: regular revenue receipts and payments; capital receipts and payments; drawings/dividends and disbursements; exceptional receipts and payments
- Form and structure of cash budgets
- Lagged receipts and payments
- Cash flow accounting and its relationship to accounting for income and expenditure
- Understanding that the accounting systems of an organisation are affected by its organisational structure, its administrative systems and procedures and the nature of its business transactions
- Understanding that recording and accounting practices may vary in different parts of the organisation
- An understanding of the organisation's relevant policies and procedures

1 Introduction

A very important aspect of this chapter is the **preparation** of cash budgets. You need to be able to prepare a budget using a receipts and payments forecast, and also profit and loss account and balance sheet information.

You must work through the example budgets carefully. You will see that you need to take a methodical approach, using supporting workings if the figures are complex.

Watch out in particular for the complications we have discussed in Chapter 1. These include **timing differences** between sales and receipts from debtors, and purchases and payments to suppliers. Also keep a look out for **non-cash items** such as depreciation and changes in provisions, which appear in the profit and loss account but are not included in a cash forecast.

You also need to know about the contents of other types of cash forecast, although you may encounter these less frequently.

Don't however spend all your time on the mechanics of budget preparation. The main purpose of preparing budgets is to measure whether there are likely to be **cash shortages** (or large surpluses). The last section of this chapter is thus very significant. Having prepared your cash flow forecast, you need to recognise if the business is likely to have problems, **and** recommend what can be done to rectify them.

2 Types of forecasts

2.1 Purpose of forecasts

Cash forecasting ensures that **funds sufficient** to sustain the activities of the business will be available when they are needed, at an acceptable cost. Forecasts provide an early warning of liquidity problems.

2: FORECASTING CASH FLOWS

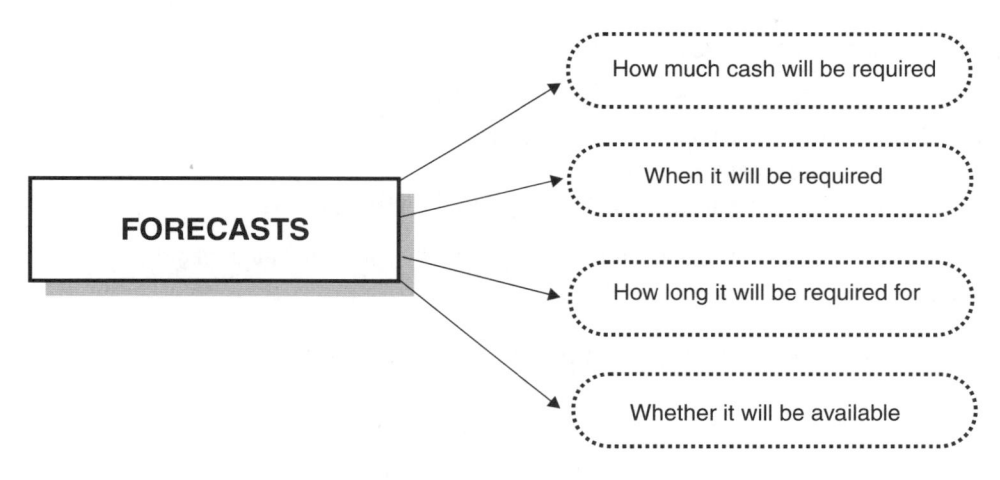

FORECASTS
- How much cash will be required
- When it will be required
- How long it will be required for
- Whether it will be available

A business must know **when** it might need funds and for how long, not just **what amount** of funding could be required. It can then decide whether to **borrow**, or whether to meet a deficiency by other means, for example **sale of investments**, **getting debtors to pay early** or **delaying payments to creditors**.

2.2 Information for banks

Banks often require customers to provide cash forecasts as a precondition of lending. A newly established business wishing to open a bank account will also normally be asked to supply a **business plan**. The cash and sales forecasts will also allow the bank to **monitor** the **progress** of the business, and **control** its **lending** more effectively.

Activity 2.1

Give examples of unforeseen changes which may affect cash flow patterns.

2.3 Types of forecast

There are two broad types of cash forecast.

- **Cash flow based forecasts** (or cash budgets) in **receipts and payments format**
- **Balance sheet and financial statement based** forecasts

2.4 Receipts and payments forecasts

Cash flow based forecasts predict a business's **receipts** and **payments**. They forecast the **amount** and **timing** of **cash receipts and payments**, **net cash flows** and **changes in cash balances**, for each time period covered by the forecast. Cash flow based forecasts include cash budgets up to a year or so ahead and short-term forecasts of just a few days.

PART A CASH MANAGEMENT

In companies that use cash flow reporting for control purposes, there will probably be:

- A **cash budget divided** into **monthly** or **quarterly periods**
- A **statement comparing actual cash flows** against the **budget**
- A **revised cash forecast**
- A **statement comparing actual cash flows** against a **revised forecast**

The cash budget is usually prepared by taking a **profits budget** for the period and **adjusting** the figures for **sales**, and **cost of sales**, into cash flows.

Cash flow control with budgets and revised forecasts

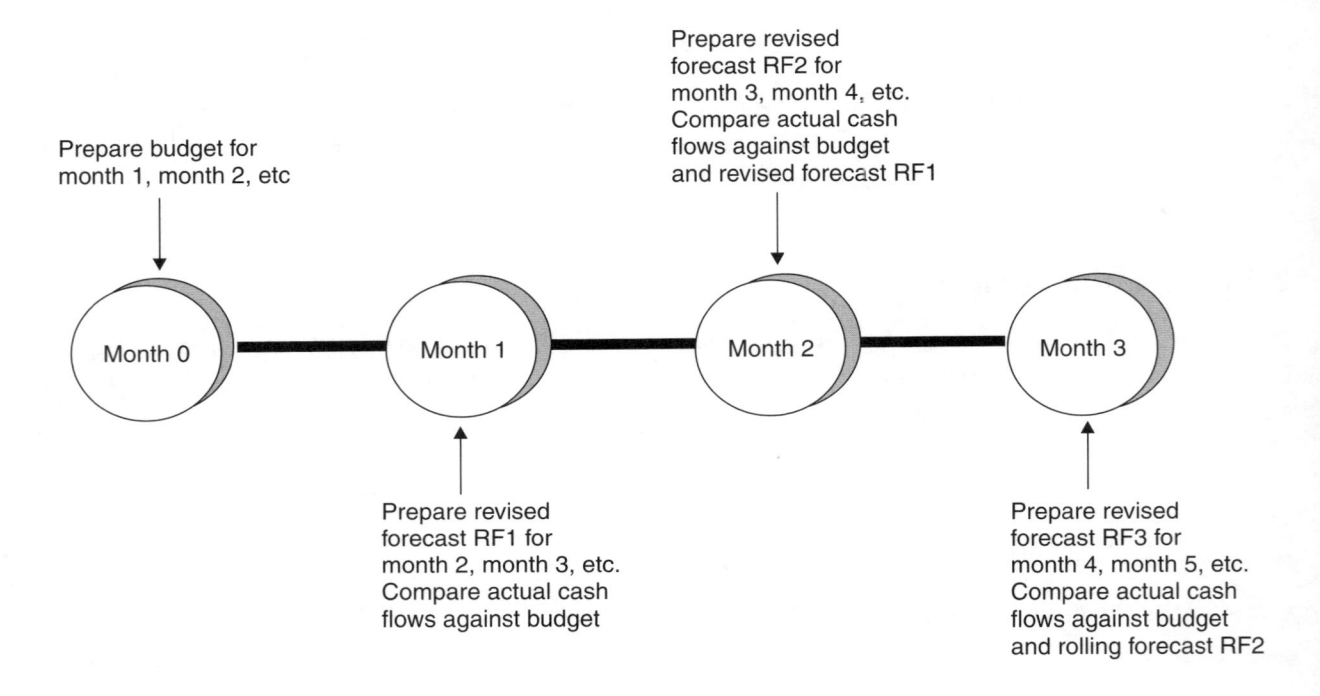

Prepare budget for month 1, month 2, etc
→ Month 0

Month 1 ← Prepare revised forecast RF1 for month 2, month 3, etc. Compare actual cash flows against budget

Prepare revised forecast RF2 for month 3, month 4, etc. Compare actual cash flows against budget and revised forecast RF1
→ Month 2

Month 3 ← Prepare revised forecast RF3 for month 4, month 5, etc. Compare actual cash flows against budget and rolling forecast RF2

2.5 Balance sheet based forecasts

In balance sheet based forecasts, a 'cash surplus' or 'funds deficit' is the **balancing item** after a forecast has been made for *all* the *other* items in the balance sheet. This method does not give the **month end** by **month end cash position** that you will often need in the workplace, and may need to show in your assessment.

For example, if a firm increases its credit period offered, leading to an increase in debtors, and intends to purchase fixed assets, what will be its requirements for cash? Such plans express the company's or group's likely future balance sheet as a consequence of adopting certain strategies.

2.6 Rolling forecasts

A rolling forecast is a forecast that **is continually updated.** A rolling forecast can be a 12-month forecast which is updated at the end of every month, with a further month added to the end of the forecast period and with figures for the intervening 11 months revised if necessary.

2.7 Preparing a forecast

The cash flow forecast should be broken down into the **shortest time periods** for which reasonably accurate information can be assembled.

- For short-term cash forecasts of up to one month or so, **weekly periods** are appropriate.
- In the very short term, up to one week or so, **daily cash forecasts** may be requested.
- For longer-term cash forecasts, periods of **a month, a quarter or longer** will be suitable.
- The **more distant the time horizon** becomes, the **longer the time periods** in the forecast should be.

2.8 Obtaining information for forecasts

Procedures should be in place to ensure that the information required to prepare forecasts is available on time. Managers should be aware of **what information** they have to **supply** and for **what periods**. A **standard form** should be provided.

Guidance should be given about the **assumptions** that should be made for calculating sales and costs, and how to highlight unusual or non-recurring payments such as capital expenditure.

If you are preparing the budget you should ensure that managers appear to have **supplied** all the **relevant information** about their areas of responsibility, and have **followed instructions** about assumptions. The information should also be checked for **consistency** – are the sales forecasts consistent with the production forecasts for example.

3 Cash budgets in receipts and payments format

3.1 Preparing a cash budget

A **cash budget** (or **cash flow budget**) normally covers one year, and is divided into shorter time periods of a month or a quarter.

A simple cash budget might just be based on a **cashier's forecast** of **receipts and payments** for the future period.

In a more sophisticated accounting system, to prepare a cash budget you would take the budgets for:

- Sales
- Cost of sales
- Profit

and **convert** the **income and expenditure items** in these budgets into cash flows by allowing for credit periods, prepayments, accruals and so on.

Adjustments are then made for:

- **Cash flow items *not* appearing** in the profit and loss account (such as expenditure on fixed assets which will be obtained from the **capital budget**)
- **Items in the profit and loss account** which do not have a **cash effect** (eg depreciation)

For forecasting purposes, it is useful to **separate exceptional** or **occasional** cash flows from regular trading cash flows (eg wages).

The forecasting method can be either one or a combination of the following:

- **Identifying a cash flow**, and scheduling when it will be received or paid
- **Projecting trends and seasonal cycles** in business activity and cash flows
- **Analysing historical payment patterns** of regular repeat payments

A broad guideline to the preparation of a cash budget is shown below.

Steps in the preparation of a cash budget

Step 1. Sort out cash receipts from debtors.

- Establish budgeted sales month by month.
- Establish the credit period(s) taken by debtors.
- Using budgeted sales and credit periods, calculate when the budgeted sales revenue will be received as cash. Deduct any discount allowed for early payment.
- Establish when the outstanding debtors at the start of the budget period will pay.

Step 2. Establish whether any other cash income will be received, and when. Put these sundry items of cash receipts into the budget.

Step 3. Sort out cash payments to suppliers.

- Establish purchase quantities each month.
- Establish the credit period(s) taken from suppliers.
- Using purchase quantities and credit periods, calculate when the cash payments to suppliers will be made.
- Establish when the outstanding creditors at the start of the budget period will be paid.

Step 4. Establish other cash payments in the month.

These will include:

- Payments of wages and salaries
- Payments for sundry expenses
- Other one-off expenditures, such as fixed asset purchases, tax payments

Payments should be scheduled into the month when they will actually occur. Items of cost not involving cash payments (eg depreciation) must be excluded.

Step 5. Set out the cash budget month by month. A commonly used general layout is as follows.

Receipts	X
Less: Payments	(X)
Net cash flow in month	X
Opening cash balance	X or (X)
Closing cash balance	X or (X)

The closing cash balance in one month becomes the opening cash balance the next month.

3.2 Assumptions

You should make clear any assumptions over and above those you're told to make when you prepare a forecast.

You can derive the total amount of receipts and payments from other budgets, such as the company's operating budgets and capital expenditure budget. However for each item of cash inflows or outflows, you need to make assumptions about the **quantity** and **timing** of the flows.

3.3 Cash payment assumptions

Assumptions about payments can take account of:

- The **credit terms** given by suppliers, company policy on purchase orders and the administration of cheque payments, etc
- Any **specific supply arrangements**, such as a delivery once every two months, with payment for each delivery at the end of the following month
- **Past practice** (eg the proportion of invoices (by value) paid in the month of supply and invoice, the proportion paid in the month following, and so on)
- The **predictable dates** for certain payments, such as payments for rent, business rates, telephones, electricity and corporation tax

If in doubt, you should budget for **earlier payments**.

Some items of expenditure will be regarded as **fixed costs** in the operating budget. Salaries, office expenses and marketing expenditure are three such items.

- With some fixed costs, you can assume that there will be an **equal monthly expenditure** on each item
- You will pay **other fixed costs once a quarter**, and will need to take into consideration large fixed sums at these points, for example for rent.

PART A   CASH MANAGEMENT

3.4 Cash receipt assumptions

You may find it more difficult to make **assumptions about receipts** than assumptions about payments.

- With consumer sales by cash, credit and debit card, the major uncertainty will be **volume of sales**. The timing of receipts will be predictable (payment with sale).
- With a mix of cash and credit sales you must **estimate** the **proportion** of each in total sales, and then make assumptions about the **timing** of receipts from credit sales.

There are several ways of estimating when receipts will occur.

(a) If your company has **specific credit terms**, such as a requirement to pay within 15 days of the invoice date, you could make various assumptions.

Assumptions
• Invoices will be sent out at the time of sale
• A proportion, say 25%, will be paid within 15 days
• A proportion, say 65%, will be paid between 16 days and 30 days
• A proportion (say 9%) will pay in the month following
• There will be some bad debts (say 1%)

(b) If your company offers cash discounts for early payment, you should provide for the **discounts allowed** in the forecasts of receipts.

(c) You can estimate the **time customers take to pay** from **past experience**. You need to take care to allow for **seasonal variations** and the possibility that **payments** are **slower** at **some times** of the year than at others (for example, delays during holiday periods).

(d) **Calendar effects** may be important. You may assume that receipts are higher on some weekdays (such as Saturday) than others, and on some working days each month (such as the first week, just after customers have been paid their salaries at the end of the last month).

(e) **Payment patterns** can also **vary from one country to another**. Companies in some European countries, for example, will often take several months after the invoice date to pay amounts due.

As with payments, if you are in doubt you should be **prudent**. The consequences of over-optimism, unplanned cash shortages, could be serious.

3.5 Mark up and margins

Having estimated sales, you may estimate cost of sales by assuming that the normal margin or mark up applies. You should hopefully remember the difference between mark up and margin:

- **Mark up** is the profit element expressed as a fraction or percentage of **cost price.**
- **Margin** is the profit element expressed as a fraction or percentage of **selling price.**

Example: Mark up and margin

The selling price of product A is £20 and the cost of sales £15. The profit made on each sale is therefore £5. What is the mark up and margin on this product?

Solution

Mark up = 5/15 = 33.3%
Margin = 5/20 = 25%

3.6 Time periods and overdraft size

When you come to divide the forecast period into smaller time periods, these smaller periods should coincide as closely as possible with **significant cash flow events**, to provide management with information about the **high or low points for cash balances**. As well as predicting the **surplus or overdraft** at the end of the forecast period, the maximum overdraft *during* the forecast period should be predicted.

Example: Timing of cash flows

Megabuy Ltd is a large retail business. Purchases are sold at a **mark up** of (cost plus) $33^{1}/_{3}$%. (Or purchases are 75% of sales, (the **margin** is 25% of sales).)

(a)

	Budgeted sales £	Labour cost £	Expenses incurred £
January	40,000	3,000	4,000
February	60,000	3,000	6,000
March	160,000	5,000	7,000
April	120,000	4,000	7,000

(b) Sufficient stock is in hand at the end of each month to meet sales demand in the next half month.

(c) Creditors for materials and expenses are paid in the month after the purchases are made or the expenses incurred. Labour is paid in full by the end of each month. Expenses include a monthly depreciation charge of £2,000.

(d) 75% of sales are for cash and 25% of sales are on one month's interest-free credit.

(e) The company will buy equipment for cash costing £18,000 in February and will pay a dividend of £20,000 in March. The opening cash balance at 1 February is £1,000.

Tasks

(a) Prepare a profit and loss account for February and March.
(b) Prepare a cash budget for February and March.

Solution

(a) PROFIT AND LOSS ACCOUNT

	February		March		Total	
	£	£	£	£	£	£
Sales		60,000		160,000		220,000
Cost of purchases (75%)		45,000		120,000		165,000
Gross profit		15,000		40,000		55,000
Less: Labour	3,000		5,000		8,000	
Expenses	6,000		7,000		13,000	
		9,000		12,000		21,000
		6,000		28,000		34,000

(b) **Workings**

(i) *Receipts:*

			£
in February	75% of Feb sales (75% × £60,000)		45,000
	+ 25% of Jan sales (25% × £40,000)		10,000
			55,000

			£
in March	75% of Mar sales (75% × £160,000)		120,000
	+25% of Feb sales (25% × £60,000)		15,000
			135,000

(ii)

	Purchases in January		Purchases in February
	£		£
Purchases:			
For Jan sales (50% of £30,000)	15,000		
For Feb sales (50% of £45,000)	22,500	(50% of £45,000)	22,500
For Mar sales	–	(50% of £120,000)	60,000
	37,500		82,500

These purchases are paid for in February and March.

(iii) *Expenses*: cash expenses in January (£4,000 – £2,000) and February (£6,000 – £2,000) are paid for in February and March respectively. Depreciation is not a cash item.

CASH BUDGET

	February £	March £	Total £
Receipts from sales	55,000	135,000	190,000
Payments			
Trade creditors	37,500	82,500	120,000
Expenses creditors	2,000	4,000	6,000
Labour	3,000	5,000	8,000
Equipment purchase	18,000	–	18,000
Dividend	–	20,000	20,000
Total payments	60,500	111,500	172,000
Receipts less payments	(5,500)	23,500	18,000
Opening cash balance b/f	1,000	(4,500)*	1,000
Closing cash balance c/f (net cash flow)	(4,500)*	19,000	19,000

Notes

(a) The cash balance at the end of February is carried forward as the opening cash balance for March.

(b) The profit in February and March does mean that there is sufficient cash to operate the business as planned.

(c) Steps should be taken either to ensure that an overdraft facility is available for the cash shortage at the end of February, or to defer certain payments so that the overdraft is avoided.

3.7 Opening debtors and creditors

You may see a cash budget where you are required to **analyse an opening balance sheet** to decide how many outstanding debtors will pay what they owe in the first few months of the cash budget period, and how many outstanding creditors must be paid.

Example: Debtors and creditors

A balance sheet as at 31 December 20X4 shows that a company has the following debtors and creditors.

Debtors	£150,000
Trade creditors	£ 60,000

You are informed of the following.

(a) Debtors are allowed two months to pay.
(b) 1½ months' credit is taken from trade creditors.
(c) Sales and materials purchases were both made at an even monthly rate throughout 20X4.

Task

Determine in which months of 20X5 the debtors will eventually pay and the creditors will be paid.

PART A CASH MANAGEMENT

Solution

(a) Since debtors take two months to pay, the £150,000 of debtors in the balance sheet represent credit sales in November and December 20X4, who will pay in January and February 20X5 respectively.

Since sales in 20X4 were at an equal monthly rate, the cash budget should plan for receipts of £75,000 each month in January and February from the debtors in the opening balance sheet.

(b) Similarly, since creditors are paid after 1½ months, the balance sheet creditors will be paid in January and the first half of February 20X5, which means that budgeted payments will be as follows.

	£
In January (purchases in second half of November and first half of December 20X4)	40,000
In February (purchases in second half of December 20X4)	20,000
Total creditors in the balance sheet	60,000

(The balance sheet creditors of £60,000 represent 1½ months' purchases, so that purchases in 20X4 must be £40,000 per month, which is £20,000 per half month.)

Activity 2.2

A shop's stock increased from £5,000 to £6,000 during June 20X1. Its trade creditors increased from £10,000 to £12,000. What payment was made to suppliers if the cost of sales for the month was £40,000?

Activity 2.3

Sarhall Ltd has budgeted sales for June of £100,000, for July of £120,000, and for August of £80,000. 20% of sales are for cash and 80% are on credit. Of the credit sales, 60% are paid within 30 days and the balance is paid in 60 days. Bad debts amount to 1% of sales. What figure for receipts from debtors should be included in the cash flow forecast for August?

Example: A month-by-month cash budget in detail

Now you have some idea as to the underlying principles, let us put these to work. The following information relates to Stringham and Templer Ltd.

(a) The company's only product, an overcoat, sells at £40 and has a variable cost of £26 made up as follows.

Material £20   Labour £4   Variable overhead £2

(b) Fixed costs of £6,000 per month are paid on the 28th of each month.

(c) Quantities sold/to be sold on credit

May	June	July	Aug	Sept	Oct	Nov	Dec
1,000	1,200	1,400	1,600	1,800	2,000	2,200	2,600

(d) Production quantities

May	June	July	Aug	Sept	Oct	Nov	Dec
1,200	1,400	1,600	2,000	2,400	2,600	2,400	2,200

(e) Cash sales at a discount of 5% are expected to average 100 units a month.

(f) Customers are expected to settle their accounts by the end of the second month following sale.

(g) Suppliers of material are paid two months after the material is used in production.

(h) Wages are paid in the same month as they are incurred.

(i) 70% of the variable overhead is paid in the month of production, the remainder in the following month.

(j) Corporation tax of £18,000 is to be paid in October.

(k) A new delivery vehicle was bought in June, the cost of £8,000 is to be paid in August. The old vehicle was sold for £600, the buyer undertaking to pay in July.

(l) The company is expected to be £3,000 overdrawn at the bank at 30 June 20X5.

(m) The opening and closing stocks of raw materials, work in progress and finished goods are budgeted to be the same.

Task

Prepare a month by month cash budget for the second half of 20X5, and add such brief comments as you consider might be helpful to management.

PART A CASH MANAGEMENT

Solution

CASH BUDGET FOR 1 JULY TO 31 DECEMBER 20X5

	July £	Aug £	Sept £	Oct £	Nov £	Dec £	Total £
Receipts							
Credit sales	40,000	48,000	56,000	64,000	72,000	80,000	360,000
Cash sales	3,800	3,800	3,800	3,800	3,800	3,800	22,800
Sale of vehicles	600						600
	44,400	51,800	59,800	67,800	75,800	83,800	383,400
Payments							
Materials	24,000	28,000	32,000	40,000	48,000	52,000	224,000
Labour	6,400	8,000	9,600	10,400	9,600	8,800	52,800
Variable overhead (W1)	3,080	3,760	4,560	5,080	4,920	4,520	25,920
Fixed costs	6,000	6,000	6,000	6,000	6,000	6,000	36,000
Corporation tax				18,000			18,000
Purchase of vehicle		8,000					8,000
	39,480	53,760	52,160	79,480	68,520	71,320	364,720
Excess of receipts over payments	4,920	(1,960)	7,640	(11,680)	7,280	12,480	18,680
Balance b/f	(3,000)	1,920	(40)	7,600	(4,080)	3,200	(3,000)
Balance c/f	1,920	(40)	7,600	(4,080)	3,200	15,680	15,680

Working

Variable overhead

	June £	July £	Aug £	Sept £	Oct £	Nov £	Dec £
Variable overhead production cost	2,800	3,200	4,000	4,800	5,200	4,800	4,400
70% paid in month		2,240	2,800	3,360	3,640	3,360	3,080
30% in following month		840	960	1,200	1,440	1,560	1,440
		3,080	3,760	4,560	5,080	4,920	4,520

Comments

(a) There will be a **small overdraft** at the end of August but a much larger one at the end of October. It may be possible to **delay payments to suppliers** for longer than two months, **reduce purchases of materials** or reduce the volume of production by running down existing stock levels.

(b) If these courses are not possible, the company may need to **negotiate overdraft facilities** with its bank.

(c) The **cash deficit is only temporary** and by the end of December there will be a comfortable surplus. The use to which this cash will be put should ideally be planned in advance.

Activity 2.4

Tony Prince has worked for some years as a sales representative, but has recently been made redundant. He intends to start up in business on his own account, using £15,000 which he currently has invested with a building society. Tony maintains a bank account showing a small credit balance, and he plans to approach his bank for the necessary additional finance. Tony asks you for advice and provides the following additional information.

(a) Arrangements have been made to purchase fixed assets costing £8,000. These will be paid for at the end of September 20X6 and are expected to have a five-year life, at the end of which they will possess a nil residual value.

(b) Stocks costing £5,000 will be acquired on 28 September and subsequent monthly purchases will be at a level sufficient to replace forecast sales for the month.

(c) Forecast monthly sales are £3,000 for October, £6,000 for November and December, and £10,500 from January 20X7 onwards.

(d) Selling price is fixed at the cost of stock plus 50%.

(e) Two months' credit will be allowed to customers but only 1 month's credit will be received from suppliers of stock.

(f) Running expenses, including rent, are estimated at £1,600 per month.

(g) Tony intends to make monthly cash drawings of £1,000.

Task

Prepare a cash budget for the 6 months October 20X6 to March 20X7.

Activity 2.5

You are presented with the following budgeted data for your organisation for the period November 20X1 to June 20X2, which has been extracted from functional budgets that have already been prepared.

	Nov X1 £	Dec X1 £	Jan X2 £	Feb X2 £	Mar X2 £	Apr X2 £	May X2 £	June X2 £
Sales	80,000	100,000	110,000	130,000	140,000	150,000	160,000	180,000
Purchases	40,000	60,000	80,000	90,000	110,000	130,000	140,000	150,000
Wages	10,000	12,000	16,000	20,000	24,000	28,000	32,000	36,000
Overheads	10,000	10,000	15,000	15,000	15,000	20,000	20,000	20,000
Dividends		20,000						40,000
Capital expenditure			30,000			40,000		

Having consulted relevant staff, you have also been told the following.

(a) Sales are 40%, cash 60% credit. Credit sales are paid two months after the month of sale.
(b) Purchases are paid the month following purchase.

PART A CASH MANAGEMENT

(c) 75% of wages are paid in the current month and 25% the following month.
(d) Overheads are paid the month after they are incurred.
(e) Dividends are paid three months after they are declared.
(f) Capital expenditure is paid two months after it is incurred.
(g) The opening cash balance is £15,000.

The managing director is pleased with the above figures as they show sales will have increased by more than 100% in the period under review. In order to achieve this he has arranged a bank overdraft with a ceiling of £50,000 to accommodate the increased stock levels and wage bill for overtime worked.

Tasks

(a) Prepare a cash budget for the six month period January to June 20X2.

(b) Comment upon your results in the light of your managing director's comments and offer advice.

(c) If you have access to a computer spreadsheet package and you know how to use it, try setting up the cash budget on it. Then make a copy of the budget and try making changes to the estimates to see their effect on cash flow.

4 Cleared funds cash forecasts

4.1 Float

Float refers to the amount of money tied up between the time a payment is initiated and **cleared funds** become available in the recipient's bank account for immediate spending.

The figure shown on the advice slip when you check your cash balance in the bank's 'hole in the wall' machine is a historic figure. It does not reflect **receipts** you have paid into the bank over the last couple of days, or **cheques** you have issued in the same period.

- The existence of float means that there will always be a **difference** between a business's **cash position** as stated in the cash book of its accounts system and its **cleared funds**.

- A business needs to know, especially for short-term cash forecasts, what cleared funds will be because this is the amount that is **available immediately** to spend or invest.

- If **cleared funds** are **negative**, the bank will use the figure to **calculate overdraft interest**.

Knowing what **cleared funds** are likely to be has a direct and immediate relevance to cash management in the **short-term**. If a business expects to have insufficient cleared funds in the next few days, it must either **borrow funds** to **meet the obligation** or (if possible) **defer the payment**.

4.2 Cleared funds cash forecast

A **cleared funds cash forecast** is a short-term cash forecast of the cleared funds available to a business in its bank accounts, or of the funding deficit that must be met by **immediate borrowing**.

There should be relatively few items in a cleared funds forecast, and each forecast should generally relate to a **particular bank account**.

A cleared funds forecast can be prepared by a combination of three methods.

- **Obtaining information** from the business's **banks**
- **Forecasting** for **other receipts and payments** that have occurred but have not yet been lodged with a bank (You should be already familiar with bank reconciliations.)
- **Adapting the cash budget** by adjusting receipts and payments for float times

The amount of payments or receipts in the clearance system can be specified, so that the forecast shows:

- Cleared funds
- Clearance float
- Unused bank facilities

Businesses should review and update cleared funds forecasts regularly, **daily** for businesses with large and uncertain cash flows. Reviewing forecasts regularly should limit delays and hold-ups in banking or paying cheques.

Activity 2.6

Kim O'Hara runs an import/export retail business, largely on a cash basis. He likes to negotiate the best possible deals from his suppliers and this generally means a strict adherence to any payment terms so as to benefit from any settlement discounts: he also orders his supplies at the last possible moment, as he is a firm believer in a 'just-in-time' philosophy. On the other hand Creighton plc is a large software house, dealing with major clients. Which type of forecast would be most appropriate to each business?

5 Cash forecasts based on financial statements

5.1 Balance sheet-based forecasts

A balance sheet based forecast is an estimate of the company's balance sheet at a future date. It is used to identify either the **cash surplus** or the **funding shortfall** in the company's balance sheet at the forecast date.

A balance sheet estimate calls for some prediction of the amount/value of each item in the company's balance sheet, **excluding cash and short-term investments**, as these are what we are trying to predict.

You then combine the various estimates into a balance sheet. The figures on each side of the balance sheet will not be equal, and there will be one of the following.

- A **surplus of share capital and reserves** over **net assets** (total assets minus total creditors). If this occurs, the company will be forecasting a **cash surplus**.
- A **surplus of net assets** over **share capital and reserves**. If this occurs, the company will be forecasting a **funding deficit**.

5.1.1 Example of balance sheet-based forecast

Blakey Limited has an existing balance sheet and an estimated balance sheet in one year's time before necessary extra funding is taken into account. The summary is as follows.

	Existing £	Forecast after one year £
Total net assets	100,000	160,000
Share capital and reserves	100,000	120,000

The company is expecting to increase its net assets in the next year by £60,000 (£160,000 – £100,000) but expects retained profits for the year to be only £20,000.

There is an **excess of net assets** over **share capital and reserves** amounting to £40,000 (£160,000 – £120,000), which is a funding deficit.

The company must consider ways of obtaining extra cash (e.g. by borrowing) to cover the deficit. If it cannot, it will need to keep its assets below the forecast amount, or to have higher short-term creditors.

Balance sheet-based forecasts have **two main uses**:

- As **longer-term (strategic) estimates**, to assess the scale of funding requirements or cash surpluses the company expects over time and provisions for doubtful debts.
- As a **check** on the **realism** of **cash flow-based forecasts** (The estimated balance sheet should be **roughly** consistent with the net cash change in the cash budget)

5.2 Deriving cash flow from profit and loss account and balance sheet information

Alternatively you can derive a forecast figure for cash flows using both the balance sheet and profit and loss account.

- The profit before interest and tax is **adjusted** first of all for **items not involving cash**, such as depreciation.
- This is further adjusted for changes in the levels of working capital (e.g. debtors and creditors) to arrive at operational cash flows.

You will also do this when preparing a cash flow statement under FRS 1 (covered in Unit 11 *Drafting Financial Statements*).

Deriving cash flow information is examined in the example below, which is based on Activity 1.7 in Chapter 1. For the time being, assume that there is no depreciation to worry about. The task is to get from profit to operational cash flow, by taking into account movements in working capital.

		Profit £	Operational cash flow £
Sales		200,000	200,000
Opening debtors (∴ received in year)			15,000
Closing debtors (outstanding at year end)			(24,000)
Cash in			191,000
Cost of sales		170,000	170,000
Closing stock (purchased, but not used, in year)			21,000
Opening stock (used, but not purchased, in year)			(12,000)
Purchases in year			179,000
Opening creditors (∴ paid in year)			11,000
Closing creditors (outstanding at year end)			(14,000)
Cash out			176,000
Profit/operational cash flow		30,000	15,000

		£	£
Profit			30,000
(Increase)/Decrease in stocks	Opening	12,000	
	Closing	(21,000)	
			(9,000)
(Increase)/Decrease in debtors	Opening	15,000	
	Closing	(24,000)	
			(9,000)
Increase/(Decrease) in creditors	Closing	14,000	
	Opening	(11,000)	
			3,000
Operational cash flow			15,000

5.3 Uses of different forecasts

Both 'receipts and payments' forecasts and forecasts based on financial statements could be used alongside each other. The cash management section and the financial controller's section should **reconcile differences** between forecasts on a continuing basis, so that the forecast can be made more accurate as time goes on.

Activity 2.7

Write down an explanation of the difference between a cash flow based forecast and a balance sheet based forecast. What are the main advantages of each method and how are they complementary?

6 Control and corrective action

6.1 Cash flow control

A forecast is of no use unless businesses compare actual figures with the forecast so that corrective action can be taken. An objective of **cash flow control** is to **achieve net cash flows** or cash balances that **satisfy a target or budget**.

Why might a forecast differ from the actual flows?

- **Poor forecasting techniques**
- **Unpredictable events or developments**, for example loss of a major customer, insolvency of a major debtor, changes in interest rates, inflation affecting certain costs or revenues

6.2 Cash flow control reports

Managers with responsibility for cash receipts, payments and balances should receive cash flow reports regularly.

Control reports could be prepared for operational cash flows. The frequency, format and structure of a control report can suit management requirements, but the purpose of the report should be to compare either:

- **Actual cash flows** against a **budget** or target (as illustrated below)
- A **current forecast** of cash flows against an **original budget** or target

Reports could be discussed at monthly management meetings (or board meetings). Managers can be asked to explain **differences or variances** that exceed a certain control limit (perhaps a percentage of the budgeted cash flow figure).

Example: Cash flow control reports

In the example below, which figures do you think needed to be explained by the managers responsible?

CASH FLOW CONTROL REPORT

Alpha Language Schools: UK Division
Month: March
Currency: Sterling

	Month Budget £'000	Month Actual £'000	Month Difference £'000	Cumulative: year to date Budget £'000	Cumulative: year to date Actual £'000	Cumulative: year to date Difference £'000
Cash receipts						
Tuition	1,100	1,150	50	2,900	2,980	80
Books	70	25	(45)	210	155	(55)
Cassettes	340	355	15	650	692	42
Sale of fixed assets	0	24	24	30	24	(6)
Other income	15	7	(8)	45	44	(1)
	1,525	1,561	36	3,835	3,895	60
Cash payments						
Staff costs: teaching	390	496	106	1,000	1,270	270
Staff costs: management	250	248	(2)	650	624	(26)
Book purchases	60	32	(28)	155	81	(74)
Materials printing	25	28	3	65	62	(3)
Origination	15	19	4	40	35	(5)
Commissions	60	61	1	155	158	3
Advertising	85	113	28	210	275	65
Marketing expenses	72	69	(3)	185	170	(15)
Travel and entertaining	216	235	19	520	499	(21)
Equipment	60	72	12	150	144	(6)
Establishment	150	146	(4)	450	435	(15)
Office expenses	42	37	(5)	100	96	(4)
Other payments	30	24	(6)	75	72	(3)
	1,455	1,580	125	3,755	3,921	166
Net cash flow	70	(19)	(89)	80	(26)	(106)
Opening cash balance	22	5	–	12	12	–
Closing cash balance	92	(14)	(89)	92	(14)	(106)

Solution

The managers responsible could be asked to explain the high payments for teaching costs in March (£106,000 or 27% above the budget amount) and advertising (£28,000 or 33% above budget). The financial controller or director might be asked to comment on the division's borrowing limits, and whether these are now expected to be sufficient.

6.3 Quality control of cash flow forecasts

When actual results differ from budget, you might conclude that plans never work out in practice. However, as planning is a vital management activity, and if actual results differ from the plan, organisations should find out whether the **planning processes** can be improved.

Accuracy of cash flow forecasts can be enhanced by:

- **Reviewing actual cash flows** against the **forecasts**, learning from past mistakes
- **Updating rolling forecasts** or revised forecasts, where useful, to replace earlier, less reliable forecasts

A constant monthly amount for receipts and payments will often indicate either **sloppy cash forecasting practice**, or a **high degree of uncertainty** in the forecast. Specific receivables and payables rarely remain unchanged except where there is a formal arrangement.

6.4 Quality control of rolling forecasts

As a financial year progresses, the actual cash flows for the past months could show **large variances** from budget, but a **rolling forecast** indicates that the original budget for the end-of-year cash balance will still be achieved. This is likely to indicate that the rolling forecast has been prepared with little thought.

Unchanged figures over a number of months of revised forecast submissions are also an indication of a **weak forecasting system**. It could be that business expectations have not changed; however there are few businesses that do not fluctuate with market conditions.

6.5 Corrective action

Businesses can take various short and long-term measures to improve their cash position.

6.6 Short-term methods of easing cash shortages

6.6.1 Improving the business

Cash deficits can arise out of **basic trading factors** underlying the business such as **falling sales** or **increasing costs**. These items can be dealt with by taking normal business measures, rectifying the fall in sales by marketing activities or by cutting costs.

6.6.2 Controlling the operating cycle: short-term deficiencies

Cash deficits can also arise out of the business's management of the operating cycle and from timing differences.

- **Short-term borrowing** from the bank is only a temporary measure. The bank might convert an overdraft into a long-term loan, or perhaps agree to new overdraft limits.
- **Sale of short-term investments** could provide liquidity.

- **Raising share capital** is expensive and should be generally used for long-term investment, not short-term cash management.
- The **nature** and **timing** of **discretionary flows** such as dividends might alter.
- **Different sources of finance** (such as leasing) might alter.
- **Stock levels** could also **decrease** to reduce the amount of money that is 'tied up' in their production cost.
- The technique of **leading and lagging,** shortening the operating cycle by **obtaining money** from **debtors** as soon as possible and **taking as much trade credit** as possible, could be used.

Example: Leading and lagging

Assume that Widmerpool Ltd is a clothing wholesaler specialising in overcoats. Each overcoat costs £50 to make and is sold for £100. The bank has refused an overdraft to Widmerpool. Creditors are normally paid at the end of Month 1; the overcoats are sold on the 15th of Month 2. Payment is received on the first day of Month 4.

Under this system we have the following forecast.

	Inflows £	Outflows £	Balance £
Month 1 (end)	–	50	(50)
Month 2	–	–	(50)
Month 3 (end)	100	–	50

In other words the cash cycle means that the firm is in deficit for all of Months 2 and 3. As the bank has refused an overdraft, the creditors will not be paid.

Task

Explain how Widmerpool could improve its current situation, and describe the problems it might face in attempting to do so.

Solution

If Widmerpool can persuade its creditors to wait for two weeks until the 15th of Month 2 and offers a settlement discount of £5 to debtors to induce them to pay on the 15th of Month 2, the situation is transformed.

	Inflows £	Outflows £	Balance £
Month 1	–	–	–
Month 2	95	50	45
Month 3	–	–	45

In practice, it may not be that simple. A firm's debtors and creditors might be 'leading and lagging' themselves.

- Creditors can object to their customers taking extra credit; and Widmerpool may lose the advantage of trade discounts. Certain creditors have to be paid early, if they are powerful.
- Debtors might refuse to pay early, despite the inducement of a discount.

Despite the problems, it is worth keeping the bank happy even if the firm loses out on a few trade discounts in the process.

6.7 Long-term methods of easing cash shortages

Shortening the operating cycle is helpful in dealing with **short-term deficiencies** and saving interest costs, but it is not necessarily a long-term solution to a business's funding problems. A shorter operating cycle time will **reduce the amount of cash** that a business needs to invest in its operating activities.

Longer-term methods of improving a business's cash position include the following.

6.7.1 Postponing capital expenditure

Some capital expenditure items are more important and urgent than others. It might be imprudent to postpone expenditure on fixed assets which are needed for the **development and growth** of the business.

On the other hand, some capital expenditure is routine and might be postponed without serious consequences. The **routine replacement** of **motor vehicles** is an example. If a company's policy is to replace company cars every two years, but the company is facing a cash shortage, it might decide to replace cars every three years.

6.7.2 Changing terms of business with customers

If a business has a formal credit policy setting down terms with debtors, it may take a long-term decision to offer **tighter terms**, to accelerate cash inflows. (Leading and lagging can be thought of as a more short-term method of improving the timing of inflows.)

Often however this policy will result in a loss of goodwill and problems with customers. There will also be very little scope for speeding up payments when the credit period currently allowed to debtors is no more than the norm for the industry.

6.7.3 Reversing past investment decisions by selling assets previously acquired

Some assets are less crucial to a business than others. If cash flow problems are severe, a business may have to consider **selling investments or property.**

6.7.4 Negotiating a reduction in cash outflows, so as to postpone or reduce payments

There are several ways in which this could be done.

- **Long-term arrangements with suppliers** might be **re-negotiated.** If the credit period allowed is already generous, creditors might be very reluctant to extend credit even further.
- **Loan repayments** could be **rescheduled** by agreement with a bank.
- The directors may decide that a **company's dividend payments** should be reduced over the next few years. However directors might be constrained by shareholders' expectations.

6.8 Overtrading

Overtrading happens when a business **tries to do too much too quickly** with too little long-term capital. It is trying to support too large a volume of trade with the capital resources at its disposal.

Even if an overtrading business operates at a profit, it could easily run into serious trouble because it is **short of money**. Liquidity troubles stem from the fact that it does not have enough capital to provide the cash to pay its debts as they fall due.

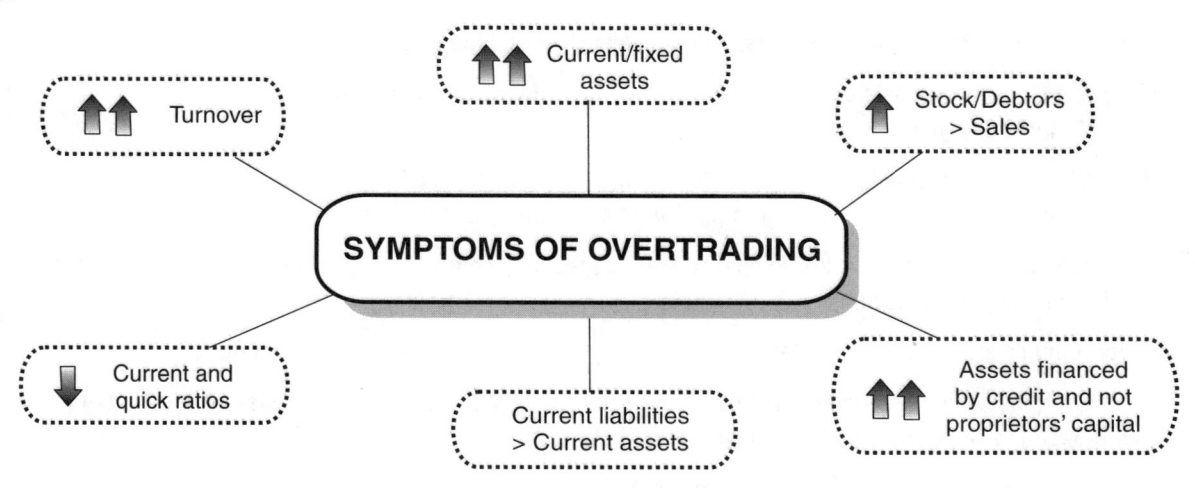

SYMPTOMS OF OVERTRADING

- ↑↑ Turnover
- ↑↑ Current/fixed assets
- ↑ Stock/Debtors > Sales
- ↓ Current and quick ratios
- Current liabilities > Current assets
- ↑↑ Assets financed by credit and not proprietors' capital

Suitable solutions to the problem would be measures to reduce the degree of overtrading. A business needs to take a long-term view of future prospects, and **avoid short-termism**.

- **New capital** from the shareholders could be injected.
- **Short-term finance** could be **converted** to longer-term finance.
- **Better control** could be applied to stocks and debtors.
- The business could **abandon ambitious plans** for increased sales and more fixed asset purchases until it has had time to build up its capital base with retained profits.

PART A   CASH MANAGEMENT

Key learning points

- ☑ **Cash forecasts** provide an early warning of liquidity problems and funding needs. **Banks** often expect business customers to provide a cash forecast as a condition of lending.

- ☑ One sort of cash forecast is a statement of **cash receipts and payments**, and **net cash flows (cash flow based forecasts)**.

- ☑ **Cash flow based forecasts** include **cash budgets and cleared funds forecasts for the short term**.

- ☑ Cash budgets and forecasts can be used for **control reporting**. Balance sheet based forecasts are used for long-term **strategic analysis.**

- ☑ A **cash budget** is a detailed forecast of cash receipts, payments and balances over a planning period. It is formally adopted as part of the business plan or master budget for the period.

- ☑ Cash budgets are prepared by taking **operational budgets** and converting them into forecasts as to when receipts and payments occur.

- ☑ **Cleared funds** are used for short-term planning. They take clearance delays into account.

- ☑ A cash surplus or funding requirement can also be prepared by constructing a **forecast balance sheet (balance sheet-based forecast),** or adjusting other financial statements.

- ☑ **Cash flow control reports** indicate differences between **expected** and **actual flows**, so that businesses can take action to improve their cash position if necessary.

- ☑ A business can alleviate cash problems in the short-term by **cost reduction, short-term borrowing, sale of short-term investments and reducing working capital levels**.

- ☑ Longer-term measures for alleviating cash problems include **postponing capital expenditure, rescheduling loan payments,** and changing the business's strategy to **increase selling and marketing activity.**

- ☑ Managers should review reports to see whether they are **misleading**, for example **assumptions are simplistic**, or reports are **not adjusted** for **changed circumstances**.

Quick quiz

1 A .... forecast is a forecast that is continually updated.

2 Why should the assumptions in a cash forecast be clearly stated?

3 List the steps in preparing a cash flow budget.

4 Operational cash flows of a business could be improved directly by:

- *Reducing/Increasing* debtors
- *Reducing/Increasing* stocks
- *Reducing/Increasing* the credit period for the company's trade creditors

Delete the word in italics that does not apply.

5 The 'float' is the time between (A) .... and (B) .... (Fill in the blanks)

6 Which of the following items is the most likely to cause 'float'?

    A   Cheque payments
    B   BACS payments
    C   Debit card payments
    D   Standing orders

7 The following items have been extracted from a company's budget for next month:

	£
Sales on credit	240,000
Expected increase in stock next month	20,000
Expected decrease in trade debtors next month	12,000

The budgeted receipt from trade debtors next month is £252,000.

☐ True

☐ False

8 The following items were extracted from a company's budget for next month:

	£
Purchases on credit	360,000
Expected decrease in stock over the month	12,000
Expected increase in trade creditors over the months	15,000

What is the budgeted payment to trade creditors for the month?

    A   £333,000
    B   £345,000
    C   £357,000
    D   £375,000

9 What is a balance sheet based forecast?

10 What is the purpose of a cash flow control report?

11 'Shortening the operating cycle by obtaining money from debtors as soon as possible, *and* taking as much trade credit from suppliers as possible.' What technique does this describe?

12 Heavy Metal Ltd is preparing its cash flow forecast for the next quarter. Which of the following items should be excluded from the calculations?

    A   The receipt of a bank loan that has been raised for the purpose of investment in a new rolling mill
    B   Depreciation of the new rolling mill
    C   A tax payment that relates to profits in a previous accounting period
    D   Disposal proceeds from the sale of the old mill

Answers to quick quiz

1 A **rolling** forecast is a forecast that is continually updated.

2 It allows the forecast to be tested for reasonableness.

3 Sort out cash receipts from debtors; cash income received; cash payments to suppliers; other cash payments; set out month by month cash budgets

4 The following words are those which you should *not* have deleted.

- *Reducing* debtors
- *Reducing* stocks
- *Increasing* credit period for the company's trade creditors

5 (A) Initiation of a payment
   (B) When cleared funds become available in the recipient's bank account

6 A Cheque payments

7 True. Receipt = Sales on credit − Change in trade debtors
             = 240,000 − (−12,000)
             = £252,000

Changes in stock were not relevant.

8 B Change in creditors = Purchases − Cash paid
     15,000   = 360,000 − Cash paid
     Cash paid = £345,000

9 An estimate of the balance sheet of the business at a future date

10 To help ensure that net cash flows or cash balances satisfy targets set by management

11 Leading and lagging

12 B Depreciation is a non-cash item and should therefore be excluded.

2: FORECASTING CASH FLOWS

Activity checklist

This checklist shows which performance criteria, range statement or knowledge and understanding point is covered by each activity in this chapter. Tick off each activity as you complete it.

Activity		
2.1	☐	This activity deals with Performance Criterion 15.1.E: identify significant deviations from the cash budget and take corrective action within defined organisational policies
2.2	☐	This activity deals with Performance Criterion 15.1.C: ensure forecasts of future cash payments and receipts are in accord with known income and expenditure trends
2.3	☐	This activity deals with Performance Criterion 15.1.C: ensure forecasts of future cash payments and receipts are in accord with known income and expenditure trends
2.4	☐	This activity deals with Performance Criterion 15.1.D: prepare cash budgets in the approved format and clearly indicate net cash requirements
2.5	☐	This activity deals with Performance Criterion 15.1.B: consult appropriate staff to determine the likely pattern of cash flows over the accounting period and to anticipate any exceptional receipts and payments
2.6	☐	This activity deals with Knowledge and Understanding 12: form and structure of cash budgets
2.7	☐	This activity deals with Knowledge and Understanding 12: form and structure of cash budgets

PART A CASH MANAGEMENT

chapter 3

Cash budgeting techniques

Contents

1. Introduction
2. Estimation problems
3. Moving averages and trend analysis
4. Inflation and cash budgeting
5. Sensitivity analysis and computer models

Performance criteria

15.1.C Ensure forecasts of future cash payments and receipts are in accord with known income and expenditure trends

15.1.E Identify significant deviations from the cash budget and take corrective action within defined organisational policies

Range statement

15.1.1 Cash flows to be monitored: regular revenue receipts and payments; capital receipts and payments; drawings or dividends and disbursements; exceptional receipts and payments

Knowledge and understanding

- The main types of cash receipts and payments: regular revenue receipts and payments; capital receipts and payments; drawings/dividends and disbursements; exceptional receipts and payments
- Form and structure of cash budgets
- Basic statistical techniques for estimating future trends: moving averages, allowance for inflation
- Computer models to assess the sensitivity of elements in the cash budget to change (eg price, wage rate changes)
- Understanding that the accounting systems of an organisation are affected by its organisational structure, its administrative systems and procedures and the nature of its business transactions
- Understanding that recording and accounting practices may vary in different parts of the organisation
- An understanding of the organisation's relevant policies and procedures

1 Introduction

This chapter covers a number of refinements to cash forecasts. You may have encountered **time series analysis** and **indexation for inflation** in your earlier studies. Even if you have, however, it is worth spending time revising these topics. Experience shows that they can cause problems in this unit.

A vital stage in preparing a cash budget is making assumptions about future receipts and payments. Because these are uncertain, or because businesses may wish to change their policies, you must understand the effect on the budget of variations from what you expected. **Sensitivity analysis** enables you to measure the effects of altering your assumptions. It is thus something that you will often be asked to do in practice, probably using a spreadsheet.

2 Estimation problems

2.1 Volatility of cash flows

Cash flow patterns vary between businesses and with time and circumstances.

- For some organisations, **operational cash flows** are **fairly stable**, subject to seasonal variations, with the organisation regularly generating surplus cash.
- Other organisations will have **much more volatile operational cash flows**, particularly if sales income is earned in irregular large amounts rather than in regular smaller amounts.

2.2 Uncertainty over time

One problem with forecasts is that the data used is **not** always **reliable**. Since the figures are compiled from estimates for the future, the accuracy of the final figures is uncertain. Cash forecasts will inevitably be **less accurate** in the **longer term**, because uncertainties grow over time.

Business planners can use various techniques to measure the degree of uncertainty in the forecast. These include the simple **'rule of thumb'** method of expressing a range of values from worst possible result to best possible result, with the best estimate lying somewhere in between.

3 Moving averages and trend analysis

3.1 Time series analysis

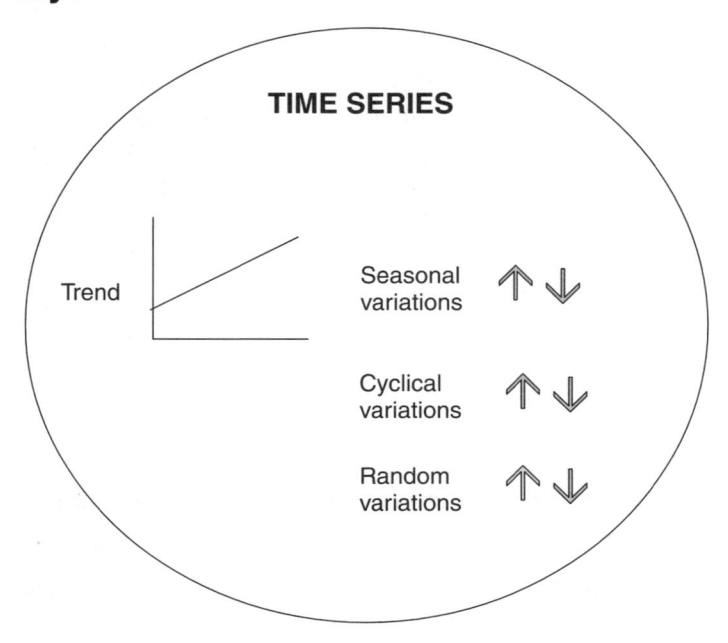

Time series analysis uses the past as a guide to the future. A **time series** is a series of figures or values recorded over time.

Examples of time series

- Output at a factory each day for the last month
- Monthly sales for the last two years
- Total annual costs for the last ten years
- The Retail Prices Index each month for the last ten years
- The number of people employed by a business each year for the last twenty years

3.2 The trend

The **trend** is the underlying long-term movement over time in the values of the data recorded.

Example: Trends

Identify the three types of trend in the following examples of time series.

	Output per labour hour Units	Cost per unit £	Number of employees
20X4	30	1.00	100
20X5	24	1.08	103
20X6	26	1.20	96
20X7	22	1.15	102
20X8	21	1.18	103
20X9	17	1.25	98
	(A)	(B)	(C)

Solution

In time series (A) there is a **downward trend** in the **output per labour hour**. Output per labour hour did go up between 20X5 and 20X6, but the long-term movement is clearly a downward one.

In time series (B) there is an **upward trend** in the **cost per unit**. Although unit costs went down in 20X7 from a higher level in 20X6, the basic movement over time is one of rising costs.

In time series (C) there is **no clear movement** up or down, and the number of employees remained fairly constant around 100. The trend is therefore a static, or level one.

3.3 Seasonal variations

Seasonal variations are **short-term fluctuations** in recorded values, due to circumstances which affect results at different times of the year, on different days of the week, at different times of day.

- Sales of ice cream will be higher in summer than in winter, and sales of overcoats will be higher in autumn than in spring.
- Shops might expect higher sales shortly before Christmas, or in their winter and summer sales.
- Sales might be higher on Friday and Saturday than on Monday.
- The telephone network may be heavily used at certain times of the day (such as mid-morning) and used less at other times (such as in the middle of the night).

In the example below, there are **seasonal fluctuations** in demand, but there is also a **basic upward trend**. The number of customers served by a company of travel agents over the past four years is shown in the following historigram. (**Historigram** is the name given to a graph of time series.)

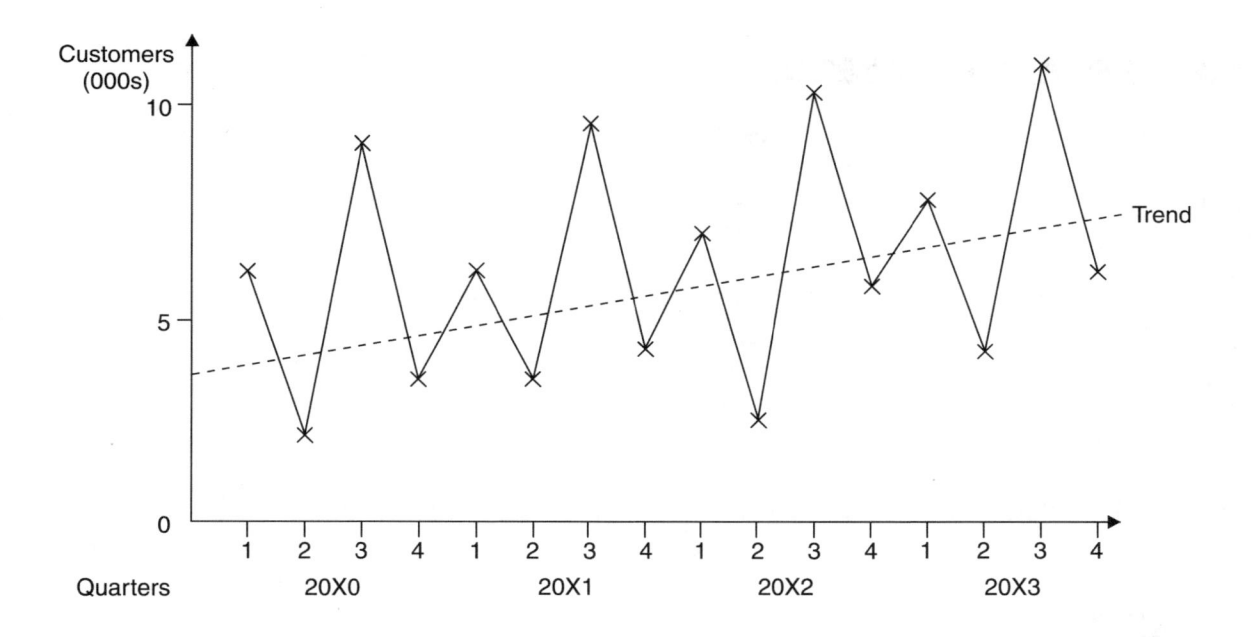

3.4 Cyclical variations

Cyclical variations are **medium-term changes in results** caused by circumstances which repeat in cycles. In business, cyclical variations are commonly associated with economic cycles, successive booms and slumps in the economy. **Economic cycles may last** a **few years**.

Cyclical variations are longer term than seasonal variations.

3.5 Finding the trend

Three methods can be used to **identify** the **trend and seasonal variations**.

Method	
Inspection	Trend line drawn by eye to lie evenly between recorded points
Regression analysis	Statistical technique to calculate trend line 'of best fit'
Moving averages	Removing seasonal or cyclical variations by averaging

3.5.1 Finding the trend by moving averages

A **moving average** is an average of the results of a fixed number of periods. Since a moving average is an average of several time periods, it relates to the mid-point of the overall period.

PART A   CASH MANAGEMENT

Example: Moving averages

Year	Sales Units
20X0	390
20X1	380
20X2	460
20X3	450
20X4	470
20X5	440
20X6	500

Task

Take a moving average of the annual sales over a period of three years.

Solution

Average sales in the **three year period 20X0 – 20X2** were:

$$\left(\frac{390 + 380 + 460}{3}\right) = \frac{1{,}230}{3} = 410$$

This average relates to the middle year of the period, 20X1.

Similarly, **average sales** in the **three year period 20X1 – 20X3** were:

$$\left(\frac{380 + 460 + 450}{3}\right) = \frac{1{,}290}{3} = 430$$

This average relates to the middle year of the period, 20X2.

The **average sales** can also be found for the periods 20X2-20X4, 20X3-20X5 and 20X4-20X6, to give the following.

Year	Sales	Moving total of 3 years sales	Moving average of 3 years sales (÷ 3)
20X0	390		
20X1	380	1,230	410
20X2	460	1,290	430
20X3	450	1,380	460
20X4	470	1,360	453
20X5	440	1,410	470
20X6	500		

The moving average series has five figures relating to the years from 20X1 to 20X5. The original series had seven figures for the years from 20X0 to 20X6.

There is an **upward trend** in sales, which is more noticeable from the series of moving averages than from the original series of actual sales each year.

This example averaged over a three-year period. In practice, the most appropriate moving average will depend on the **circumstances** and the **nature** of the time series.

(a) A moving average which takes an **average** of the **results** in **many time periods** will represent results over a longer term than a **moving average** of **two or three periods**.

(b) With a moving average of results in many time periods, the **last figure** in the series will be **out of date** by several periods. In our example, the most recent average related to 20X5. With a moving average of five years' results, the final figure in the series would relate to 20X4.

(c) When there is a **known cycle** over which seasonal variations occur, such as the days in the week or the seasons in the year, the best moving average would be one which covers one full cycle.

3.5.2 Moving averages of an even number of results

In the previous example, we took moving averages of the results in an **odd** number of time periods, and the average then related to the mid-point of the overall period.

If we take a moving average of results in an **even** number of time periods, the basic technique would be the same, but the mid-point of the overall period would not relate to a single period. For example, suppose an average were taken of the following four results.

Spring	120	
Summer	90	average 115
Autumn	180	
Winter	70	

The average would relate to the **mid-point** of the period, between summer and autumn.

The trend line average figures need to relate to a **particular time period,** so that seasonal variations can be calculated. To overcome this difficulty, we take a **moving average** of the moving average.

Example: Trend line – even number of periods

Calculate a four-quarter moving average trend line of the following results.

Year	Quarter	Volume of sales '000 units
20X5	1	600
	2	840
	3	420
	4	720
20X6	1	640
	2	860
	3	420
	4	740
20X7	1	670
	2	900
	3	430
	4	760

PART A   CASH MANAGEMENT

Solution

A **moving average of four** will be used, since the volume of sales would appear to depend on the season of the year, and each year has four quarterly results.

The moving average of four does not relate to any specific period of time; therefore a second moving average of two will be calculated on the first moving average trend line.

Year	Quarter	Actual volume of sales '000 units (A)	Moving total of 4 quarters' sales '000 units (B)	Moving average of 4 quarters' sales '000 units (B ÷ 4)	Mid-point of 2 moving averages Trend line '000 units (C)
20X5	1	600			
	2	840			
			2,580	645.0	
	3	420			650.00
			2,620	655.0	
	4	720			657.50
			2,640	660.0	
20X6	1	640			660.00
			2,640	660.0	
	2	860			662.50
			2,660	665.0	
	3	420			668.75
			2,690	672.5	
	4	740			677.50
			2,730	682.5	
20X7	1	670			683.75
			2,740	685.0	
	2	900			687.50
			2,760	690.0	
	3	430			
	4	760			

By taking a mid point (a moving average of two) of the original moving averages, we can relate the results to specific quarters (from the third quarter of 20X5 to the second quarter of 20X7).

3.6 Finding the seasonal variations

Once you have established a trend, you can find the seasonal variations. You can use one of two methods:

- **Additive** model
- **Multiplicative** model

3.6.1 Seasonal variations using the additive model

The example below shows how you can find the seasonal variations, using a technique known as the **additive model**.

Example: The trend and seasonal variations

Output at a factory appears to vary with the day of the week. Output over the last three weeks has been as follows.

	Week 1 '000 units	Week 2 '000 units	Week 3 '000 units
Monday	80	82	84
Tuesday	104	110	116
Wednesday	94	97	100
Thursday	120	125	130
Friday	62	64	66

The trend line calculated from this output is given by the formula $y = 92.7 + 0.42x$. This shows that, in a historigram of given output, the trend line begins at 92.7 on the y axis and increases by 0.42 for each day of output. The resultant trend is a straight line.

Task

Find the seasonal variation for each of the 15 days, and the average seasonal variation for each day of the week.

Solution

The regression line indicates an **upward trend** in daily output. Actual results fluctuate up and down according to the day of the week.

The **difference** between the **actual result** on any one day and the **trend figure** for that day will be the **seasonal variation** for the day.

The **trend figures** themselves are found simply by putting the **day numbers** (0 to 14) as values of x in the equation $y = 92.7 + 0.42x$.

The seasonal variations for the 15 days are as follows.

PART A CASH MANAGEMENT

		Actual	Trend	Seasonal variation
Week 1	Monday	80	92.70	− 12.70
	Tuesday	104	93.12	+ 10.88
	Wednesday	94	93.54	+ 0.46
	Thursday	120	93.96	+ 26.04
	Friday	62	94.38	− 32.38
Week 2	Monday	82	94.80	− 12.80
	Tuesday	110	95.22	+ 14.78
	Wednesday	97	95.64	+ 1.36
	Thursday	125	96.06	+ 28.94
	Friday	64	96.48	− 32.48
Week 3	Monday	84	96.90	− 12.90
	Tuesday	116	97.32	+ 18.68
	Wednesday	100	97.74	+ 2.26
	Thursday	130	98.16	+ 31.84
	Friday	66	98.58	− 32.58

The variation between the **actual results** on any one particular day and the **trend line average** is not the same from week to week, but an average of these variations can be taken.

	Monday	Tuesday	Wednesday	Thursday	Friday
Week 1	− 12.70	+ 10.88	+ 0.46	+ 26.04	− 32.38
Week 2	− 12.80	+ 14.78	+ 1.36	+ 28.94	− 32.48
Week 3	− 12.90	+ 18.68	+ 2.26	+ 31.84	− 32.58
Total	− 38.40	+ 44.34	+ 4.08	+ 86.82	97.44
Average	− 12.80	+ 14.78	+ 1.36	+ 28.94	− 32.48

Our estimate of the **'seasonal' or daily variation** is almost complete, but there is one more important step to take.

Variations around the basic trend line should cancel each other out, and add up to 0. At the moment, they do not. We therefore **spread** the **total of the daily variations** (−0.2) across the five days (0.2 ÷ 5) so that the **final total** of the **daily variations** goes to **zero**.

	Monday	Tuesday	Wednesday	Thursday	Friday	Total
Estimated daily variation	− 12.80	+ 14.78	+ 1.36	+ 28.94	− 32.48	− 0.2
Adjustment to reduce total variation to 0	+ 0.04	+ 0.04	+ 0.04	+ 0.04	+ 0.04	+ 0.2
Final estimate of daily variation	− 12.76	+ 14.82	+ 1.40	+ 28.98	− 32.44	0.0

These might be rounded up or down as follows.

Monday −13; Tuesday +15; Wednesday +1; Thursday +29; Friday −32; Total 0.

3.6.2 Seasonal variations using the multiplicative model

An alternative technique to the additive model is the **multiplicative model** (or **proportional model**) where each figure is expressed as a **percentage of the trend**.

> **LINK TO UNIT 9**
>
> Time series analysis is based on the following elements
>
> Y = the actual time series
> T = the trend series
> S = the seasonal component
> C = the cyclical component
> I = the random non-recurring component
>
> Ignoring the longer-term cyclical component the **additive** model expresses a time series as
>
> Y = T + S + I
>
> The **multiplicative** (proportional) model expresses a time series as
>
> Y = T × S × I
>
> Further details are given in the BPP Study Text for Units 8/9 *Managing Costs and Allocating Resources*.

The above example can be reworked on the basis of the multiplicative model. Each actual figure is expressed as a percentage of the trend.

		Actual	Trend	Seasonal percentage
Week 1	Monday	80	92.70	86.3
	Tuesday	104	93.12	111.7
	Wednesday	94	93.54	100.5
	Thursday	120	93.96	127.7
	Friday	62	94.38	65.7
Week 2	Monday	82	94.80	86.5
	Tuesday	110	95.22	115.5
	Wednesday	97	95.64	101.4
	Thursday	125	96.06	130.1
	Friday	64	96.48	66.3
Week 3	Monday	84	96.90	86.7
	Tuesday	116	97.32	119.2
	Wednesday	100	97.74	102.3
	Thursday	130	98.16	132.4
	Friday	66	98.58	67.0

The summary of the seasonal variations expressed in proportional terms is as follows.

	Monday %	Tuesday %	Wednesday %	Thursday %	Friday %
Week 1	86.3	111.7	100.5	127.7	65.7
Week 2	86.5	115.5	101.4	130.1	66.3
Week 3	86.7	119.2	102.3	132.4	67.0
Total	259.5	346.4	304.2	390.2	199.0
Average	86.5	115.5	101.4	130.1	66.3

PART A CASH MANAGEMENT

Instead of summing to zero, as with the absolute approach, these should sum (in this case) to 500 (an average of 100%).

They actually sum to 499.8 so 0.04% has to be added to each one. This is too small to make a difference to figures rounded to one decimal place, so we should add 0.1% to each of two seasonal variations.

3.6.3 Comparison of additive and multiplicative model

The multiplicative model is better than the additive model where the trend is increasing or decreasing over time. In this case, the actual variations will tend to increase (or decrease) so absolute seasonal adjustments will become out of date, unlike percentage adjustments.

Activity 3.1

Clare, the finance director of Crisroe Ltd, has become concerned about how the output of one of the company's factories has varied according to the day of the week. She has analysed output over the last three weeks.

	Week 1 Units	Week 2 Units	Week 3 Units
Monday	560	574	588
Tuesday	840	875	910
Wednesday	728	770	812
Thursday	658	679	700
Friday	434	448	462

Clare has used regression analysis to calculate a trend line for output of:

$y = 2.94x + 648.9$

Task

Find the seasonal variation for each of the fifteen days, and the average seasonal variation for the week using:

(a) The additive model
(b) The multiplicative model

Assume Monday of the first week is 0, Friday of the third week is 14.

3.7 Forecasting

Businesses can use time series analysis to forecast cash or other transactions, not by removing seasonal data, but by **adding it back** in.

Extending a trend line outside the range of known data, in this case forecasting the future from a trend line based on historical data, is known as **extrapolation**. The technique involves extrapolating a trend and then adjusting for seasonal variations:

Step 1   Calculate average increases in **trend line values**.

Step 2   Use the **trend line** to **forecast future trend line values**.

Step 3   **Adjust these values** by the **average seasonal variation** applicable to the future period, to determine the forecast for that period. With the additive model, add (or subtract for negative variations) the variation. With the multiplicative model, multiply the trend value by the variation proportion.

Example: Forecasting

Sales of product X each quarter for the last three years have been as follows (in thousands of units). Trend values, found by a moving averages method, are shown in brackets.

Year	1st quarter	2nd quarter	3rd quarter	4th quarter
1	18	30	20 (18.75)	6 (19.375)
2	20 (20)	33 (20.5)	22 (21)	8 (21.5)
3	22 (22.125)	35 (22.75)	25	10

Average seasonal variations for quarters 1 to 4 are –0.1, +12.4, +1.1 and –13.4 respectively.

Task

Use the trend line and estimates of seasonal variations to forecast sales in each quarter of year 4.

Solution

Step 1. Calculate average increase in trend line value

The trend line indicates an increase of about 0.6 per quarter. This can be confirmed by calculating the average quarterly increase in trend line values between the third quarter of year 1 (18.75) and the second quarter of year 3 (22.75). The average rise is:

$$\frac{22.75 - 18.75}{7} = \frac{4}{7} = 0.57, \text{ say } 0.6$$

Although there are eight trend figures, there are only seven increases so the total increase has been divided by seven.

Step 2. Use the trend line to forecast future trend line values

Taking 0.6 as the quarterly increase in the trend, the forecast of sales for year 4, before seasonal adjustments (the trend line forecast), would be as follows.

Year	Quarter			Trend line	
3	*2nd	(actual trend)	22.75, say	22.8	* last known trend line value.
	3rd			23.4	
	4th			24.0	
4	1st			24.6	
	2nd			25.2	
	3rd			25.8	
	4th			26.4	

PART A   CASH MANAGEMENT

Step 3. Incorporate seasonal variations to obtain final forecast

	Quarter	Trend line forecast '000 units	Average seasonal variation '000 units	Forecast of actual sales '000 units
Year 4	1st	24.6	–0.1	24.5
	2nd	25.2	+12.4	37.6
	3rd	25.8	+1.1	26.9
	4th	26.4	–13.4	13.0

If we had been using the multiplicative model, with an average variation for quarter 3 of, say, 105.7%, our prediction for the third quarter of year 4 would have been 25.8 × 105.7% = 27.3.

3.7.1 Problems with forecasts

All forecasts are subject to error, but the likely errors vary from case to case.

- The **further** we forecast into **the future**, the more unreliable it is likely to be.
- The **less data available** on which to base the forecast, the less reliable the forecast will be.
- The **pattern** of trend and seasonal variations **may not continue** in the future.
- **Random variations** might upset the pattern of trend and seasonal variation.

3.7.2 Residuals

Residual = Predicted results – Actual results

where predicted results are **results** which would have been **predicted** by the trend line adjusted for the average seasonal variation.

The residual is the difference which is *not* explained by the trend line and the seasonal average variation. The residual gives some indication of how much **actual results** were **affected** by **other factors**. Large residuals suggest that any forecast is likely to be unreliable.

In the example above the 'prediction' for the third quarter of year 1 would have been 18.75 + 1.1 = 19.85. As the actual value was 20, the residual was only 20 – 19.85 = 0.15. The residual for the fourth quarter of year 2 was 8 – (21.5 – 13.4) = 8 – 8.1 = –0.1

3.8 Trend analysis in cash forecasting

Businesses can use trend analysis to predict their **overall level of activity**, and can therefore derive their **cash requirements**. **Seasonal factors** giving rise to peaks or troughs (eg in raw materials or commodity prices) can be introduced to the forecast model over a period.

Activity 3.2

The quarterly sales of a division of Sarhall Ltd in recent years have been as follows.

Quarter	1 Units	2 Units	3 Units	4 Units
20X2	200	110	320	240
20X3	214	118	334	260
20X4	220	124	340	278

Tasks

(a) Calculate a moving average of quarterly sales.

(b) Calculate the average seasonal variations.

(c) Using the results of (a) and (b) and the three step process in para 3.7, predict the sales in the third quarter of 20X5.

4 Inflation and cash budgeting

4.1 Effects of inflation

If a business achieves an increase in sales of 10% in monetary (cash) terms over a year, this result becomes less impressive if we know that there was general price inflation of 15% over the year. The business is now **selling less** at the new higher prices.

Other consequences of inflation include the **value of financial assets**, such as debt, **declining**.

- Companies will try and **collect their debts** even **more quickly**, so that the cash can be reinvested.
- Delaying payments to creditors **reduces** the **underlying value** of the debt.
- A company's forecasts become **out of date** very quickly.
- Interest rates might be **very high**, in the short term, and so a treasurer will invest cash on short-term deposit.

4.2 Indices

An **index** is a measure, over a period of time, of the average **changes** in the values (prices or quantities) of a group of items.

An index may be a **price index** or a **quantity index**.

- A **price index** measures the change in the money value of a group of items over a period of time.

- A **quantity index** measures the change in the non-monetary values of a group of items over a period of time, for example a productivity index.

For the purpose of **internal management reporting**, results recorded over a number of periods can be adjusted using an appropriate price index to convert the figures from money to 'real' terms. One well-known index is the UK's **Retail Prices Index**, which measures changes in the costs of items of expenditure in the average household.

4.3 The base period, or base year

Index numbers are normally expressed as percentages, taking the value for a **base date** as 100. The base date or base year should normally be '**representative**', that is not one in which there were abnormally high or low prices for any items in the 'basket of goods' making up the index.

Example: Calculation of an index

Suppose sales for a company over the last five years were as follows.

Year	Sales (£'000)
20X5	35
20X6	42
20X7	40
20X8	45
20X9	50

The managing director decided that he wanted to set up a sales index (i.e. an index which measures how sales have done from year to year), using 20X5 as the base year. The £35,000 of sales in 20X5 is given the index 100%. What are the indices for the other years?

Solution

If £35,000 = 100%, then:

20X6   £42,000 = $\frac{42,000}{35,000} \times 100\% = 120\%$

The same calculation can be applied to other figures, and the table showing sales for the last five years can be completed, taking 20X5 as the base year.

Year	Sales (£'000)	Index
20X5	35	100
20X6	42	120
20X7	40	114
20X8	45	129
20X9	50	143

4.4 Indices of more than one item

In practice, indices generally consist of **more than one item**. For example, suppose that the cost of living index is calculated from only three commodities: bread, tea and caviar, and that the prices for 20X1 and 20X5 were as follows.

	20X1	20X5
Bread	20p a loaf	40p a loaf
Tea	25p a packet	30p a packet
Caviar	450p an ounce	405p an ounce

The prices above are in different units, and there is no indication of the **relative importance** of each item. In formulating index numbers, these aspects can be overcome by using **weighting**. To determine the weighting, we need information about the **relative importance** of each item, such as the price × quantity consumed in the base month.

Example: Weighted index

A company wishes to construct a price index for three commodities, A, B and C. The prices in March (the base period) were £2, £3 and £5 respectively and quantities consumed in the same period were 5,000, 6,000 and 3,000 respectively. The prices of the items in April and May were as follows.

	April	May
	£	£
A	2.00	2.20
B	3.24	3.45
C	4.50	5.00

Using the amount spent on an item in March as that item's weighting, construct a price index for April and May.

Guidance notes

1. Begin by calculating a price relative for each item in each month. A price relative is the price of the item in April (or May) as a percentage of its price in March.
2. Calculate the weightings (price in March × quantity consumed in March).
3. For each month, multiply each item's weighting by the price relative and add the result.
4. Calculate the April and May index numbers by dividing the April and May totals by the March total.

Solution

Step 1

Price relative for each item in April and May (price in month as a percentage of the base month price)

	April	May
A	100 (£2/£2 × 100%)	110 (£2.20/£2)
B	108 (£3.24/£3 × 100%)	115 (£3.45/£3)
C	90 (£4.50/£5 × 100%)	100 (£5/£5 × 100%)

PART A CASH MANAGEMENT

Step 2

Weightings for each item (price in March × quantity consumed in March)

				Weight
A	£2 × 5,000	=	£10,000	10
B	£3 × 6,000	=	£18,000	18
C	£5 × 3,000	=	£15,000	15

Use 10, 18 and 15 as weights.

Step 3

Construct price indices (weighting × prices relative. Then total)

	Price relative × weight			
Period	A	B	C	Total
March	1,000	1,800	1,500	= 4,300
April	1,000 (10 × 100)	1,944 (18 × 108)	1,350 (15 × 90)	= 4,294
May	1,100 (10 × 100)	2,070 (18 × 115)	1,500 (15 × 100)	= 4,670

Price index for April = $\frac{4,294}{4,300} \times 100 = 99.9$

Price index for May = $\frac{4,670}{4,300} \times 100 = 108.6$

4.5 The use of index numbers in cash forecasting and budgeting

How are index numbers useful in **cash budgeting and forecasting**? If you're preparing a cash budget you may not be particularly interested in prices in 'real terms'. Instead you will be interested in the **exact monetary amount**.

Index numbers are still useful, however.

- You can use index numbers to **predict future cash inflows**. For example, if 500,000 units will be sold in three or four months time, an estimate of future monetary prices gives some idea of the amount of sales **in cash**.

- Similarly, with cash outflows, an **estimated future price index** can suggest the likely size of cash payments.

Different items, such as capital items, costs of various kinds, and revenues, are likely to be subject to differing rates of inflation, and **different indices** may therefore be appropriate for different items.

Activity 3.3

You are assisting with the work on the maintenance department's budget for the next quarter of 20X4. The maintenance department's budget for the current quarter (just ending) is £200,000.

	Quantity used in current quarter	Average price payable per unit	
		Current quarter	Next quarter
	Units	£	£
Material A	9	10.00	10.20
Material B	13	12.00	12.50
Material C	8	9.00	9.00
Material D	20	25.00	26.00

A base weighted index for the next quarter stands at 103.5, compared to 100 for this quarter, for the price of input quantities.

Tasks

(a) Estimate the budget for the next quarter, assuming that the quantities of each material to be used:

    (i) Remain the same
    (ii) Increase by 10%

(b) Give reasons why your budget estimate could be in error.

5 Sensitivity analysis and computer models

5.1 Sensitivity analysis

Sensitivity analysis is a method commonly used in planning, especially by companies using a **spreadsheet model** or other **financial modelling package**. Sensitivity analysis tests the **'responsiveness'** of profitability or cash flow to changes in one of the budget variables.

For example, it would be possible to test the cash budget for:

- An unforeseen 10% rise in material costs
- An unforeseen 5% drop in productivity
- A shortfall in sales volumes of, say, 10%
- A labour strike of, say, one month
- A delay of six months in opening a new plant or operation

Example: Sensitivity analysis

Julatkins Ltd recently set up a new operation and prepared a cash budget. As with many start-ups, initial expenditures were expected to be high in comparison with first year revenues. The company's budget year ended on 31 March and the operation was planned to commence on 1 June of the previous year. Selling to customers would not begin until 1 September. Revenue was forecast at £2 million for the period to 31 March.

The initial cash budget, illustrated below, indicated a maximum deficit of about £750,000–£800,000 in September and October. The main areas of uncertainty were

PART A CASH MANAGEMENT

- Sales revenue
- One major item of production cost
- Marketing costs

Original cash budget	Jun £'000	Jul £'000	Aug £'000	Sept £'000	Oct £'000	Nov £'000	Dec £'000	Total £'000
Sales	0	0	160	210	280	360	490	1,500
Total inflows	0	0	160	210	280	360	490	1,500
Set-up costs	120	20	0	0	0	0	0	140
Production	100	100	100	100	100	100	100	700
Distribution	0	0	20	20	20	20	20	100
Marketing and advertising	0	150	150	75	75	75	75	600
Staff costs	10	20	24	24	24	24	24	150
General overheads	6	14	16	16	16	16	16	100
Accommodation	0	25	0	0	25	0	0	50
Capital equipment	30	0	0	10	0	0	0	40
Total outflows	266	329	310	245	260	235	235	1,880
Net inflow/(outflow)	(266)	(329)	(150)	(35)	20	125	255	(380)
Cumulative cash flow	(266)	(595)	(745)	(780)	(760)	(635)	(380)	(380)

Management was aware that lower than anticipated revenues, and excessive production costs, would possibly create a bigger cash deficit than the company could afford. Management believed, however, that controls over marketing expenditure would ensure that such costs should not exceed budget.

Task

Using the original cash budget, make the following changes to assumptions and produce a revised forecast:

- Reduce estimated sales revenue by 25%
- Increase production costs increased by 50%.

Solution

Revised cash budget	Jun £'000	Jul £'000	Aug £'000	Sept £'000	Oct £'000	Nov £'000	Dec £'000	Total £'000
Sales	0	0	120	158	210	270	367	1,125
Total inflows	0	0	120	158	210	270	367	1,125
Set-up costs	120	20	0	0	0	0	0	140
Production	150	150	150	150	150	150	150	1,050
Distribution	0	0	20	20	20	20	20	100
Marktg & advertising	0	150	150	75	75	75	75	600
Staff costs	10	20	24	24	24	24	24	150
General overheads	6	14	16	16	16	16	16	100
Accommodation	0	25	0	0	25	0	0	50
Capital equipment	30	0	0	10	0	0	0	40
Total outflows	316	379	360	295	310	285	285	2,230
Net inflow/(outflow)	(316)	(379)	(240)	(137)	(100)	(15)	82	(1,105)
Cumulative cash flow	(316)	(695)	(935)	(1,072)	(1,172)	(1,187)	(1,105)	(1,105)

5.2 Spreadsheets

You should be familiar with spreadsheets already. We provide below an example of how a spreadsheet can be used in cash budgeting and forecasting.

Example: Preparing a cash flow projection

A loan officer of a bank advising a small company wishes to assess the company's cash flow using a spreadsheet model. The cash flow projection is to provide a monthly cash flow analysis over a 5 year period. The following data is relevant.

(a) On 1 January 20X4 the company expects to have £15,000 in the bank. Sales in January are expected to be £25,000, and a growth rate of 1.25% per month in sales is predicted throughout the forecast period.

(b) The company buys stock one month in advance and pays in cash. All sales are on credit. There are no bad debts.

(c) On average, payment is received from customers as follows.
- 60% is one month in arrears
- 40% is two months in arrears

(d) The cost of sales is 65% of sales value. Overhead costs (cash expenses) are expected to be £6,500 per month, rising by 5% at the start of each new calendar year.

(e) Purchases of capital equipment and payments of tax, interest charges and dividends must also be provided for within the model. The loans officer has advised the company that the interest rate on bank overdrafts is expected to be 1.695% per month.

PART A — CASH MANAGEMENT

The loans officer has decided to label the spreadsheet rows and columns as follows.

	A	B	C	D	E	F
1:		20X4				
2:		Jan	Feb	March	April	May
3:		£	£	£	£	£
4:	Sales					
5:	Cash receipts:					
6:	One months in arrears					
7:	Two months in arrears					
8:	Three months in arrears					
9:	Total receipts					
10:						
11:	Cash payments:					
12:	Stock					
13:	Overheads					
14:	Interest					
15:	Tax					
16:	Dividends					
17:	Capital purchases					
18:	Total payments					
19:						
20:	Cash receipts less payments					
21:	Balance b/f					
22:	Balance c/f					

Task

Your task is to construct the formulae necessary.

Solution

The formulae can be constructed in a variety of ways. One way would be to insert some 'constant' values into cells of the spreadsheet and then cross-refer each formula to these constants, or absolutes.

Row	Column A	B
23:	Sales growth factor per month	1.0125
24:	Interest rate per month	0.01695
25:	Debts paid within 1 month	0.6
26:	Debts paid within 2 months	0.4
27:	Debts paid within 3 months	0
28:	Bad debts	0
29:	Cost of sales as proportion of sales	0.65

Alternatively, these values could be specified in the formulae in the spreadsheet. The advantage of setting up key data like this separately is that in the event of a change in interest rates, only one figure needs to be changed and there is no need for a search through the spreadsheet for relevant formulae.

Examples of constructing formulae for the spreadsheet are as follows.

- The formulae for sales in February 20X4, in this example, would be (+B4 * B23), in March 20X1 (+C4 * B23), in April 20X4 (+D4 * B23) etc. Replication of the formula could be used to save input time.

- The formula for cash receipts in April 20X4 would be:

    E6 = D4 * B25
    E7 = C4 * B26
    E8 = B4 * B27
    E9 = + E6 + E7 + E8

- Cash payments for stock would be expressed as the cost of sales in the next month; for February 20X4, the formula in cell C12 would be:

    + D4 * D29

- Total cash payments in May 20X4 would be the sum of cells F12 to F17, i.e. the formula in cell F18 would be:

    @ SUM (F12..F17)

    and so on.

- Input data would include:

    (i)   The opening cash balance on 1 January 20X4
    (ii)   Dividend and tax payments
    (iii)   Capital purchases
    (iv)   Sales in January 20X4
    (v)   The constant values (in our example in column B, rows 23 to 29)
    (vi)   The other data establishing movements in the first month

With this input data, and the spreadsheet formulae, a full cash flow projection for the five year period can be produced and, if required, printed out.

Activity 3.4

Whenever a forecast or budget is made, management should consider asking 'what if' questions, and so carry out a form of sensitivity analysis. Using the example above, how would you take account of the following changed assumptions? Describe what amendments would need to be made to the contents of individual cells.

(a) What if the payment pattern from debtors is:

    1 month in arrears   40%
    2 months in arrears   50%
    3 months in arrears   10%?

(b) What if sales growth is only ½% per month?

ATTENTION!

If you require practice in spreadsheet construction and use, practical, hands-on examples are available in the BPP Publication *Excel Exercises for Technician*. The book is accompanied by a CD containing Excel spreadsheets.

Note that *Excel Exercises for Technician* assumes you already have basic Excel skills (to AAT Foundation Level).

PART A   CASH MANAGEMENT

Key learning points

- **Cash flow patterns** vary between businesses and with time and circumstances. Management should minimise volatility, to avoid over-stretching borrowing requirements.
- **Time series analysis** is used to analyse trends, seasonal and cyclical patterns and so help predict the future results of the business.
- Trends can be found by **inspection**, **regression analysis** or a **moving average**. A **moving average** is based on a group of periods, updated over time.
- **Seasonal patterns** can vary with the time of a quarter, month, day etc. **Cyclical variations** are longer term changes.
- Time series analysis can be used for forecasting in a three step approach.
- Step 1: **Calculate average increase** in **trend line values**.
- Step 2: **Use trend line** to **forecast future trend line values.**
- Step 3: **Adjust future trend values** by **average seasonal variation**.
- An **index** is a measure over a period of time of the **average changes in prices** of items or a group of items.
- **Indices** can be used in cash forecasts to **predict future cash flows**.
- **Sensitivity analysis** tests the results of a forecast to see how sensitive the results are to changes in inputs (eg lower or higher interest rates). **Spreadsheet modelling** is used for this purpose.

Quick quiz

1   Give three examples of time series.

    1 ....

    2 ....

    3 ....

2   What are seasonal variations?

3   What are the three steps involved in making forecasts of future values using time series analysis?

    Step 1

    Step 2

    Step 3

4   What is the name for a series of numbers showing the relative value of a group of items over time?

    A   Trend numbers
    B   Index numbers
    C   Base numbers
    D   Time series numbers

5   In the context of budgeting, what is sensitivity analysis used for?

Answers to quick quiz

1   Examples might include: the monthly Retail Prices Index over a period of years; daily factory output over a period of a month; total annual costs over a ten-year period.

2   Short-term fluctuations in recorded values due to circumstances which affect the values at different points in each period, eg at different times of the year.

3   **Step 1.** Calculate average increases in trend line values
    Step 2. Use the trend line to forecast future trend line values
    Step 3. Adjust these values by the average seasonal variation applicable to the future period

4   B   **Index numbers** are series of numbers showing the relative values of a group of items over a period of time.

5   It can be used to test the responsiveness of profitability or cash flow to changes in one of the budget variables.

PART A CASH MANAGEMENT

Activity checklist

This checklist shows which performance criteria, range statement or knowledge and understanding point is covered by each activity in this chapter. Tick off each activity as you complete it.

Activity

3.1 □ This activity deals with Knowledge and Understanding 14: basic statistical techniques for estimating future trends: moving averages, allowances for inflation

3.2 □ This activity deals with Knowledge and Understanding 14: basic statistical techniques for estimating future trends: moving averages, allowances for inflation

3.3 □ This activity deals with Performance Criterion 15.1.C: ensure forecasts of future cash payments and receipts are in accord with known income and expenditure trends

3.4 □ This activity deals with Performance Criterion 15.1.E: identify significant deviations from the cash budget and take corrective action within defined organisational policies

chapter 4

Banks and economic policy

Contents

1 Introduction
2 The banking system
3 Financial markets
4 Government monetary policy

Performance criteria

15.2.A Arrange overdraft and loan facilities in anticipation of requirements and on the most favourable terms available

15.2.D Ensure account is taken of trends in the economic and financial environment in managing cash balances

Knowledge and understanding

- The basic structure of the banking system and the money market in the UK and the relationships between financial institutions
- Government monetary policies

PART A CASH MANAGEMENT

1 Introduction

This chapter provides the knowledge and understanding you need to have of the banking system, the relationship between different financial institutions and the most significant elements of government policy. Try when you're reading this chapter to think of how the economic environment can affect businesses, through, for example, a change in interest rates or an increase in tax rates.

Certain topics introduced in this chapter, relations with banks and different types of financial instrument, will be discussed further in the next few chapters.

2 The banking system

2.1 Banks and businesses

Businesses have bank accounts. Banks, like other businesses, are profit-making organisations.

Activity 4.1

What do you think are the main factors that influence a bank's policy towards its customers?

2.2 Financial intermediation

A **financial intermediary** brings together providers and users of finance, as:

- Broker (an agent handling a transaction on behalf of others)
- Principal (eg holding money balances of lenders for re-lending on to borrowers)

Banks are an example of financial intermediaries. They borrow money in order to lend it out to receive a return.

Types of intermediary		
Bank intermediaries	Barclays Lloyds TSB HSBC Nat West Royal Bank of Scotland Abbey National	Alliance & Leicester Halifax Co-operative Bank Girobank Merchant banks Investment banks
Other financial intermediaries	Building societies Finance houses	

Financial intermediaries make their profit by obtaining funds from lenders at **one rate of interest** and re-lending to borrowers at a **higher rate**.

2.3 Importance of financial intermediation

Financial intermediation is necessary as it is easier for savings to be loaned to borrowers via intermediaries than directly. Some large companies borrow millions of pounds at a time. Few **individuals** have that sort of money to lend. It would be a long, complex, and expensive matter for a firm to canvass potential savers. The bank does this job by **aggregating** individual savings.

In theory, banks should be better at **assessing credit risk** (the risk that the borrower will default on the loan) than individuals. With financial intermediation, an individual's savings are also not tied directly to the fate of one borrower. Risks are therefore **reduced** and **pooled**.

Many lenders or depositors want a **reasonable degree of liquidity**, while borrowers may need loans over a long period. A financial intermediary can provide long-term funds to borrowers and also facilities to meet lenders' or depositors' needs for liquidity.

2.4 Banks in the UK

Types of banks	
Primary banks	Operate money transmission. Known as • Commercial banks • Retail banks • High street banks
Secondary banks	• Merchant banks • Other British banks • Foreign banks in the UK • Consortium banks

2.5 Retail banking

Retail banking is the banking activity of the traditional **'high street' bank**, dealing with relatively small deposits and small loans to customers. Retail services are also now conducted over the telephone or the Internet by many banks. Retail banks have extensive branch networks and the bulk of their business is in sterling.

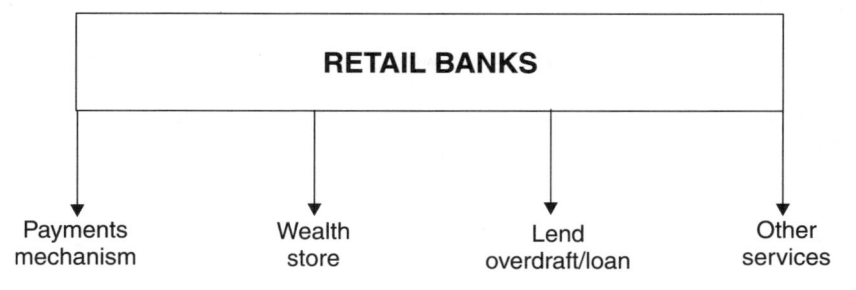

```
                    RETAIL BANKS
        ┌───────────┬──────────┬──────────┬──────────┐
        ↓           ↓          ↓          ↓
   Payments      Wealth      Lend       Other
   mechanism     store    overdraft/loan services
```

PART A CASH MANAGEMENT

2.6 Assets and liabilities of banks

ASSETS		LIABILITIES	
• Notes and coin	X	• Current accounts	X
• Balances with the Bank of England	X	• Time deposits	X
• Treasury bills	X	• Currency deposits	X
• Local authority bills	X		
• Commercial bills of exchange	X		
• Money market bills	X		
• Money market loans	X		
• Loans to customers	X		
• Overdrafts	X		
• Gilts and shares	X		

Activity 4.2

Do you know what

(a) Time deposits
(b) Balances with the Bank of England
(c) Bills

are?

Don't worry too much at this stage if you don't.

Activity 4.3

In the balance sheet of a retail bank, which one of the following items do you think would constitute the largest asset?

(a) Customers' overdrafts and bank loans
(b) Customers' deposits
(c) Land and buildings

2.7 Income and expenses of a bank

Income		Expenses	
• Interest received	X	• Interest paid	X
• Charges on current accounts	X	• Staff wages/salaries	X
• Commissions and fees on other financial services such as insurance, pensions	X	• Maintenance of premises and equipment	X
• Activities on the foreign exchange markets	X	• Other running costs of branches and head office	X
• Mortgage lending	X	• Advertising	X
		• Bad debts	X

2.8 The central bank

A **central bank** is an institution which typically has the roles of controlling the monetary system of a country, acting as banker to the banks, and acting as a lender of last resort.

The **Bank of England** ('the Bank') is a public corporation and is the central bank of the UK.

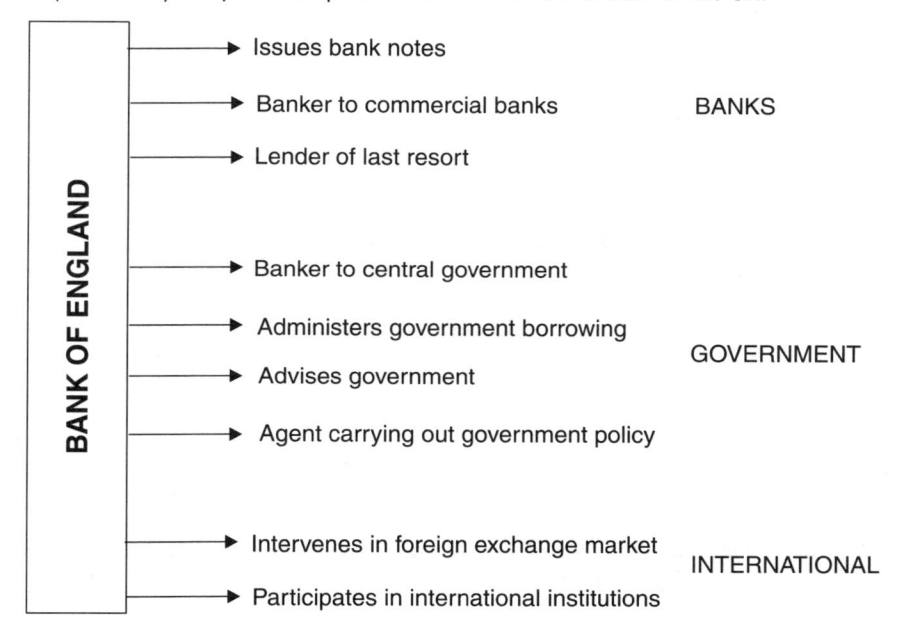

BANK OF ENGLAND:
- Issues bank notes
- Banker to commercial banks } BANKS
- Lender of last resort

- Banker to central government
- Administers government borrowing } GOVERNMENT
- Advises government
- Agent carrying out government policy

- Intervenes in foreign exchange market } INTERNATIONAL
- Participates in international institutions

2.9 Merchant banks

Merchant banking (or wholesale banking) involves small numbers of customers who have larger deposits or who require larger loans. Because large sums are involved, customers expect the banks to trim their profit margins and offer a cheaper, more competitive service.

Merchant banks offer many specialist financial management services including management of stocks and shares, advice on corporate financial matters and arranging leases.

2.10 Building societies

Building societies are important deposit-taking institutions and compete with clearing banks and other financial institutions to obtain deposits from customers.

Building societies offer a **wide range** of **savings schemes** to attract deposits, aimed mainly at the personal sector. Some are for **fixed terms**, but most provide for **withdrawal on demand**, possibly with some interest penalty. Some offer current account services similar to banks.

Most building society assets take the form of **mortgages** – ie loans to borrowers for house purchase, over periods of up to 25 years.

3 Financial markets

3.1 The money markets

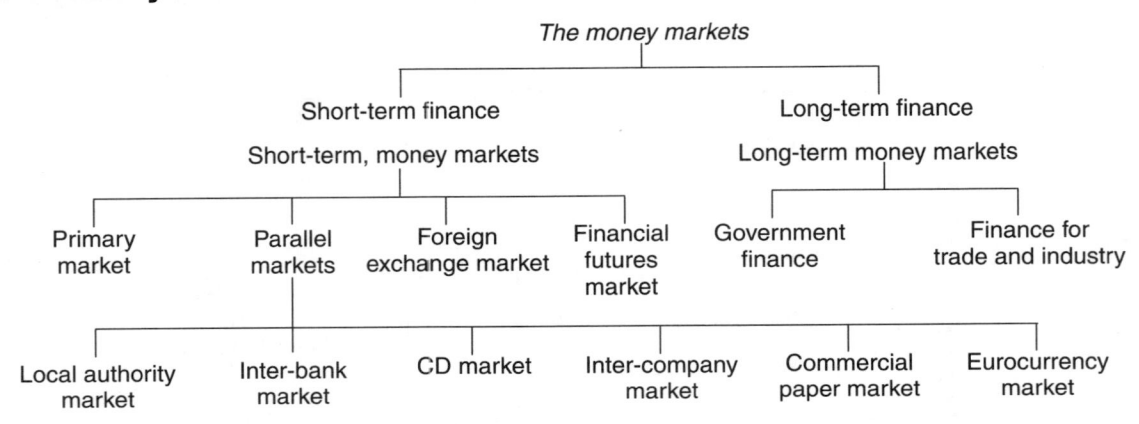

```
                            The money markets
                    ┌───────────────┴───────────────┐
              Short-term finance              Long-term finance
            Short-term, money markets       Long-term money markets
     ┌────────┬────────┬────────┐            ┌─────────┬─────────┐
  Primary  Parallel  Foreign  Financial   Government   Finance for
  market   markets   exchange  futures     finance    trade and industry
                     market    market
           ┌────┬────┬────┬────┬────┐
        Local  Inter- CD   Inter-  Commercial  Eurocurrency
      authority bank market company paper       market
       market  market      market  market
```

The **money markets** are just like any other markets with buyers, sellers and traders. The commodity traded in these markets is, however, very specific – money, which is lent and borrowed in wholesale amounts.

The money markets provide financial institutions with a means of covering deficits (shortages of money), and also providing profitable ways of lending surplus funds especially in the short term.

3.2 Money market financial instruments

Types of instrument	
Deposits	Deposits in bank accounts and with other financial intermediaries
Bills	Short-term financial assets convertible into cash at very short notice
Short-term IOUs	Issued by large companies which can be held to maturity or sold to others
Certificate of deposits	Fixed-term large amount instruments which can be sold on the CD market

3.3 The primary market

The **primary money market** consists of approved banks and securities firms.

The primary market is a money market in which the banks can place surplus funds in a very **liquid form**. They can draw on these funds to make **settlements** with other banks or the government when their operational deposits get too low.

The primary market is also used by the Bank of England to **correct cash shortages** in the economy or withdraw surplus cash, by buying and selling bills.

3.4 Local authority markets

Local authorities have a special wholesale market in which they can borrow short term funds.

3.5 Inter-bank market

The inter-bank market is an important market in unsecured loans between banks, used to:

- **Smooth out fluctuations** in receipts and payments by the bank
- **Borrow funds** in banks' own names and lend the funds to a less well-established bank at a higher rate of interest
- **Sound out the market** for the likely future trends in rates

The interest rate charged in the largest inter-bank market is the **London Inter-Bank Offered Rate (LIBOR).** Individual banks use this rate to determine their own base rates, and so the rate of interest at which they will lend to their own customers.

3.6 Certificates of deposit market

Certificates of deposit (CDs) are explained in detail in a later chapter of this text.

3.7 Inter-company market

In this much smaller market, companies with surplus funds lend direct (through a broker) to companies which need to borrow money.

3.8 Commercial paper market

Commercial paper is an IOU issued by a company, when it wants to raise short term money. It is not for a specific debt.

3.9 Eurocurrency markets

A **eurocurrency deposit** is a deposit of funds with a bank **outside the currency's country of origin**. A deposit of US dollars with a bank in London, or a deposit of Japanese Yen with a bank in Paris, is a eurocurrency deposit. A eurocurrency loan is a loan of eurocurrency by the bank with which the money has been deposited.

The **'euro-' prefix** does not mean that a European currency or bank must be involved in a 'eurocurrency' transaction. The term 'eurocurrency' has nothing to do with the European single currency, the 'euro', either.

3.10 Long-term money markets

The most important long-term money market in the UK is the London Stock Exchange. This is a capital market where firms obtain **long-term finance** by issuing shares to investors in return for money. Investors can sell shares or buy them. Government bonds, also known as gilt-edged securities or **gilts**, can be bought or sold on the Stock Exchange.

3.11 Financial futures market

The **financial futures market** is centred in the London International Financial Futures and Options Exchange (LIFFE). The idea behind **financial futures** is that a deal for a loan or deposit of money to take place sometime in the future can be made now.

4 Government monetary policy

4.1 The quantity of money

The amount of money in an economy is measured in a number of ways from the 'narrow' definition M0 (comprising mainly notes and coin) to the 'broader' definition M4 (in the UK). Money supply is increased in various ways.

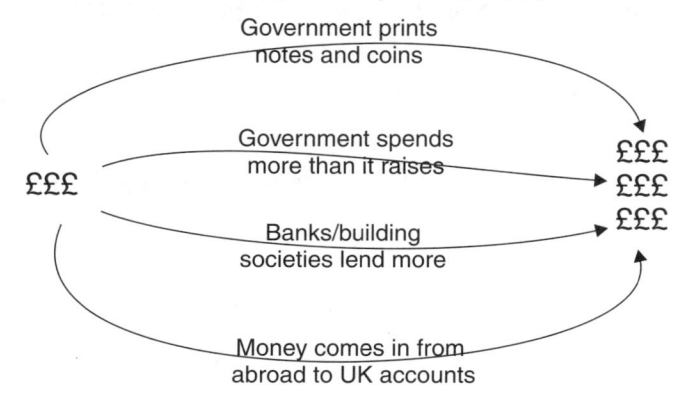

- Government prints notes and coins
- Government spends more than it raises
- Banks/building societies lend more
- Money comes in from abroad to UK accounts

4.2 Government monetary policy

The government of a country intervenes in its economy for a number of reasons. The UK Government has objectives for price stability, economic growth, and employment, which a government can influence in two ways.

- **Fiscal policy** is concerned with government spending and taxation.
- **Monetary policy** is described in more detail below.

4.3 Monetary policy

Monetary policies are policies implemented by the Treasury and the Bank of England. They influence:

- **Quantity of money**
- **Price of money** (interest rates)
- **Availability of credit** in the economy.

Some economists have argued that the money supply is important because too much money in the economic system causes inflation.

4.4 The availability of credit in the economy

Bank lending, and hence the amount of money people and businesses can borrow, can be controlled by

- **Reserve requirements** (ratios)
- **Other direct controls**
- **Interest rate policy**

4.4.1 Reserve requirements

These require that a certain proportion of a bank's assets are held in reserve, and are not used for lending.

4.4.2 Other types of control

Governments can place **upper limits** on the amount of lending by banks, or can ask that lending to specific sectors be restricted.

Governments can also **intervene in the markets**, by selling treasury bills or gilts, and hence taking cash out of the system.

The **regulatory structure** imposed by governments, requiring banks to have adequate capital structure and methods of limiting risk, also limit the amount of lending by banks.

Activity 4.4

Why might a government seek to control the growth of bank lending?

4.5 Interest rate policy

Interest rate policy controls the growth in **demand** for loans rather than the **supply** of bank lending. The interest rate is the price of money. Increasing this price should reduce the demand for money, depending on how sensitive borrowers are to an interest rate increase.

4.6 Effects of higher interest rates

If higher interest rates do reduce the demand for borrowing, they will have a dampening effect on consumer demand. Consumers will **buy less on credit**, and the knock-on effect for many companies is that fewer of their products will be **purchased**. Companies may also be squeezed by increased costs on any **variable rate finance** which they have.

Higher interest rates can also have a significant effect on the **housing market** because potential house buyers may be deterred from buying a house on mortgage finance. Businesses closely connected with house purchase, such as estate agents and home improvements companies, may be particularly affected.

4.7 PSBR and PSDR

An excess of public sector spending over revenue – a **Public Sector Borrowing Requirement (PSBR)** – feeds directly into increases in the money supply. The bigger the PSBR, the bigger the **increase** in the **money supply**.

If the government wishes to control the money supply it will wish to keep the size of the PSBR within a certain limit.

A **PSDR (public sector debt repayment)** – occurring when public sector revenue is greater than public sector expenditure – has a negative effect on money supply growth.

Activity 4.5

Suppose that interest rates fall significantly and unexpectedly. Identify the effects on a furniture store which has a large overdraft.

Key learning points

- **Financial intermediaries** exist to smooth the flow of funds in the economy.
- **Primary (commercial, clearing) banks** are banks that offer facilities for making payments.
- **Secondary banks** deal mostly with wholesale business in the secondary money markets, not in the high street.
- The balance sheet of a bank consists of its liabilities (mostly **deposits** of one sort or another) and its assets (mostly **loans** to customers of one sort or another).
- Banks make a **profit** by lending at a higher rate of interest than the rate they pay for deposits. Other forms of income, such as fees and commissions, are increasingly important sources of income for banks.
- The **central bank** (the Bank of England in the UK) has various roles and is particularly important for the government's monetary policy.
- The **money markets** consist of a **primary market,** which the Bank of England uses to regulate interest rates, and **secondary markets,** which deal principally with the short-term finance of banks, governments, and large commercial organisations.
- **Fiscal policy** deals with taxation, government spending and government borrowing.
- **Monetary policy** deals with the supply of money, the price of money (interest) and the availability of credit (to make borrowing harder or easier).
- The UK government prefers to regulate the price of money, through **interest rates**, rather than **quantitative or qualitative controls** over amounts that can be lent.
- **Higher interest rates** should reduce the **demand for borrowing**, resulting in a **decrease in consumer demand** and an **increase in businesses' cost of capital**.

Quick quiz

1 Which of the following are financial intermediaries?

☐ Retail banks

☐ Merchant banks

☐ Building societies

☐ Finance houses

☐ Insurance companies

☐ Pension funds

☐ Unit trust companies

☐ Investment trust companies

2 For whom does the Bank of England operate as banker?

3 Identify the main wholesale money markets.

4 Are (a) a deposit of US dollars with a Japanese bank; and (b) a deposit of pounds sterling with a bank in the USA, 'eurocurrency' deposits?

5 Monetary policy is mainly concerned with government spending and taxation.

☐ True

☐ False

6 If interest rates have risen, what, in effect, is the change in monetary policy?

7 Primary banks operate the money transmission mechanism in the UK. Which of the following is not a primary bank?

A High street bank
B Merchant bank
C Commercial bank
D Retail bank

8 ……………is the interest rate charged in the largest inter-bank market in the UK.

PART A CASH MANAGEMENT

Answers to quick quiz

1   All of them.
2   The government, and other banks.
    The Bank of England also operates some (but very few) accounts for individuals.
3   The primary market; the local authority market; the inter-bank market; the certificates of deposit market; the inter-company market; the commercial paper markets; the eurocurrency markets.
4   Yes – both are deposits of funds with banks outside the country's currency of origin. (The 'euro' prefix, remember, does not mean that a European country or currency must be involved.)
5   False. The description given is of fiscal policy.
6   Monetary policy has been tightened: money is more expensive.
7   B   Merchant bank
8   **LIBOR** (London Inter-Bank Offered Rate) is the interest rate charged in the largest inter-bank market.

Activity checklist

This checklist shows which performance criteria, range statement or knowledge and understanding point is covered by each activity in this chapter. Tick off each activity as you complete it.

Activity

4.1	☐	This activity deals with Performance Criterion 15.2.A: arrange overdraft and loan facilities in anticipation of requirements on the most favourable terms available
4.2	☐	This activity deals with Knowledge and Understanding 2: the basic structure of the banking system and the money market in the UK and the relationships between financial institutions
4.3	☐	This activity deals with Knowledge and Understanding 2: the basic structure of the banking system and the money market in the UK and the relationships between financial institutions
4.4	☐	This activity deals with Knowledge and Understanding 5: government monetary policies
4.5	☐	This activity deals with Performance Criterion 15.2.D: ensure account is taken of trends in the economic and financial environment in managing cash balances

chapter 5

Dealing with banks

Contents

1 Introduction
2 Your relationship with banks
3 Services offered by banks

Performance criteria

15.2.A Arrange overdraft and loan facilities in anticipation of requirements and on the most favourable terms available

Range statement

15.2.1 Maintain liquidity through the management of cash, loans and overdrafts

Knowledge and understanding

- The main types of cash receipts and payments: regular revenue receipts and payments; capital receipts and payments; drawings/dividends and disbursements; exceptional receipts and payments
- Bank overdrafts and loans; terms and conditions; legal relationship between bank and customer
- Liquidity management
- Understanding that the accounting systems of an organisation are affected by its organisational structure, its administrative systems and procedures and the nature of its business transactions
- An understanding that practice in this area will be determined by an organisation's specific financial regulations, guidelines and security procedures

1 Introduction

In the previous chapter, we identified the role of banks as **financial intermediaries** in the **economy** as a whole. From the point of view of a business or individual who uses the services of a bank, a **bank** provides:

- A safe place where money can be deposited
- Short-term finance
- Other financial services

In this chapter we look at how a customer should deal with its bank, and the **rights** and **responsibilities** of the bank and the customer. You may encounter a situation where this relationship has run into trouble.

The last section of this chapter deals with the different ways of **transmitting money.** This is an important aspect of cash and credit management; selection of the right means of payment can simplify the administration of cash and credit.

2 Your relationship with banks

2.1 What is a customer?

You become a **customer** as soon as the bank opens an account for you in your name. In any other situation, you become a customer as soon as the bank accepts your instructions and undertakes to provide a service.

Your relationship with the bank arises from a legal **contract** between you. There are four main types of **contractual relationship** which may exist between bank and customer.

2.2 Debtor/creditor relationship

You deposit money with the bank. These funds go into your account and can be withdrawn at any time. **The bank is the debtor** (for the money owed to you) and you are **the creditor**. However, there are circumstances where this relationship can be reversed. If, for example, your account is overdrawn, then you owe money to the bank.

The *Joachimson v Swiss Bank Corporation (1921)* case laid down the essential terms of this area of the bank/customer relationship.

- The bank **undertakes to receive money**, cheques etc for its customer's account.
- The bank **borrows the proceeds** and undertakes to repay them.
- The bank will **not cease to do business** with the customer except upon reasonable notice.
- The bank is **not liable to pay** until the **customer demands payment** from the bank.
- The customer undertakes to **exercise reasonable care** in executing his written orders so as not to mislead the bank or to facilitate forgery.

2.3 Bailor/bailee relationship

Banks have safes or strong rooms and will usually be willing to offer a **safe deposit service** to customers. A **bailment** exists if you (the **bailor**) deliver personal property to the bank (the **bailee**). The bank must take **'reasonable'** care to **safeguard** your property against damage or loss, and **re-deliver it only** to **you** or someone authorised by you.

2.4 Principal/agent relationship

Often in business one person (the **agent**) acts for another (the **principal**). At a basic level when you receive a crossed cheque, you must pay it into a bank account to receive the proceeds. You will employ the bank as your agent to present the cheque for payment and credit the proceeds to your account. Where the bank arranges insurance such as household contents insurance, the bank is acting as an insurance broker and is the agent of its customer.

2.5 Mortgagor/mortgagee relationship

On some loans you will be asked to give assets as **security.** If you do not repay the loan, the bank can sell the asset and use the proceeds to pay off or reduce the outstanding loan. If the loan is secured by a mortgage on assets such as property, you are the **mortgagor**, granting the mortgage, while the bank is the **mortgagee**, accepting the mortgage.

2.6 Rights of banks

The bank has certain rights in its relationship with its customers on the basis of legal rules or justice.

2.6.1 Charges and commissions

The bank may charge you bank charges and commissions over and above interest on advances, provided these are 'reasonable'.

2.6.2 Use of customers' money

The bank can use your money in any way which is legally and morally acceptable. However your money must be available for withdrawal in line with the terms of your deposit. For example, banks must allow the money in a **current account** to be available for **withdrawal on demand.**

2.6.3 Overdrawn balances

The bank has a right to be **repaid overdrawn balances** on **demand**, except where the terms of the overdraft require a period of notice.

2.6.4 Customers drawing cheques

You owe a duty of care to the bank when drawing cheques to attempt to prevent fraud by for example **not signing blank cheques**.

2.6.5 Lien over securities

A lien is a right to **retain possession** of **someone else's property** to clear a debt. For example, if you have an overdrawn account, and deposit cheques into it, instead of paying you the proceeds of the cheques, the bank can use the cheques to clear the debt owed to it. The principle would not apply to items held in safe custody, such as jewellery.

2.6.6 Indemnification

Indemnification refers to a bank being secured against possible loss when acting on your behalf.

2.7 Banks' fiduciary duty

Because the bank is in a position of trust, and can exert influence on its customers, the law expects the bank to act with **utmost good faith**, particularly when advising a customer.

2.8 Other duties of banks

2.8.1 Honour cheques

The bank has a duty to honour your cheques as long as:

- The cheques are **correctly made out** and **properly drawn**.
- You have **sufficient funds** in your account or payment of the cheque would not exceed an agreed overdraft limit.
- There is **no legal reason** why the **cheques should not be paid**.

2.8.2 Receipt of customer's funds

The bank has a duty to **credit cash** or **cheques paid** into your account.

2.8.3 Repayment on demand

The bank must repay funds on demand provided that:

- You have made a **written** request in the form of a cheque or as otherwise agreed.
- The transaction takes place during the **bank's opening hours**.
- The transaction takes place either at your home branch or at another **agreed branch or bank**.

2.8.4 Comply with instructions

The bank must comply with your instructions to pay funds through a direct debit mandate or standing order, provided that you have **sufficient funds** in your account.

2.8.5 Provide a statement

A bank must provide a statement showing transactions on your account in a **'reasonable time'**. The bank must also provide details of the **balance on your account** on request.

2.8.6 Confidentiality

A bank should keep confidential what it knows about your affairs. There are four recognised exceptions where a bank may disclose what it knows about your affairs.

- **Legal requirement** to disclose
- **Public duty** to disclose
- When the **interest of the bank** requires disclosure (for example the bank suing you to recover what you owe it)
- When you have given express or implied **consent**

2.8.7 Advice of forgery

A bank must advise you if cheques bearing a **forgery** of your signature are being drawn on your account.

2.8.8 Care and skill

Banks should use **care and skill** in their actions, for professional reasons and to gain the benefits of certain legal protections.

2.8.9 Closure of accounts

A bank must provide **reasonable notice** if it wishes to close your account, say because of your misuse of it. The period of notice is needed to allow you to make other financial arrangements.

2.9 Customer's duties

Just as the bank has certain legal duties, so do you as its customer. However the duties you have do **not** include checking the bank statements for incorrect entries.

2.9.1 A duty of care

You must **exercise care** in drawing cheques, so that fraud is not facilitated. For example, you should not issue blank cheques or write cheques out in pencil.

2.9.2 Advice of forgery

You must tell the bank **of any known forgeries** on your account.

2.10 Maintaining a good relationship with the bank

As well as fulfilling its duties, a bank's personal and business customers should try to maintain a good relationship with it.

Activity 5.1

Can you think of some ways in which your organisation might maintain a good relationship with its bank?

Activity 5.2

Your managing director is concerned about the circumstances in which a bank may legitimately disclose information about a customer's affairs. Explain this matter to her.

3 Services offered by banks

3.1 Cheques

A **cheque** is a written instruction to a bank authorising and requiring the bank to make a payment to a third party or to the customer. Cheques are one of the most significant means by which a business's customers will pay their debts, and by which a business will pay its suppliers.

3.2 Dates on cheques

Banks can refuse to pay cheques that don't have the date written in, as their authority is uncertain.

Banks consider that the customer's authority to pay the cheque expires after six months from the date of issue. The bank would return it marked **'stale cheque'** or 'out of date' so that the drawer may either confirm authority to pay it or issue a fresh cheque bearing a current date.

A **post-dated cheque** is a cheque that bears a future date which has not arrived when the cheque is presented for payment. If a cheque is post-dated and presented for payment before the date inserted on it, the bank should refuse to pay it until the date arrives. Credit controllers should be wary of customers sending post-dated cheques.

3.3 Crossings on cheques

A **general crossing** is usually shown by two lines on the face of the cheque (generally pre-printed on the cheques). A general crossing instructs the paying bank to make payment **only to another bank**.

A **special crossing** is the name of the collecting bank (and often its branch address) written across the cheque. This is an instruction to the paying bank to make payment **only to the bank designated by the special crossing.**

A general or special crossing may be combined with either or both of **'not negotiable'** or **'a/c payee'** crossings.

The words **not negotiable** may be written between the lines of the crossing, primarily for protection against theft. The 'not negotiable' crossing on a cheque does not prevent its transfer. It ensures that the transferee has no better rights than his transferor had.

The **a/c payee** crossing is an instruction to the collecting bank to collect payment **only** for the original payee.

In the example below a general crossing has been combined with an a/c payee.

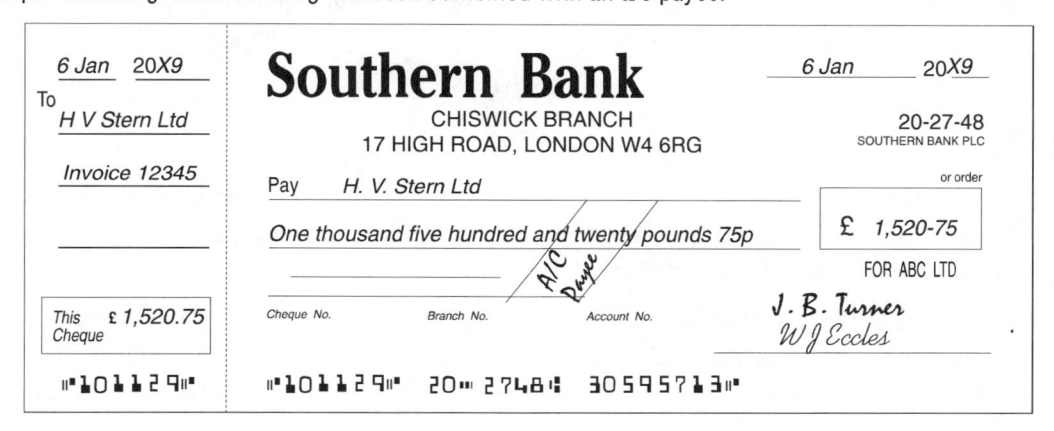

3.4 Bars to payment of cheques

Legal bars to payment of a cheque include:

- The customer's subsequent death
- The customer's bankruptcy
- Court orders against the customer

You can **stop payment** of a cheque by giving instructions, confirmed in writing, to the bank before the cheque is paid. However if you use a cheque guarantee card, you will commit the bank to honouring the cheque and it cannot be stopped.

3.5 Sufficiency of funds

A bank need not honour your cheque if you do not have a credit balance or an agreed overdraft which suffices to provide funds for the payment of the cheque. However cheques issued under the **cheque guarantee scheme** must be honoured even if you have an unauthorised overdraft. The cheque guarantee scheme requires the bank to pay the holder of the cheque the lesser of its value or a fixed amount (£50, £100 or £250, as shown on the cheque card).

Problems with payments usually occur when there are insufficient funds available to the customer to meet the cheque.

3.6 Debit cards

Debit cards are designed for customers who like paying by plastic card but do not want credit. These can be used to withdraw money from a current account in three ways.

- Cash
- Payment by debit card to a third party accepting such cards
- Payment by cheque, supported by the debit card as a guarantee card

You can use a debit card in EFTPOS systems (**Electronic Funds Transfer at Point of Sale**). An EFTPOS system can initiate an immediate transfer of funds from your account to that of the person providing you with goods or services.

3.7 Credit cards

Credit cards provide **credit to** cardholders. A credit card holder uses the card to purchase goods or services within a **total credit limit**. A monthly statement will be issued to the cardholder by the card company. The cardholder must pay at least a **certain minimum amount**. Interest is charged on unpaid amounts.

Credit cards also provide a **means of payment**. Traders who sell goods or services to customers with a bank's credit card are reimbursed by the card company, which takes a **commission**. Thus the banking organisations give the credit, and not the traders. The trader forwards his credit card sales vouchers and has to pay a **service charge** (averaging about 1.8% of the sales value).

Credit cards differ from **charge cards**, such as American Express, whose balance must be paid in full every month.

3.8 Banker's draft

This method of payment eliminates the risk of a cheque being 'bounced'. The **banker's draft** is effectively a cheque drawn on the bank by itself, payable to a person specified by the customer. An alternative to a banker's draft is the **building society cheque**.

3.9 Standing orders

Standing (or banker's) orders are a method of making a series of payments at a known date to a known recipient.

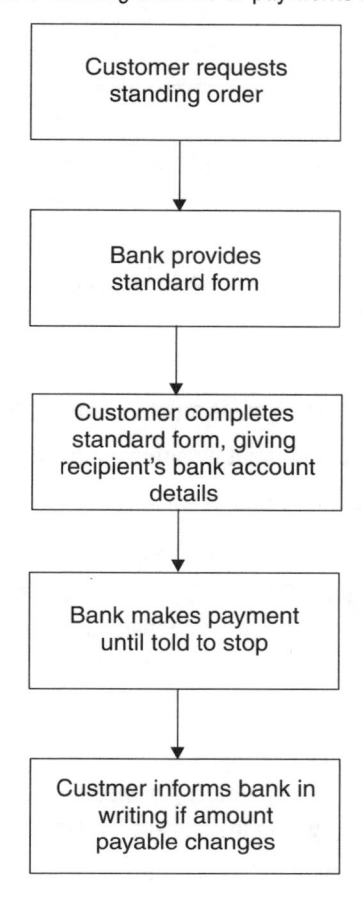

```
┌─────────────────────────┐
│   Customer requests     │
│    standing order       │
└───────────┬─────────────┘
            ↓
┌─────────────────────────┐
│    Bank provides        │
│    standard form        │
└───────────┬─────────────┘
            ↓
┌─────────────────────────┐
│  Customer completes     │
│  standard form, giving  │
│  recipient's bank account│
│       details           │
└───────────┬─────────────┘
            ↓
┌─────────────────────────┐
│   Bank makes payment    │
│    until told to stop   │
└───────────┬─────────────┘
            ↓
┌─────────────────────────┐
│  Custmer informs bank in│
│   writing if amount     │
│   payable changes       │
└─────────────────────────┘
```

Manual orders are used for complicated transactions or where the bank wants to be sure that funds are available to cover the transaction before it is debited to the customer's account.

3.10 Direct debits

Direct debits are similar to standing orders in that they allow the customer to make regular payments automatically. However, as well as authorising the bank to make the payment, the customer gives his **bank details** to the **creditor** which then tells the bank how much to debit to the customer's account.

Direct debits are used for payments which are likely to vary (for example, because of changes in interest rates or the basic rate of tax), and so the alternative would often be to pay by cheque or cash rather than standing order. One example of a payment where direct debits would normally be used is a **mortgage repayment.**

PART A CASH MANAGEMENT

Activity 5.3

Can you think of other examples of payments frequently made by direct debit?

Many **firms receiving regular payments** from customers prefer to collect by direct debit. A large organisation with hundreds of thousands of similar amounts to collect will spend less on administration if it initiates (and can therefore identify) all the credits to its account.

When the amount to be collected changes, the change is made centrally without delay. The creditor knows the timing of its receipts, enhancing its cash management.

Safeguards are built into the system to protect the public.

- All **changes in amount** and collection dates must be **notified to** the payers 14 days in **advance**.
- The customer can **cancel the direct debit** by notifying the bank.
- The bank will make an **immediate refund** of any incorrect debit notified by customers.
- Only **approved organisations** sponsored by banks can **operate a direct debit** scheme.
- The creditor must provide an **indemnity** to its **sponsoring bank** so that the banks are guaranteed a refund of incorrect debits which they have refunded to their customers.

3.11 BACS

Bankers' Automated Clearing Services (BACS) is a company owned by the high street banks which operates the **electronic transfer of funds** between accounts within the banking system.

When a business uses BACS, it sends information to BACS for processing.

The most important **advantage** of the BACS system is that it operates with very **reduced amounts** of paperwork. BACS is widely used for **monthly salaries** paid by an employer into employees' bank accounts, for standing order payments and for payments to suppliers.

3.12 Clearing House Automated Payments System (CHAPS)

The **Clearing House Automated Payments System** is a computerised system to enable **same-day** clearing, guaranteed if instructions are received from the banks involved before 2pm. Each bank transmits and receives payment instructions through its gateway computer. Messages, once accepted by CHAPS, are **irrevocable. Payment is certain.**

Activity 5.4

Outline the main services offered by banks to the small or medium-sized business.

5: DEALING WITH BANKS

Key learning points

- ☑ The principal **legal relationships** which may exist between bank and customer are **debtor/creditor, principal/agent, bailor/bailee and mortgagor/mortgagee**.

- ☑ A bank's **rights** include **using** its **customers' money** in a way acceptable to the bank, being **repaid on demand** for overdrawn balances and expecting customers to take **reasonable care** in drawing cheques.

- ☑ A bank's **duties** include **honouring a customer's cheques** properly drawn, **repaying a customer's funds** on demand, **providing a statement of account** to the customer and **maintaining confidentiality** about a customer's affairs.

- ☑ Banks provide a number of **clearing and money transmission services**, and are increasingly using IT.

- ☑ **Direct debits** are useful for companies which sell goods on credit, as they can collect amounts directly from customers' accounts.

PART A   CASH MANAGEMENT

Quick quiz

1   Banks act as a link between borrowers and savers. What is this role called?

    A   Financial intervention
    B   Financial interposition
    C   Financial intermediation
    D   Financial interlineation

2   A .... is an arrangement in which one person (the bailor) delivers personal property to another person (the bailee) as, for example, with a bank's safe deposit service.

3   A bank's loan to a customer is secured by a charge on the customer's house. Who is the mortgagor and who is the mortgagee?

4   What is a fiduciary relationship?

5   Banks consider that a customer's authority to pay a cheque expires a year after the date of issue.

    ☐ True

    ☐ False

6   With a ...., the customer authorises the bank to make a series of payments. With a ...., the creditor is authorised to tell the bank how much to debit to the customer's account.

7   What safeguards are given to customers with regard to direct debits?

8   Which of the following types of payment are often made by direct debit?

    ☐ Mortgage repayment

    ☐ Purchase of property

    ☐ Insurance premium

    ☐ Equipment rental

Answers to quick quiz

1   C   Financial intermediation.

2   A **bailment** is an arrangement in which one person (the bailor) delivers personal property to another person (the bailee) as, for example, with a bank's safe deposit service.

3   The customer is the mortgagor and the bank is the mortgagee.

4   A relationship based on trust in which the superior party must act in good faith.

5   False. Banks consider that authority to pay expires six months after the date of issue of the cheque.

6   With a **standing order**, the customer authorises the bank to make a series of payments. With a **direct debit**, the creditor is authorised to tell the bank how much to debit to the customer's account.

7   Charges and payment dates must be notified to the payer 14 days in advance; the customer can cancel the direct debit at any time; the bank may refund amounts incorrectly debited directly to the customer; only approved organisations can operate a direct debit scheme.

8   Mortgage repayment; insurance premium; equipment rental. All of these are regular payments whereas purchase of property is a one-off payment.

Activity checklist

This checklist shows which performance criteria, range statement or knowledge and understanding point is covered by each activity in this chapter. Tick off each activity as you complete it.

Activity

5.1	☐	This activity deals with Performance Criterion 15.2.A: arrange overdraft and loan facilities in anticipation of requirements and on the most favourable terms available
5.2	☐	This activity deals with Knowledge and Understanding 3: bank overdrafts and loans; terms and conditions; legal relationship between bank and customer
5.3	☐	This activity deals with Knowledge and Understanding 1: the main types of cash receipts and payments: regular revenue receipts and payments; capital receipts and payments; drawings/dividends and disbursements; exceptional receipts and payments
5.4	☐	This activity deals with Performance Criterion 15.2.A: arrange overdraft and loan facilities in anticipation of requirements and on the most favourable terms available

PART A CASH MANAGEMENT

chapter 6

Raising finance

Contents

1. Introduction
2. Borrowings
3. Banks' criteria for lending
4. Overdrafts
5. Medium and long-term loans
6. Leasing as a source of finance
7. Other forms of finance

Performance criteria

15.2.A Arrange overdraft and loan facilities in anticipation of requirements and on the most favourable terms available

15.2.E Maintain an adequate level of liquidity in line with cash forecasts

Range statement

15.2.1 Maintain liquidity through the management of cash overdrafts and loans

Knowledge and understanding

- Bank overdrafts and loans; terms and conditions; legal relationship between bank and customer
- Managing risk and exposure
- Liquidity management
- Understanding that the accounting systems of an organisation are affected by its organisational structure, its administrative systems and procedures and the nature of its business transactions
- An understanding that practice in this area will be determined by an organisation's specific regulations, guidelines and security procedures
- An understanding that in public sector organisations there are statutory and other regulations relating to the management of cash balances

PART A CASH MANAGEMENT

1 Introduction

When they are considering raising funds, businesses need to take into account:

- The **bank's attitude** to their request for funds
- The **best source of funds** for the purposes that the business needs money.

You therefore need to be able to identify:

- What **finance sources** are **available**
- **How suitable** the different sources are for the business

This involves being aware of the **advantages** and **disadvantages** of each source of finance and being able to **recommend** the best source of finance in a specific set of circumstances.

In this chapter we cover various different ways of funding a business's demand for cash. The distinction between bank **loans** and **overdrafts** is particularly important in this unit.

2 Borrowings

2.1 Why organisations need to borrow

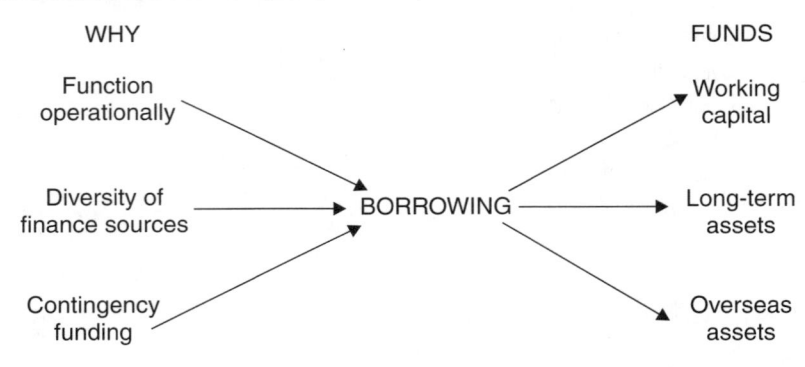

```
WHY                                          FUNDS
Function                                     Working
operationally  ─┐                         ┌─ capital
                │                         │
Diversity of    ├──► BORROWING ──────────┼─► Long-term
finance sources │                         │   assets
                │                         │
Contingency   ─┘                         └─ Overseas
funding                                      assets
```

2.2 Types of bank borrowing

Types of facility	
Overdraft facility	Short-term borrowings up to a certain amount, repayable on demand
Term loan	Fixed amount repaid with interest over or at end of set period
Committed facility	Bank agrees to make a certain amount available to borrowers on demand
Revolving facility	Facility renewed after a certain period
Uncommitted facility	Bank makes funds available but has no obligation to lend

3 Banks' criteria for lending

3.1 Costs of bad loan debts

If the bank makes a loan which is not repaid, a bank's profits suffer in a number of ways.

- The **expected interest** from the loan may not be earned.
- The amount advanced and not recoverable **is written off** as a **bad debt.**
- The **costs of administering the account** are much **increased**.
- There are **legal costs** in chasing the debt.

Banks therefore have to set criteria that borrowers must fulfil if they are to lend money.

3.2 Lending criteria

A bank's decision whether or not to lend will be based on the following factors. The mnemonic is **CAMPARI**.

- **C**haracter of the customer
- **A**bility to borrow and repay
- **M**argin of profit
- **P**urpose of the borrowing
- **A**mount of the borrowing
- **R**epayment terms
- **I**nsurance against the possibility of non-payment.

3.3 Character of the borrower

Banks use various sources of information to judge the character of borrowers:

```
INFORMATION SOURCES

Borrower's
past record
                        Personal
                        interviews
Key business
ratios
                        Credit
```

3.4 Ability to borrow and repay

The bank will look at a business customer's **financial performance** as an indication of **future trends**. The bank needs some reassurance that the loan will be invested in a way that will generate profit. Bankers will look at financial statements for signs of:

- Low/declining profitability
- Increased dependence on borrowing
- Overtrading
- Inadequate control over working capital
- Sudden provisions
- Delays

Re-investment of retained profits is a sign of the owner's commitment to making the business successful. (In other words, the owner does not take out all profits as dividends or drawings.)

The bank will also assess whether the schedule for re-paying the loan is **viable**; will the business generate sufficient receipts to meet the requirements?

The bank should check whether the company has the **legal capacity** to borrow. A company might be prohibited by its articles of association (the legal instrument setting it up) from certain types of borrowing.

3.5 Margin of profit

Remember, banks want to lend money to make money! Decisions on interest are thus most important.

The lending policies of most banks stipulate **different rates** for different purposes of borrowing (see below). Individual banks will also have **discretion** depending on the return required from each customer. A loan for a risky venture (such as a new business) will typically be offered at a higher rate of interest, so as to compensate the bank for the **risk** it takes.

3.6 Purpose of the borrowing

The customer must specify the **purpose of the borrowing**.

Loans for certain purposes will normally not be granted at all. A loan which is for an **illegal purpose**, such as drug smuggling, obviously must be refused.

Some loans will be granted only on **certain conditions**. Lending money (usually on overdraft) to finance some of the working capital of a business is quite normal. However banks may be concerned about excessive increases in non-cash assets (stock or debtors). Conditions may be imposed on the levels of **liquidity** the business must have, including ratios of assets to liabilities, and levels of **cash flows.**

3.7 Amount of the borrowing

The lending proposition must state exactly **how much** the customer needs to borrow.

The bank will check that the customer is **not asking** for **too much**, or **more than is needed** for the particular purpose, This links with the customer's **wealth** and **ability to repay.**

The banker will also check that the customer has not asked for **less than** he or she really needs. Otherwise the bank may later have to lend more, purely to safeguard the original advance.

3.8 Repayment terms

The likelihood that the **advance** will be **repaid** is the most important requirement for a loan. A bank should not lend money to a person or business who has not got the resources to repay it with interest, even if it has **security** for the loan.

The timescale for repayment is very important. Overdrafts are technically repayable **on demand** (though it is rare for a bank to insist on this without first having discussed a different timescale). Other loans might be payable in instalments, especially loans to acquire assets.

3.9 Insurance against the possibility of non-payment

If a **bank needs** to take **insurance** against the possibility that the loan will not be repaid, then the loan should not be made. That said, many **customers** might take out payment protection insurance, for peace of mind.

3.10 Security for lending

The **security for a loan** should have the following characteristics.

Characteristics	
Easy to take	Bank will want **title** for the property or be able to obtain it easily
Easy to value	Security should have an **identifiable value** which is stable or increasing, and fully covers lending plus a margin
Easy to realise	Security should be **sold easily** and quickly convertible to cash.

Activity 6.1

Why do you think banks will want to have security that is easy to realise?

PART A CASH MANAGEMENT

Security may take the form of either a **fixed charge** or a **floating charge**.

Types of charges	
Fixed charge	Security related to specific asset or group of assets (land and buildings). Borrower cannot dispose of asset without lender's consent, and will need to provide substitute asset in its place
Floating charge	Security related to class of assets (stocks or debtors). If default occurs, security is whatever assets are in that class at time of default. Borrower can freely dispose of assets if there is no default

3.11 Personal guarantees

Sometimes the bank will insist that a business loan is supported by a **personal guarantee**. Such requirements are mainly a concern of smaller or medium sized businesses.

For example, Mr Quiggin is Managing Director of Members Ltd. Members Ltd has an overdraft arrangement with the bank, but Mr Quiggin has to give a personal guarantee of the overdraft. This means that if Members Ltd fails to pay its debt **to the bank**, the bank can call in the guarantee, and Mr Quiggin will have to pay the debt out of his own resources.

Activity 6.2

Recently a number of thefts and unexplained account movements have reduced the size of Crisroe Ltd's surplus. The managing director has recently decided that she wants to move house. Rather than take out a mortgage, she suggests to the bank that the company borrows money, on overdraft, to buy her a house. She will personally guarantee the loan, although at the moment the only asset she can pledge as security is a bar in Spain, which she inherited from her mother; her brothers and sisters are suing her for a share of it.

What chance do you think Crisroe Ltd has of obtaining the loan?

Activity 6.3

Tarquin Devonshire-Smythe is the wealthy director of a major public company, which has business accounts at other branches of a bank at which you are employed. He does not have a personal account with your bank, but he approaches the bank with a banking proposition.

He has been reliably informed about an investment which promises to yield a very good return in the next few years, and he has the opportunity now to purchase £15,000 of shares, with tax advantages to himself.

He asks the bank for a personal loan of £15,000, the full amount of the investment cost. He would like to repay the loan as follows:

(a) Interest payments only until the end of the term of the loan
(b) Capital repayment in full at the end of the term

He would like the term of the loan to be 5 years. He would make the interest payments out of his regular income, and would repay the capital by selling off the shares after 5 years.

He will offer no security, other than the shares themselves. He also asks for a favourable rate of interest, only 2½% above the bank's base rate.

Explain what answer the bank will give to his proposition.

4 Overdrafts

4.1 Overdrafts as finance source

An overdraft is a form of **short-term lending**, available to both personal and business customers, when a current account shows a negative balance.

The distinction between an **overdraft** and an **overdraft facility** is important.

- An **overdraft** is the actual amount that the bank has lent to a customer.
- An **overdraft facility** is the opportunity given to the customer to obtain a short-term loan up to a certain limit. The customer does not necessarily make full **or any** use of this opportunity.

By providing an overdraft facility to a customer, the bank commits itself to provide an overdraft to the customer up to the agreed limit. The bank will earn interest on the lending, but only to the extent that the customer **uses the facility** and goes into overdraft.

4.2 Characteristics of overdraft

Overdraft	
Amount	Overdraft should not go above a set amount, determined by borrower's income
Margin	Interest will be charged on daily amount overdrawn at margin over base rate
Commitment fee	Commitment fee may be payable if overdraft facility is large
Purpose	Overdrafts normally cover short-term deficits, period before income comes in
Repayment	Overdrafts are technically repayable on demand
Security	If overdraft facility is large, bank may require security
Benefits	Bank has to accept that customer will benefit from overdraft being varying amount

4.3 Overdrafts and the operating cycle

Many businesses require their bank to provide financial assistance for normal trading over the **operating cycle**.

The amount of the overdraft required at any time will depend on the **cash flows of the business** – the timing of receipts and payments, seasonal variations in trade patterns and so on. The purpose of the overdraft is to bridge the gap between cash payments and cash receipts, which means that it must by its very nature be short-term.

For example, suppose that a business has the following working capital.

	£	£
Stocks and debtors		10,000
Bank overdraft	1,000	
Creditors	3,000	
		4,000
Working capital		6,000

It now buys stocks costing £2,500 for cash, using its overdraft. Working capital remains the same, £6,000, although the bank's financial stake has risen from £1,000 to £3,500.

	£	£
Stocks and debtors		12,500
Bank overdraft	3,500	
Creditors	3,000	
		6,500
Working capital		6,000

A bank overdraft provides support for normal trading finance. In this example, finance for normal trading rises from £(10,000 − 3,000) = £7,000 to £(12,500 − 3,000) = £9,500 and the bank's contribution rises from £1,000 out of £7,000 to £3,500 out of £9,500.

4.4 Hard core overdrafts

When a customer has an overdraft facility, and the account is always in overdraft, then it has a **hard core** overdraft.

If the hard core element of the overdraft appears to be becoming a long-term feature of the business, the bank might wish to convert the hard core of the overdraft into a **medium-term loan**, thus giving formal recognition to its more permanent nature. Otherwise the bank will normally demand **annual reductions** in the hard core of an overdraft.

4.5 Using overdrafts to increase business assets

If a business is seeking an increased overdraft to increase the business assets, a bank will first check whether the purpose is to acquire more **fixed assets** or more **current assets**.

There is nothing wrong with asking a bank for a loan to help with the purchase of fixed assets. However using an overdraft to purchase a fixed asset reduces the liquidity of the business, and might even make it illiquid.

Businesses should be requesting an overdraft facility:

- Either to **increase total current assets**
- Or to **reduce other current liabilities**

4.5.1 Increasing total current assets

A business may wish to use its overdraft facility

- To increase its stock levels
- To increase its overall debtors
- To increase its overall sales turnover

A business may wish to **increase its stock levels** without increasing its total sales for a number of reasons.

Stock increases	
Large order	Need to produce goods to order for customer before customer will pay for them. Temporary finance, overdraft is appropriate
Seasonal peak	Need for stocks to meet seasonal demand for goods. Temporary finance, overdraft is appropriate
Speculative purchase	Taking advantage of one-off opportunity, for example purchase of raw materials at favourable price. Overdraft is appropriate provided build-up temporary and not unduly risky
Permanent increase	Permanent increase without turnover increase will mean risk of obsolescence is greater. Overdraft unlikely to be suitable

A business may want to **increase its total debtors** without increasing its sales turnover due to:

- A loss of **efficiency** in the **credit control**, invoicing and debt collection procedures of the business
- The **inability** of existing customers **to pay** without being allowed more credit

In both cases, the bank will be cautious about agreeing to an increased overdraft facility.

When a business **increases its sales turnover**, it will almost certainly have to increase its investment in stocks and debtors. A danger with business expansion is **overtrading**. A bank will be wary of requests to support ambitious expansion schemes.

4.5.2 Using an overdraft to reduce other current liabilities

An extension of an overdraft to reduce trade creditors balances may be requested:

(a) **To take advantage of attractive purchase discounts offered by suppliers for early settlement of debts**. This should be acceptable to a bank, because taking the discount would reduce the costs and so increase the profits of the business.

(b) **To pay creditors who are pressing for payment**. If the business **customer** is in difficulties, a bank would take the view that granting an increased overdraft would mean taking over debts that would not be paid, and so may not allow an increase.

PART A   CASH MANAGEMENT

Activity 6.4

The directors of Crisroe Ltd have asked their bank for a £50,000 overdraft which they say will be used for normal trading operations. They present two balance sheets, one indicating the firm's position before the loan and one after. What do you think the bank's response will be?

CRISROE LIMITED – BALANCE SHEET (BEFORE)

	£	£
Fixed assets		200,000
Current assets	120,000	
Current liabilities: trade creditors	60,000	
Working capital		60,000
		260,000
Share capital and reserves		260,000

CRISROE LIMITED – BALANCE SHEET (AFTER)

	£	£	£
Fixed assets (200,000 + 50,000)			250,000
Current assets		120,000	
Current liabilities: bank overdraft	50,000		
trade creditors	60,000		
		110,000	
Working capital			10,000
			260,000
Share capital and reserves			260,000

A business may want an overdraft facility to enable it to **pay its tax bills**. An overdraft facility to help a business to pay tax is a 'legitimate' purpose for an overdraft, although the bank might want to know why the business had not set funds aside to pay the tax.

5 Medium and long-term loans

5.1 Uses of loans

The main advantage of lending on a loan account for the bank is that it makes **monitoring** and **control** of the advance much easier. The bank can see immediately when the customer is falling behind with repayments, or struggling to make the payments.

5.2 Features of loans

Certain features about a medium-term loan differentiate it from lending on overdraft.

(a) The customer knows what he will be **expected** to pay back at regular intervals and the bank can also predict its future income with more certainty (depending on whether the interest rate is fixed or floating).

(b) Once the loan is agreed, the **term** of the loan must be **adhered** to, provided that the customer does **not fall behind** with **repayments.** It is not repayable on the bank's demand.

(c) As the bank will be committing funds to a customer for a number of years, it may **build certain written safeguards** into the loan agreement, to prevent the customer from becoming over-extended with borrowing during the course of the loan.

(d) Interest payments on a loan are based on the **full amount borrowed**. The loan is repayable not later than the date agreed in the loan agreement, or at an earlier date if the borrower breaks a '**loan covenant'**.

5.3 The term of the loan

The term of the loan will depend on four factors.

(a) The need for the loan, which should **not exceed** the **useful life of the asset** to be purchased. The customer will expect to repay the loan whilst he is still using the asset and enjoying any profits it might be earning

(b) The **internal guidelines** of the individual bank

(c) Government **regulations**, if any, on the maximum term for certain types of lending

(d) **Negotiations** between customer and bank, which involve the opinion of the customer about what term of loan he would like, and the bank's judgement about what term it would be willing to offer

5.4 Loan repayment profiles

Loans can be repaid in three ways.

Methods of repayment	
Bullet	Borrower does not repay any of the loan principal until end of loan period; for example if £100,000 is loaned for 5 years, only interest is payable during 5 years and £100,000 repayable at end
Balloon	Some of loan principal paid during term of loan, but most is repaid at end
Amortising	Loan principal is repayable gradually over term of loan. Loan repayments at regular intervals during loan term partly consist of interest, partly repayment and amount of principal owed is zero at end of loan term

5.5 Loan interest

The interest rate on a loan can be:

- **Fixed** throughout the period of the loan
- **Variable**, depending on interest rates obtainable in the money markets

In addition to the interest payable, a business might have to pay:

- An **arrangement fee** to the bank, for considering the loan application
- **Legal costs**
- **Commitment fees**

Activity 6.5

Why do you think banks often charge higher rates of interest on overdrafts than on loans?

5.6 Loan covenants

Taking out a loan often means certain obligations are placed on the borrower over and above repaying the loan on demand. These obligations are called **covenants**.

Types of covenant	
Positive covenants	Require borrower to **do something**, such as provide the bank with financial or management accounts, or submit certificates that loan agreement is being followed
Negative covenants	Borrower promises **not to do something**, for example not borrow money until current loan repaid
Quantitative covenants	Set **limitations on financial position**, such as total borrowings not to exceed 100% of shareholders' funds

Activity 6.6

Describe the main advantages of overdraft and loan finance for small businesses, and indicate when each might be the most appropriate source of finance.

6 Leasing as a source of finance

6.1 The nature of leasing

Rather than buying an asset outright, a business may lease an asset. **Leasing** has become a popular source of finance in the UK.

Leasing can be defined as a **contract** between **lessor** and **lessee** for hire of a specific asset, selected from a manufacturer or vendor of such assets by the lessee.

- The **lessor retains ownership** of the asset.
- The **lessee has possession** and **use** of the asset on payment of rentals.

Many lessors are **financial intermediaries** such as banks and insurance companies. The range of assets leased is wide, including office equipment and computers, cars and commercial vehicles, aircraft, ships and buildings.

6.2 Types of leases

6.2.1 Operating leases

Operating leases are rental agreements between a lessor and a lessee where:

(a) The **lessor supplies** the **equipment** to the lessee.

(b) The **lessor is responsible** for **servicing and maintaining** the leased equipment.

(c) The period of the lease is less than the **expected economic life** of the asset, so that at the end of a lease, the lessor can lease the same equipment to someone else, and obtain a good rent for it, or sell the equipment second-hand.

6.2.2 Finance leases

Finance leases are lease agreements where the lessee has use of the asset for most or all of the **asset's expected** useful life.

There are other important characteristics of a finance lease.

(a) The **lessee is responsible** for the **upkeep**, servicing and maintenance of the asset. The lessor is not involved in this at all.

(b) The lease has a **primary period**, which covers all or **most of the useful economic life** of the asset. The lease payments during the primary period should **pay** for the **full cost** of the asset and provide the lessor with a **suitable return** on his investment.

(c) The lessee can usually continue to lease the asset for an indefinite **secondary period**, in return for a very low nominal rent. Alternatively, the lessee might sell the asset on a lessor's behalf and keep most of the sale proceeds.

Under a car lease, the primary period of the lease might be three years, with an agreement by the lessee to make three annual payments of £6,000 each. The lessee will be responsible for repairs and servicing, road tax, insurance and garaging.

6.2.3 Sale and leaseback

Sale and leaseback is when a business which already owns an asset, for example a building, agrees to sell the asset to a financial institution and to lease it back. The business has the benefit of the funds from the sale while retaining use of the asset, in return for regular payments to the financial institution.

6.3 Advantages of leasing

There are various advantages of leasing for the **lessee** and the **lessor**.

The **lessor invests finance** by purchasing assets from suppliers and makes a return out of the lease payments from the lessee. He will also get **capital allowances** on his purchase of the equipment.

Leasing might be attractive to the lessee if the lessee **does not have the cash** to pay for the asset, and would have difficulty obtaining a bank loan to buy it. Alternatively **finance leasing** may be **cheaper** than a bank loan.

6.4 Hire purchase

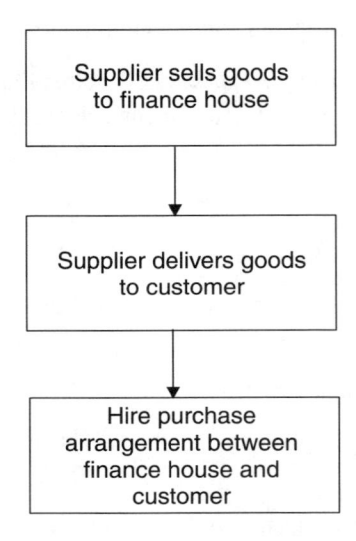

```
┌─────────────────────────┐
│  Supplier sells goods   │
│     to finance house    │
└─────────────────────────┘
             │
             ▼
┌─────────────────────────┐
│ Supplier delivers goods │
│       to customer       │
└─────────────────────────┘
             │
             ▼
┌─────────────────────────┐
│     Hire purchase       │
│  arrangement between    │
│    finance house and    │
│        customer         │
└─────────────────────────┘
```

Hire purchase is another form of credit finance with which leasing can be contrasted.

The finance house will nearly always insist that the hirer should pay a **deposit** towards the purchase price, perhaps as low as 10%, or as high as 33%.

Goods bought by businesses on hire purchase include:

- Company vehicles
- Plant and machinery

- Office equipment
- Farming machinery

When a company acquires a capital asset under a hire purchase agreement, it will eventually obtain **full legal title** to the asset. The HP payments consist partly of 'capital' payments towards the purchase of the asset, and partly of interest charges.

For example, if a company buys a car costing £10,000 under an HP agreement, the car supplier might provide HP finance over a three year period at an interest cost of 10%, and the HP payments might be, say, as follows.

	Capital element £	Interest element £	Total HP payment £
Year 0: down payment	2,540	0	2,540
Year 1	2,254	746	3,000
Year 2	2,479	521	3,000
Year 3	2,727	273	3,000
Total	10,000	1,540	11,540

The **tax position** on a hire purchase arrangement is as follows.

- The buyer obtains whatever **capital allowances** are available, based on the capital element of the cost.
- The hirer's **interest payments** within the HP payments are an **allowable** expense against tax, spread over the term of the HP agreement.
- **Capital payments** within the HP payments, however, are **not allowable** against tax.

Activity 6.7

Explain the advantages of leasing assets from the viewpoint of managing an organisation's cash balances.

7 Other forms of finance

7.1 Issuing securities

A security is a financial instrument such as **shares** or **loan stocks**, which a company may issue and which can be traded.

7.2 Loan stocks

Investors holding **loan stocks** are creditors, who are entitled to **interest**. They are like IOUs which can be sold.

A **debenture** is, legally speaking, a **written acknowledgement** of a debt incurred by a company. However the term is generally used to describe loans that are secured on the company's assets.

Unsecured loan stocks are loans with no greater security than the company's ordinary creditors. However, conditions attached to the loan often place some restrictions upon the company's future borrowing powers.

Convertible loan stock is loan stock which is convertible into ordinary shares.

The rate of interest on loan stock is normally **fixed**, although a few companies have issued variable (or floating) rate stocks, with interest linked to movements in an interest rate such as the 3-month London Inter-Bank Offered Rate (**LIBOR**).

7.3 Equities

Equity capital (shares) should finance long-term investment. For the **company**, equity is the least risky form of finance, whereas for the investor it offers the **highest return** for the **highest risk**. The return to shareholders (dividends) is, in theory, at the discretion of the directors who can **vary the dividend** if they so choose.

7.4 Trade creditors

Rather than rely on the bank overdraft as a source of working capital, businesses frequently use **trade creditors** as a source of short-term borrowing. The use of trade credit as short-term borrowing has advantages from the borrower's point of view.

- Many suppliers offer **60-day terms**, with the possibility of a settlement discount for early payment.
- Whilst a firm has relationships with only a few banks, it has relationships with **many suppliers**, few of whom have the sort of clout that the bank has.
- Trade creditors have an **interest** in the **commercial relationship**.

That said, later in this Interactive Text, we look at the measures that creditors can take to enforce payment.

7.5 Not-for profit organisations

A **not-for-profit organisation**, such as a **charity,** may be able to call upon government grants, charitable donations or bank loans.

Key learning points

- Companies often have to rely on **bank finance**, but it is important that the right type of finance is obtained.
- **Temporary shortfalls** require short-term financial solutions, such as an **increased overdraft**.
- The acquisition of fixed assets on the other hand requires **matching long-term loan** or **equity finance**.
- **Overdrafts** are subject to an **agreed limit**, and are repayable on demand. The customer has a flexible means of short term borrowing. Overdrafts can be renewed. **Interest** is only payable when the **account** is **overdrawn**.
- An overdraft is best considered as support for **normal working capital**. A customer's account can be expected to swing between **surplus and overdraft**.
- A **term loan** is drawn in full at the beginning of the loan period and repaid at a specified time or in defined instalments.
- The term of the loan will be determined by the **useful life** of the asset purchased, the guidelines of the bank, and the results of any negotiations.
- Term loans are offered with a variety of **repayment schedules** (eg bullet, balloon, amortising). Often, the **interest and capital repayments** are **predetermined**.
- **Other sources of finance** (medium-term) include **hire purchase**, **finance leases** and **operating leases**.
- Some businesses obtain extra finance by **taking longer credit from suppliers.** This can be a cheap source of finance, but businesses may **lose supplier goodwill** and the **benefit of discounts**.

PART A   CASH MANAGEMENT

Quick quiz

1 A .... is a loan for a fixed amount for a specified period.

2 In the following mnemonic, concerning a bank's decision to lend, what does each of the letters stand for?

   C   ....
   A   ....
   M   ....
   P   ....
   A   ....
   R   ....
   I   ....

3 What is a commitment fee?

4 How is the loan principal repaid in the case of an amortising loan?

   A   Repaid gradually throughout the loan term
   B   Some is repaid during loan term, but most is repaid at end of loan term
   C   Majority of principal is repaid during loan term, whatever is left at end of loan term is repaid then
   D   No loan principal is repaid until end of loan term

5 A .... charge relates to a specific asset or group of assets.

6 An overdraft facility is the amount of short-term funds that a bank has lent to a customer.

   ☐ True
   ☐ False

7 With a finance lease, who is responsible for upkeep of the asset?

   ☐ The lessor
   ☐ The lessee

8 A .... is a written acknowledgement of a debt incurred by a company, generally a loan that is secured on the company's assets.

Answers to quick quiz

1. A **term loan** is a loan for a fixed amount for a specified period.

2. **C**haracter of the customer
   Ability to borrow and repay
   Margin of profit
   Purpose of the borrowing
   Amount
   Repayment terms
   Insurance against possible repayment.

3. A fee charged by a bank to increase an overdraft facility.

4. A Principal is repaid gradually during loan term.

5. A **fixed** charge relates to a specific asset or group of assets.

6. False. An overdraft facility is the opportunity given to the customer to borrow up to a certain amount. The customer does not necessarily make use of that opportunity.

7. The lessee.

8. A **debenture** is a written acknowledgement of a debt incurred by a company, generally a loan that is secured on the company's assets.

PART A　CASH MANAGEMENT

Activity checklist

This checklist shows which performance criteria, range statement or knowledge and understanding point is covered by each activity in this chapter. Tick off each activity as you complete it.

Activity

6.1	☐	This activity deals with Performance Criterion 15.2.A: arrange overdraft and loan facilities in anticipation of requirements and on the most favourable terms available.
6.2	☐	This activity deals with Knowledge and Understanding 3: bank loans and overdrafts; terms and conditions; legal relationship between bank and customer.
6.3	☐	This activity deals with Knowledge and Understanding 3: bank loans and overdrafts; terms and conditions; legal relationship between bank and customer.
6.4	☐	This activity deals with Performance Criterion 15.2.E: maintain an adequate level of liquidity in line with cash forecasts.
6.5	☐	This activity deals with Performance Criterion 15.2.A: arrange overdraft and loan facilities in anticipation of requirements and on the most favourable terms available.
6.6	☐	This activity deals with Performance Criterion 15.2.A: arrange overdraft and loan facilities in anticipation of requirements and on the most favourable terms available.
6.7	☐	This activity deals with Performance Criterion 15.2.E: maintain an adequate level of liquidity in line with cash forecasts.

chapter 7

Investing money

Contents

1. Introduction
2. Budgeting for surpluses
3. Cash investments: bank and building society accounts
4. Marketable securities: prices and interest rates
5. Government securities
6. Local authority and other public sector stocks
7. Certificates of deposit
8. Bills of exchange
9. Other commercial stocks
10. Making investments

Performance criteria

15.2.B Invest surplus funds in marketable securities within defined financial authorisation limits

15.2.C Ensure the organisation's financial regulations and security procedures are observed

15.2.D Ensure account is taken of trends in the economic and financial environment in managing cash balances

15.2.E Maintain an adequate level of liquidity in line with cash forecasts

Range statement

15.2.1 Maintain liquidity through management of cash, overdrafts and loans

Knowledge and understanding

- Bank overdrafts and loans: terms and conditions; legal relationship between bank and customer
- Types of marketable security (Bills of exchange, certificates of deposit, government securities, local authority short term loans); terms and conditions; risks
- Managing risk and exposure
- Liquidity management
- Understanding that the accounting systems of an organisation are affected by its organisational structure, its administrative systems and procedures and the nature of its business transactions

PART A CASH MANAGEMENT

- An understanding that practice in this area will be determined by an organisation's specific financial regulations, guidelines and security procedures
- An understanding that in public sector organisations there are statutory and other regulations relating to the management of cash balances

1 Introduction

You may face a situation where your organisation has a cash surplus. That surplus needs to be used in the best way, and this will often mean **investing** it.

In this chapter therefore we consider the different types of marketable security that are available for investment. A key aspect in the choice of which instrument to use is the trade-off between:

- The **risks** to balances invested
- The **returns** that can be achieved from investing funds

Although you do not have to become an expert investment manager, you may be asked to identify problems with an **investment policy**, and **recommend improvements**. The **security** of investments is important as they are a key business asset.

2 Budgeting for surpluses

2.1 Management of surpluses

Many businesses have temporary cash surpluses which they need to manage to earn a return. Cash is an asset of a business; if it is to be invested it must be invested profitably and the investment must be **secure**.

Banks provide one avenue for investment, but larger firms can invest in other forms of financial instrument in the money markets. Generally speaking, the greater the return offered, the riskier the investment.

2.2 Motives for holding cash

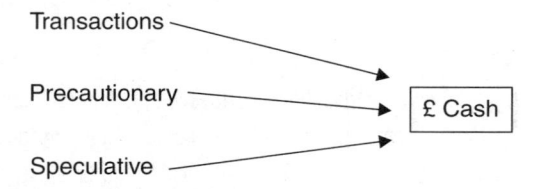

Transactions ⟶ £ Cash
Precautionary ⟶
Speculative ⟶

The economist J M Keynes identified three reasons why a business may wish to hold cash – the **transactions**, **precautionary** and **speculative** motives. In addition a business will need to consider whether it will need large amounts of cash for **investment** purposes.

2.2.1 The transactions motive

The **transactions motive** is when a business needs cash to meet its **regular commitments** of paying its creditors, its employees' wages, its taxes, its annual dividends to shareholders and so on.

2.2.2 The precautionary motive

The **precautionary motive** is when a business maintains a 'buffer' of cash for **unforeseen contingencies**. This buffer may be provided by an **overdraft facility**, which has the advantage that it will cost little or nothing until it is actually used.

Many larger companies use **cash management models** to determine the **optimal cash balance**. In a medium-sized or small business, deciding how to manage cash balances is often left to the judgement and skill of the financial manager.

2.2.3 The speculative motive

Keynes identified the **speculative motive** as a third motive for holding cash. However, most businesses do not hold surplus cash as a speculative asset (eg in the hope that interest rates will rise).

2.2.4 Cash balances and investment

If a company is planning future major **fixed asset purchases**, or if it is planning to **acquire another business**, it will consider whether any cash surplus should be **retained** and **invested** in marketable securities until it is needed.

If a company has **no plans to grow** or to invest, then surplus cash not required for transactions or precautionary purposes should be returned to shareholders. Surplus cash may be returned to shareholders by:

- Increasing the usual level of the **annual dividends** which are paid
- Making a one-off **special dividend payment**
- Using the money to **buy back its own shares** from some of its shareholders

Activity 7.1

Thinking back to what we covered earlier in this Interactive Text, state what characteristics an asset must possess in order to be considered liquid.

2.3 Liquidity

We need to consider what we mean by surplus. Take the following example.

PART A　CASH MANAGEMENT

Example: Liquidity

Overdrawn Ltd receives money every month from cash sales and from debtors for credit sales of £1,000. It makes payments, in the normal course of events of £800 a month. In January, the company uses an overdraft facility to buy a car for £4,000.

	Jan £	Feb £	March £
Brought forward	-	(3,800)	(3,600)
Receipts	1,000	1,000	1,000
Payments	(800)	(800)	(800)
Car	(4,000)	-	-
Overdrawn balance	(3,800)	(3,600)	(3,400)

The company has been left with a persistent overdraft, even though, in operating terms, it makes a monthly surplus of £200.

Surplus Ltd, on the other hand, has monthly cash receipts of £1,200 and monthly cash payments of £1,050. The company sets up a special loan account: it borrows £5,000 to buy a car. This it pays off at the rate of £80 a month.

	Jan £	Feb £	March £
Brought forward	-	70	140
Receipts	1,200	1,200	1,200
Payments	(1,050)	(1,050)	(1,050)
Loan repayment	(80)	(80)	(80)
Balance at bank	70	140	210

Which do you consider has the healthier finances?

Solution

Clearly Overdrawn Ltd produces an **operating surplus** (before the motor purchase) of £200 (£1,000 – £800) a month, which is more than Surplus's £150 (£1,200 – £1,050). Furthermore Surplus Ltd has a higher net debt, the loan for the car being £5,000 as opposed to £4,000.

Yet, in effect, the financing arrangements each have chosen have turned the tables. Overdrawn Ltd is relying on normal overdraft finance which will be **repayable on demand**. Its normal **operating surplus** of receipts from sales and debtors over payments for purchases and to creditors has been completely swamped by the long-term financing of a car.

On the other hand Surplus Ltd, by arranging a separate term loan which is more secure from its point of view, is able to run a cash surplus of £70 a month. It has effectively separated this from its cash requirements for capital investment in the car, a **financial inflow**.

A more complex example might have included a **seasonal surplus**, where surpluses generated in good months are used to cover shortfalls later. The mere existence of a surplus in one or two months in a row is no guarantee of liquidity in the long term.

2.4 Safety

Considerations of **safety** are also important. Cash surpluses are rarely hoarded on the company's premises where they can be stolen. But what should be done with them in the short term?

- They are **assets** of the company, and do need to be looked after as well as any other asset.
- In time of inflation, **money** effectively **falls in value**.
- Any surplus must be kept **secure**: some banks are not as secure as others and some investments are riskier than others.

2.5 Profitability

We can approach this aspect by means of the example below.

Example: Profitability

Compare the following two situations. Steve and Andy are both in the car repair business. Both own equipment worth £4,000 and both owe £200 to creditors. Steve, however, has accumulated £1,000 in cash which is deposited in a non interest bearing current account at his bank. Andy has £100 in petty cash.

	Steve £	Andy £
Fixed assets	4,000	4,000
Cash at bank	1,000	100
Creditors	(200)	(200)
Net assets	4,800	3,900
Profit for the year	1,200	1,200

Which would you say is the more profitable?

Solution

(a) Both obviously have made the same amount of profit in the year in question. In absolute terms they are equal.

(b) However, if we examine them more closely, we find that the relative performance of Steve and Andy differs.

$$\frac{\text{Profit}}{\text{Net assets}} \qquad \text{Steve} \quad \frac{£1,200}{£4,800} = 25\% \qquad \text{Andy} \quad \frac{£1,200}{£3,900} = 30.8\%$$

In other words, Andy is making the same amount out of more limited resources. Steve could have easily increased his profit if he had invested his spare cash and earned interest on it.

In the short term, surplus funds need to be **invested** so that they can **earn a return** when they are not being used for any other purpose.

(a) A return can be earned perhaps by an **earlier payment** of **business debts**. The return is the 'interest' saved.

(b) Otherwise, there are a **variety of accounts** and financial instruments which can earn a return on the cash surpluses. These are discussed in the next section of this chapter.

2.6 Risk and return

Any business will normally have a number of guidelines as to how the funds are invested. A business will try and maximise the return for an **acceptable** level of risk. The risk of an investment is its tendency to fluctuate in value. Assume you have £100 to invest.

(a) **Shares**. The price of shares on the stock market can 'go down as well as up'. For example, on Day 1 you might have paid £100 for shares which on Day 2 had fallen in value to £90, whereas on Day 3 their value might have increased to £120.

(b) **Deposit**. The amount of money you deposit in your bank account will not change, ie £100 will still be £100, and there will be an amount of accrued interest.

(c) Shares would obviously be a **riskier investment** than a deposit.

Certain corporate treasury departments have taken too many risks with their organisations' funds, investing them in risky financial instruments to gain a profit. These went sour, and the organisations have been left with large losses, arising solely out of treasury operations, with little relevance to the firm's main business.

We shall consider the risk and return of particular investments at the end of this chapter.

2.7 Guidelines for investing

Guidelines can cover issues such as the following.

(a) Surplus funds can only be invested in **specified types of investment** (eg no equity shares).

(b) All investments must be **convertible** into cash within a set number of days.

(c) Investments should be **ranked,** surplus funds to be invested in higher risk instruments only when a sufficiency has been invested in lower risk items (so that there is always a cushion of safety).

(d) If a firm invests in certain financial instruments, a **credit rating** should be obtained. Credit rating agencies issue gradings according to risk.

The major factors affecting choice are these.

- Whether the investor is looking for **income** or **capital appreciation**
- The investor's **tax position**
- The investor's **attitude** to the **market price fluctuations** resulting from changes in interest rates
- **Other aspects** of the **investor's business**

2.8 Legal restrictions on investments

The type of investments an organisation can make is restricted by law in certain special cases:

- Where public (ie taxpayers') money is invested by a **public sector** (central or local government) institution
- Where the money is invested by a company on behalf of personal investors in cases such as **pension schemes**
- In the case of **trusts** (as determined by the Trustee Investment Act)

Activity 7.2

The treasurer of Sarhall plc has forecast that, over the next year, the company will generate cash flows in excess of its requirements.

List *four* possible reasons for such a surplus, and explain the circumstances under which the board of directors might decide to keep the excess in liquid form.

3 Cash investments: bank and building society accounts

3.1 High street bank deposits

All of the 'High Street' banks offer a wide range of different types of interest-earning account. The variety has **increased** in recent years in competition with the building societies. The main High Street banks and many building societies also pay interest on some types of current account.

If you have a larger amount of money to invest (typically a minimum of £500), you can place the money in a **high interest account**. Access is usually still immediate, but the rate of interest offered will be higher. Cheque facilities may be available.

All banks can offer special facilities for very large amounts. For example, with amounts of, say, over £50,000 it is usually possible to get fixed rate quotes for **money market deposits** for varying intervals from seven days up to eighteen months or longer.

Activity 7.3

Why do you think that a commercial bank might operate with various different rates of interest?

3.2 Building societies deposits

The Building Societies Act 1986 allowed building societies to compete with banks over a much wider range of activities than they used to, and increasingly the societies are offering **cheque or credit card facilities.** Like the banks, the building societies have developed a wide range of different investment facilities, which are mainly for non-corporate investors.

3.3 Interest

If interest on an account is paid more frequently than annually, the annual return is higher than available from an account paying interest at the same rate at the end of each year. This is because **some interest** can be **earned** in the year **on the interest** which is **paid before** the end of the year.

You can compare the interest available on accounts by calculating the compound annual rate of interest (CAR).

If x% interest is paid n times per year, then the compound annual rate of interest is given by the following.

$$CAR = \left(\left(1+\frac{x}{n}\right)^n - 1\right) \times 100$$

For example, Account A offers 5.3% gross payable annually, while Account B offers 5.25% gross, payable quarterly. The CAR for B is:

$$\left(\left(1+\frac{0.0525}{4}\right)^4 - 1\right) \times 100 = 5.35\%$$

This is higher than the annual return on Account A.

Interest rates on cash investments may or may not vary, depending on the terms of the account.

Activity 7.4

An account in the West Sussex Building Society offers 6.0% gross payable every six months, whereas an account in the East Sussex Building Society offers 5.9% gross payable every three months. Which account offers the higher compound annual return?

4 Marketable securities: prices and interest rates

4.1 Types of marketable securities

Marketable securities, such as gilts, bills and certificates of deposit, are bought and sold on the open market, as well as earning interest.

4.2 Prices of fixed interest stocks

The price of marketable securities is affected by the following:

- The **interest rate** on the stock compared with other interest rates
- The **risk** associated with the payment of interest
- The **length of time** till redemption

4.2.1 Interest rate

The **interest rate** on a stock is normally fixed at the outset. However it may become more or less attractive when compared with the interest rates in the money markets as a whole.

Suppose that investors in the market expect a return of 6.47%. $2^{1}/_{2}$% Consolidated Stock was issued in 18X3, paying £2.50 interest for every £100 of the stock's nominal value. However, the increased return demanded means that investors will push down the price of the stock until the return on the investment reflects the market rate.

$$\frac{£2.50}{\text{Price of £100 nominal}} = 6.47\% \therefore \text{the price of £100 nominal is £2.50/0.0647 = £38.64}$$

So where general interest rates rise, the price of stocks will fall, and vice versa.

4.2.2 Risk

The **risk** associated with the payment of interest and the **eventual repayment of capital** influence the price. British Government securities are considered virtually risk free but other fixed interest stocks may not be.

4.3 Length of time till redemption

Suppose the following market values were quoted on 25 March 20X1:

9% Exchequer Stock 20X4 £113.8029
9% Treasury Stock 20X9 £142.6311

The two stocks have the same 'coupon' rates and are in other respects similar except for the redemption dates. The first stock is due to be redeemed in 20X4, whereas the second will not be redeemed until the year 20X9.

In both cases, the stocks will be redeemed at their nominal value of £100. The closer a stock gets to its redemption date the closer will the price approach £100. This is known as the **pull to maturity**.

4.4 Interest yield

The **interest yield** is the **interest or coupon rate** expressed as a **percentage** of the **market price**.

The yield for a particular investment is an expression for the **return on the stock** if it was bought at the **price ruling** and **held** for one year.

Activity 7.5

On 19 March 20X0 the market price of 9% Treasury Stock 20X9 is £134.1742. What is the interest yield?

The interest yield in practice is influenced by two other factors.

- Accrued interest
- Cum div and ex div

4.4.1 Accrued interest

The interest on 10% Treasury Stock 20X3, is paid in two equal instalments on 8 March and 8 September each year. Thus, if an investor were to sell stock on 1 June 20X1, the investor would not receive on 8 September the earned interest which the purchaser will receive. The price paid by the purchaser must reflect this amount of accrued interest.

4.4.2 Cum div (int) and Ex div (int)

For administrative reasons, issuers of securities must close their books some time before the due date for the payment of interest or dividends. This enables them to send out the warrants in time for them to reach the registered owner of the security before the due dates.

- Any person who buys investments ex dividend (**ex div**) or ex interest (**ex int**) will not receive the next payment.
- The purchaser of investments **cum int** or **cum div** will receive the next payment.

4.5 Redemption yields

The **gross redemption yield** takes account of both the **interest payable until redemption** and the **redemption value**.

Yields are determined by **market prices** which in turn reflect the demand for particular stocks. Thus, if a yield is relatively low it can be concluded that the price is relatively high and that the demand for the stock is also relatively high. Conversely, a high yield means that a stock is relatively unpopular.

5 Government securities

5.1 Gilts

Gilts is short for **'gilt-edged securities'**. These are marketable British government securities. These stocks dominate the fixed interest market.

Classification of gilts	
Shorts	Lives up to 5 years
Mediums	Lives from 5 to 15 years
Longs	Lives of more than 15 years
Undated stocks	Irredeemable or one-way option stocks eg War Loan
Index-linked stocks	Interest and redemption value linked to inflation

'Life' means the number of years before the issuer repays the principal amount.

5.2 Fixed interest gilts

Most gilts are fixed interest, and their prices and yields follow the principles outlined in the previous Section. There are some other types of gilt, outlined below.

5.3 Index-linked stocks

Various **index-linked Treasury stocks** are in issue. Both the interest and the eventual redemption value are linked to inflation. This guarantees a **real return equal to the redemption rate.**

The half yearly interest payment is calculated on the basis of the **value of the Retail Prices Index eight months before the interest payment date**.

Thus if a 2% index-linked stock was issued 8 months after the index had stood at 100 and the index stood at 150 eight months before a particular interest payment date, then the interest payable would be:

Interest payable = $\frac{1}{2} \times \frac{150}{100} \times 2\% = 1.5\%$

The ½ is needed as the **interest is payable half-yearly**. The redemption value is similarly indexed.

5.4 Convertible gilts

Convertible gilts are redeemable on the date shown or, at the holder's option, **convertible** into a new **longer dated stock**.

5.5 Gilt prices in the Financial Times

Gilt prices are to be found in the *Financial Times*. For all categories other than index-linked gilts, the information is presented as follows.

PART A CASH MANAGEMENT

Monday edition

Notes	Price (£)	Wk% +/-	Amount £m	Interest due	Last xd
Treas 10pc 20X5	121.0801	0.4	2,506	Mr 8 Se 8	22.2

Tuesday to Saturday editions

	Yield				52 week	
Notes	Int	Red	Price (£)	+ or −	High	Low
Treas 10pc 20X5	8.27	4.72	120.9273	+0.0600	123.52	115.44

The first (Monday) example above shows that 10% Treasury Stock 20X5 was quoted at £121.0801 at the close of business on the previous Friday, a change of +0.4% in the week. £2,506 million of the stock was in issue, and interest is due on 8 March and 8 September. The stock last went **ex-dividend** on 22 February. In other words, if you bought the stock after 22 February, you will not receive the interest due on 8 March. This interest will be paid to whoever held the stock up to 22 February.

The second (Tuesday to Saturday) example shows that the current price of the same stock was £120.9273 at the close of business on the previous day, which is £0.06 higher than the price on the day before. The highest quoted price in the 52 weeks to date is £123.52; the lowest is £115.44. The gross interest yield and the gross redemption yield are given in the first two columns.

Activity 7.6

Suppose that a client wishes to purchase 13¾% Treasury Stock 20X0-X3 with a nominal value of £5,000. The transaction is executed by a stockbroker, who charges commission of 0.8%, in March 20X0 at a price of £111.5064. Accrued interest is 56 days. What will be the total cost?

5.6 Purchase, sale and issue of gilts

Gilt-edged stocks may be purchased or sold through the following means.

- Through a **stockbroker**, who deals on the stock exchange and who receives commission
- Through a **registered agent** (normally a bank, solicitor or accountant) who will, in turn, act through a stockbroker
- Through **larger post offices** acting as agents for the Bonds and Stock Office

Activity 7.7

Your Managing Director tells you that he has read of how the British Government has issued a number of index-linked stocks. Explain to him why these stocks are likely to be attractive to potential investors.

6 Local authority and other public sector stocks

6.1 Local authority stocks

Marketable local authority securities may be **issued** by any **size of authority** from County Councils to Borough Councils. These stocks may, in most respects, be considered as being very similar to British Government Stocks. The main differences are as follows.

- The security of a local authority is not considered as good as the central government's.
- The market in most of the stocks is much thinner.

The **yield** on local authority stocks thus tends to be rather higher than on gilts.

In addition to the longer term loan stocks, many local authorities issue bonds which are redeemable after one or two years. These are commonly known as **yearlings**.

6.2 Public board loans

There are a number of loans from other 'public' bodies from the UK and overseas such as the Agricultural Mortgage Corporation, the Port Authorities and organisations such as Investors in Industry.

7 Certificates of deposit

7.1 CDs

Certificates of deposit (CDs) are issued by an institution (bank or building society), certifying that a **specified sum** has been **deposited** with the issuing institution, to be **repaid** on a **specific date**. The term may be as short as seven days, or as long as five years. Most are for a term of six months. The minimum nominal amount is usually £50,000.

7.2 Trading CDs

A **certificate of deposit (CD)** is a **negotiable instrument**, meaning it can be bought or sold. Title belongs to the holder (a CD is in **bearer form**). Ownership is transferred by physical delivery from buyer to seller.

As CDs are negotiable, if the holder of a CD wants cash immediately, the CD can be sold. The certificates of deposit market is one of the London money markets.

7.3 Obtaining payment on CDs

The CD recognises the obligation to the **bearer** (with or without interest) at a future date. The holder of a certificate is therefore entitled to the money on deposit, usually with **interest**, on the stated date. The holder obtains payment by presenting the CD on the appropriate date to a recognised bank.

7.4 Advantages of CDs

A CD offers an **attractive rate of interest**, *and* can be **easily sold**. Unlike a money market deposit which cannot be terminated until it matures, CDs can be **liquidated at any time** at the prevailing market rate. There is a large and active **secondary market** in bank and building society CDs. Hence they are an ideal way to invest funds in the short term while retaining the flexibility to convert into cash at short notice if the need arises.

8 Bills of exchange

8.1 Types of bill

A bill of exchange is an **unconditional order in writing** from one person or company to another, requiring the person or company to whom it is addressed to pay a **specified sum of money**:

- On demand (**sight bill**)
- At a future date (**term bill**)

A **bill of exchange** is similar to a cheque although, strictly speaking, a cheque is a type of bill of exchange. Bills may be drawn **in any currency**.

8.2 Term bills

Term bills of exchange have the following features.

- Their **duration** or **maturity** may be from **two weeks** to **six months**.
- They can be **denominated in any currency**.
- They can be for a value of up to **£500,000** per bill.

8.3 Drawing of bills

- The **bill** is **drawn** on the company or person who is being ordered to pay.
- The **drawer** orders payment of the money.
- The **drawee** is the party who is to pay, and to whom the bill is addressed.
- The **payee** receives the funds.

8.4 Details on bills

The **date of the bill** is normally the date when it is signed by the drawer. The **place of drawing** is also included. The **amount payable** must be shown in **words and figures**. The bill must also **specify** the **name of the payee,** which might be the **drawer** or a **third party.**

There are three ways of specifying the **due date for payment** of a term bill.

- On a **stated date**
- A **stated period after sight** (sight is when the drawee signs acceptance of the bill)
- A **stated period** after the **date of the bill**

A bill is an **unconditional order to pay**, and it will always include the word 'pay' and be phrased so as to make it clear that the order is unconditional.

For a term bill with a future payment date, the **drawee** signs acceptance of the order to pay (**accepts the bill**/ agrees to pay) and returns the bill to the drawer or the drawer's bank. When a bill is accepted, it becomes an IOU or promise to pay.

8.5 Example of bill

An example of an accepted bill is shown below. The name of the drawee is shown in the example on the bottom left-hand side.

8.6 Discounting bills

As an IOU, an accepted bill of exchange is a form of debt. The holder of the bill can hold on to the bill until **maturity**, then present it to the specified bank for payment. Alternatively, the bill holder can **sell the bill** before maturity, for an amount below its payment value (ie at a **discount**).

If the bill is sold, an authorised signatory of the drawer or bill holder **signs the back of the bill**, and gives the bill to the buyer. The buyer, as the new bill holder, will claim **payment at maturity,** unless the bill is sold on again.

The ability of a bill holder to sell the bill for a reasonable price depends on:

- The **credit quality** of the drawee
- The existence of a **liquid secondary market** in bills. Larger financial institutions are able to operate a liquid two-way market for accepted term bills.

The **buyer** of a bill expects to make a profit by purchasing the bill at a **discount** to its face value and then either **receiving full payment** at maturity on presenting the bill for payment, or **reselling the bill** before maturity. The profit from buying a bill therefore represents an **interest yield** on a short-term investment (to maturity of the bill).

The **seller** obtains immediate cash from the buyer of the bill, but in effect is borrowing short-term funds, with the interest rate for borrowing built into the discount price.

8.7 Bills as sources of finance

Bills of exchange are also used extensively to finance domestic and international trade, because they are tradeable instruments for short-term credit. There are two main types of sterling-denominated bills of exchange.

- **Trade bills** are bills drawn by one non-bank company on another company, typically demanding payment for a trade debt.
- **Bank bills** are bills drawn and payable by a bank. A **banker's acceptance** is where a bank accepts a bill on behalf of a customer, and promises to pay the bill at maturity.

9 Other commercial stocks

9.1 Bonds

Bond is a term for any fixed interest (mostly) security, whether it is issued by the government, a company, a bank or other institution. (Gilts are **UK government bonds**.) Businesses also issue bonds. They are usually for the long term, and may be **secured**.

9.2 Commercial paper

Commercial paper (CP) is the term for certificates **issued by a company**, promising to pay a fixed sum to the person bearing the note on a specified date. Like a gilt, CP is traded, often at a **discount** reflecting the yield required. Companies find them useful for short term borrowing (usually 3 months).

CP is unsecured and it is therefore risky. A firm's CP is therefore given a credit rating by **third party agencies** to assess its risk. Large companies might therefore restrict investment in CP.

9.3 Debenture stocks

Debenture stocks are issued in return for loans **secured on a particular asset of the business**. A factory, for example, may be offered as **security**. The loan is for the **long term**. Debenture holders take priority over other creditors when a business is wound-up. They can force a liquidation.

9.4 PIBS

Permanent interest bearing shares (PIBS) are a type of security specially created to enable **building societies** to raise funds while improving their capital ratios. PIBS are quoted on the London Stock Exchange and the market totals about £1 billion.

10 Making investments

10.1 Risk and exposure

All investments possess some degree of **risk**. In some cases this may be very small indeed. Risk may be considered in terms of its effect on **income**, **capital** or **both**.

10.1.1 Risk to income

Cash investments which carry a **variable rate of income** also carry the **risk** that the rate will fall in line with conditions prevailing in the market.

10.1.2 Risk to capital

With an **investment in gilts** or other **'undoubted' marketable fixed interest stocks**, there is always a risk of a **capital loss** if **prices fall**, even though the payment of interest is completely secure.

10.1.3 Risk to capital and income

For **many investments both income and capital are at risk**. Often a loss of income will precede a loss of capital. A company may reduce its ordinary share dividend, precipitating a fall in the share price.

10.2 Risk factors

Risk may be caused by:

- **General factors**
- **Factors specific** to an individual security or sector

10.2.1 General factors

All investments are affected, to some extent, by **changes in the political** and **economic climate**. In October 1987 all major stock markets fell dramatically, apparently taking their cue from one another.

Inflation will lead to a **fall in the value of money**, which may **affect both income and capital**. Cash and other non-equity investments are particularly susceptible, although the high yield may provide some compensation.

10.2.2 Special factors

The results of an individual company will be affected not only by general economic conditions but also by:

- Its type of products or services
- Its competitive position within the industry
- Management factors

10.3 The relationship between risk and return

The return expected by an investor will depend on the level of risk. The higher the risk, the higher the required return. This is illustrated in the diagram below.

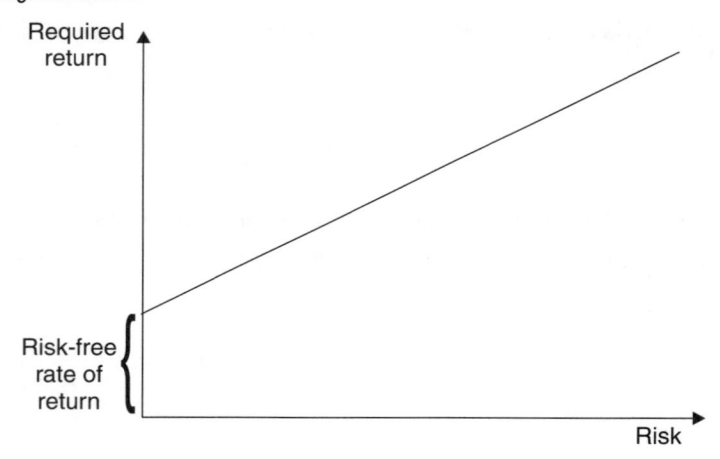

10.4 Risk on individual securities

Marketable UK securities can be ranked in order of increasing risk and increasing expected return.

- Government securities
- Local authority stocks
- Other 'public' corporation stocks
- Company mortgage debentures
- Other secured debentures
- Unsecured loans
- Convertible loan stocks
- Preference shares
- Equities

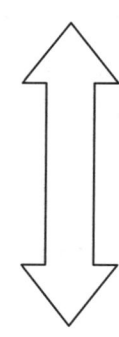

Low risk ↑↓ *High risk*

The riskiness of CDs and bills of exchange varies with the **creditworthiness of the issuers**. They are riskier than government (and probably local government) securities, but less risky than shares.

10.5 What combination of risk and return is appropriate?

Given that an investor is faced with a range of investments with differing risk/return combinations, what sort of investment should he choose?

Whilst most investors are **risk-averse** (they prefer less risk to more risk, given the same return), the intensity of that aversion varies between individuals. Some are quite happy to take a bit of a gamble in the hope of achieving a higher return.

10.6 Diversification and holding a portfolio

Holding more than one investment always carries less risk than holding only one. If only one investment is held, the investor could lose a lot if this one investment fails.

The extent to which risk can be reduced will depend on the relationship which exists between the different returns. The process of reducing risk by increasing the number of separate investments in a portfolio is known as **diversification**.

10.7 Positive and negative correlation

Where the returns from two investments have **perfect positive correlation**, this means that either both will have good results or both will have bad results.

Where the returns from two investments have **perfect negative correlation**, this means that if one has good results, the other is certain to have bad results.

Risk can be reduced by investing in securities where returns are **not** perfectly **positively correlated**. While it is not usually possible to find investments whose returns have perfect negative correlation, some degree of negative correlation is often possible.

10.8 Interest yield and risk

A company's finance director or treasurer must decide on a **target interest rate yield** for investments. One element of skill or judgement is to predict the likely movement in interest rates. The directors must decide what is an acceptable level of risk.

10.9 Timing and expectations

Timing is also important. Making an investment at the best time, even during the course of a single day, can earn a company substantial profits.

If **interest rates** are expected to **rise** in the near future, a company might prefer to hold all surplus cash temporarily on **short-term deposit.** They should only invest in **longer-term money market instruments** (eg three-month CDs) after allowing time for interest rates to rise, with the aim of profiting from the higher interest yields that would then be obtainable.

If rates are expected to **fall**, a company is more likely to **invest earlier** for **fixed terms** of several months, rather than to invest in shorter-term instruments or deposits.

Example: Choosing investment instruments

Suppose that a company has prepared a forecast of its sterling cash flows as follows.

Date	Cash in £'000	Cash out £'000	Cash balance £'000
Week 1			
Start of week			50
Day 1	1,000	100	950
Day 2	850	300	1,500
Day 3	600	500	1,600
Day 4	1,200	1,600	1,200
Day 5	1,500	600	2,100
Week 2	6,000	4,000	4,100
Week 3	5,000	5,000	4,100
Week 4	5,000	5,100	4,000

The finance director has decided to invest the company's cash surpluses in the money markets. Advise him on possible investments.

Solution

The company's cash forecast will extend beyond Week 4. If the finance director is reasonably confident that the minimum surplus for at least three months from Day 2 of Week 1 will be £1,200,000, she might decide to invest this amount in a money market instrument, such as three-month CDs. The balance of surplus funds in Week 1 might be held on deposit with a bank at the most favourable rate obtainable for money at call.

From Day 5 of Week 1, the finance director can review the cash situation again, in more detail for Week 2 and beyond, with a view to making further investment decisions for the cash surplus currently expected to build up.

Activity 7.8

Your supervisor is unclear about the risks involved in holding each of:

(a)   Ordinary shares in UK quoted companies
(b)   Bank deposit accounts
(c)   Redeemable British Government stocks

Draft a note to her, describing the relative risks and suggesting how these risks may be minimised.

10.10 Buying and selling marketable securities through brokers

For most companies buying gilts, shares and so on is effected through specialist firms of intermediaries, **brokers**. In practice, these brokers buy and sell on their clients' behalf in the various investment markets that are available. The procedure for Stock Exchange investments will be as follows:

- The client **contacts the broker** with a specific instruction.
- The broker will send a **contract note**, once the transaction has been completed, and the date at which settlement must be made.

10.11 Dealing guidelines

Before telephoning a bank to ask for an interest rate, it is a good idea to calculate the financial impact of each $1/8$% or $1/16$% on the planned transaction.

- For example, an additional $1/16$% on a £10 million investment for one year equates to £6,250 – a significant amount.
- An additional $1/16$% on a £1 million overnight deposit produces only £1.71 of extra interest, and it is not worth spending time trying to insist on a higher yield.

When a transaction is agreed by telephone, have a calculator ready, in order to agree the amount of interest receivable or payable. The interest figure verifies three elements in the transaction:

PART A   CASH MANAGEMENT

- The amount invested
- The interest rate
- The term of the loan

A company planning an investment should be comfortable with the **additional risks** associated with the higher yields on offer from any investment that might seem attractive. **Spreading the investment risk** over a number of different banks or instruments is equally important.

10.12 Smaller companies

Smaller companies that make money market investments through their local bank, or their bank liaison officer, can use many of the same dealing tips. These companies should check with their bank that the interest rate is as close to market levels as possible.

10.13 Safe custody

Purchased investments, with a few exceptions, can require **safe custody**. This is very important for bearer securities such as **Treasury bills**, **bills of exchange** and **eurobonds**, for which physical possession is taken as evidence of ownership.

Safe custody is also required for **commercial paper**, but this will usually be warehoused, free of charge, with the bank selling it.

Activity 7.9

What security procedures would be appropriate for:

(a)   A bank current account
(b)   A share certificate evidencing ownership of another company's shares?

Key learning points

- A company has a variety of opportunities for using its **cash surpluses**, but the choice of obtaining a return is determined by considerations of **profitability**, **liquidity** and **safety**.

- Surplus funds can be deposited in **interest bearing accounts** offered by banks, finance houses or building societies.

- Generally speaking interest bearing accounts are for a **fixed period** of time. Withdrawal may **not** be **permitted**, or may result in a penalty. The amount invested (principal) does not decline in monetary value.

- **Securities** (ie financial instruments) can be bought or sold, and in London the markets in the main stocks are very liquid.

- The **yield** (profitability) of a money market instrument depends on its **face value**, the **interest rate** offered and the **period of time** before it is redeemed (ie converted into cash) by the issuer.

- **Gilts** are securities issued by the UK government. Other fixed interest marketable securities include **local authority bonds**, and **corporate debt**.

- **Commercial paper** and **debenture stock** are debt instruments issued by companies. Commercial paper is unsecured.

- A **certificate of deposit** is a certificate indicating that a sum of money has been deposited with a bank and will be repaid at a later date. As CDs can be bought and sold, they are a liquid type of investment.

- A **bill of exchange** is like a cheque, only it is not drawn on a bank. It orders the drawee to pay money.

- The relative attractiveness of investing in any of these securities derives from their **return** and their **risk**. **Diversification** across a range of separate investments can reduce risk for the investor.

- The organisation's **procedures and guidelines** need to be followed when making investments, taking into account any legal restrictions.

PART A   CASH MANAGEMENT

Quick quiz

1   Which of the following investments offers the higher compound annual rate of interest?
    - Investment A offering 3.5% gross payable every six months
    - Investment B offering 3.4% gross payable monthly

2   What sort of investment opportunities are offered by high street banks?

    ☐ Deposit account

    ☐ High interest cheque accounts

    ☐ High interest deposit accounts

    ☐ Exchange equalisation accounts

    ☐ Regular income accounts

    ☐ Cash ratio deposits

    ☐ Option deposits

    ☐ Money market deposits

3   What are gilts?

4   How can gilts be bought and sold?

5   What is the advantage of a certificate of deposit over a time deposit?

    A   Profitability
    B   Maturity
    C   Security
    D   Liquidity

6   A .... is an unconditional order in writing from one person or company to another, requiring the person or company to whom it is addressed to pay a specified sum of money on demand or at a future date.

7   What factors affect the riskiness of investments?

8   Starting with the lowest risk investment, rank the following investments in order of riskiness.

    ☐ Unsecured loan stocks

    ☐ Preference shares

    ☐ Local authority stocks

    ☐ Equities

    ☐ Government securities

    ☐ Company debentures

Answers to quick quiz

1 $$\text{CAR} = \left(\left(1+\frac{x}{n}\right)^n - 1\right) \times 100$$

   $$\text{A CAR} = \left(\left(1+\frac{0.035}{2}\right)^2 - 1\right) \times 100$$

   $$= 3.53\%$$

   $$\text{B CAR} = \left(\left(1+\frac{0.034}{12}\right)^{12} - 1\right) \times 100$$

   $$= 3.45\%$$

   A has the highest compound annual rate of interest.

2 Deposit accounts, high interest cheque accounts, high interest deposit accounts, regular income accounts, option deposits, money market deposits. (For information, the exchange equalisation account is used by the Bank of England to stabilise the exchange rate of sterling; cash ratio deposits are deposits maintained by commercial banks with the Bank of England.)

3 Marketable British Government securities.

4 Through a stockbroker, a registered agent or at post offices (through the National Savings Stock Register).

5 D CDs can be liquidated at any time at the prevailing market rate.

6 A **bill of exchange** is an unconditional order in writing from one person or company to another, requiring the person or company to whom it is addressed to pay a specified sum of money on demand or at a future date.

7 (a) Market sentiment about the general political and economic climate
   (b) The rate of inflation, and the future outlook for inflation
   (c) Factors relating to the products, competitive position and management of the enterprise

8 1. Government securities
   2. Local authority stocks
   3. Company debentures
   4. Unsecured loan stocks
   5. Preference shares
   6. Equities

PART A CASH MANAGEMENT

Activity checklist

This checklist shows which performance criteria, range statement or knowledge and understanding point is covered by each activity in this chapter. Tick off each activity as you complete it.

Activity

7.1	☐	This activity deals with Performance Criterion 15.2.E: maintain an adequate level of liquidity in line with cash forecasts
7.2	☐	This activity deals with Performance Criterion 15.2.E: maintain an adequate level of liquidity in line with cash forecasts
7.3	☐	This activity deals with Knowledge and Understanding 3: bank overdrafts and loans; terms and conditions; legal relationship between bank and customer
7.4	☐	This activity deals with Performance Criterion 15.2.D: ensure account is taken of trends in the economic and financial environment in managing cash balances
7.5	☐	This activity deals with Performance Criterion 15.2.B: invest surplus funds in marketable securities within defined authorisation limits
7.6	☐	This activity deals with Performance Criterion 15.2.B: invest surplus funds in marketable securities within defined authorisation limits
7.7	☐	This activity deals with Knowledge and Understanding 4: types of marketable security (bills of exchange, certificates of deposit, government securities, local authority short-term loans); terms and conditions; risks
7.8	☐	This activity deals with Performance Criterion 15.2.C: ensure the organisation's financial regulations and security procedures are observed
7.9	☐	This activity deals with Performance Criterion 15.2.C: ensure the organisation's financial regulations and security procedures are observed

PART B

Credit control

chapter 8

Credit control: policies and procedures

Contents

1. Introduction
2. What is credit control?
3. Total credit
4. The credit control department
5. Legal aspects of granting credit
6. Payment terms and settlement discounts

Performance criteria

15.3.A Agree credit terms with customers in accordance with the organisation's policies

15.3.B Identify and use internal and external sources of information to evaluate the current credit status of customers and potential customers

Range statement

15.3.1 Internal information derived from: analysis of the accounts; colleagues in regular contact with current or potential customers or clients

15.3.2 External information derived from: credit rating agencies; supplier references; bank references

Knowledge and understanding

- Legal issues: basic contract; terms and conditions of contracts relating to the granting of credit, data protection legislation and credit control information
- Sources of credit status information
- External sources of information: banks, credit agencies and official publications
- Legal issues: remedies for breach of contract
- Discounts for prompt payment
- Interpretation and use of credit control information

- Methods of analysing information on debtors: age analysis of debtors; average periods of credit given and received; incidence of bad and doubtful debts
- Understanding that the accounting systems of an organisation are affected by its organisational structure, its administrative systems and procedures and the nature of its business transactions
- Understanding that recording and accounting practices may vary in different parts of the organisation
- Understanding that practice in this area will be determined by an organisation's credit control policies and procedures
- An understanding of the organisation's relevant policies and procedures

1 Introduction

The remaining chapters of this text deal with the topic of credit management. The **monitoring** of **total credit** is a vital part of liquidity management.

Key topics in this chapter are :

- The role of the **credit control department** – note the different ways in which the department polices total credit
- **Payment terms** – you may be asked to discuss the implications of a change in payment terms
- **Settlement discounts** – you may be asked to calculate the effects of settlement discounts, and also **why** businesses offer discounts to credit customers

2 What is credit control?

2.1 Giving credit

When we have talked about managing cash, you will have noticed the **time lag** between the provision of goods and services and the receipt of cash for them. This time lag can result in a firm making considerable demands on its bank to finance its working capital. Many businesses, however, cannot demand payment on delivery, especially for larger items. They have to give **credit**.

2.2 Trade credit

Trade credit is credit **given by a business** to **another business**. For example, many invoices state that payment is expected within thirty days of the date of the invoice. In effect this is giving the customer thirty days credit. The customer is effectively borrowing at the supplier's expense.

2.3 Consumer credit

Consumer credit is credit **offered by businesses** to the **end-consumer.**

Many businesses offer **hire purchase terms** when the consumer takes out a loan to pay for the goods purchased. Failure to repay will result in the goods being repossessed.

In practice, much of the growth in consumer credit has been driven not so much by retailers as by banks. **Credit cards** are largely responsible for the explosive growth in consumer credit.

2.4 Importance of credit control

Credit control issues are closely bound up with a firm's management of liquidity. Credit is offered to **enhance turnover** and **profitability.** However a company should not become illiquid and insolvent as a result of offering credit.

Economic conditions can influence the type and amount of credit offered.

- In boom times it should be easy to attract new customers and hence new customers can be asked for **security**.
- In recessions credit is a means of enticing customers in, and so the credit manager's job is to **control risk**.

High-risk (or marginal) customers require flexible payment arrangements. High risk customers are often profitable, but the risk has to be managed. The customer may require a credit limit of £50,000, on standard terms, but may only deserve £30,000. The supplier might choose to offer a £30,000 credit limit, together with a discount policy to encourage early payment.

2.5 Credit control and marketing

Just as there is a relationship between offering credit and securing sales, there also has to be a suitable working relationship between **credit control personnel** and **sales and marketing staff**. As we shall see in Chapters 10 and 11, the cost of chasing after slow payers and doubtful debts is considerable.

2.6 Credit control policies

The various aspects of credit control are summarised in the diagram below.

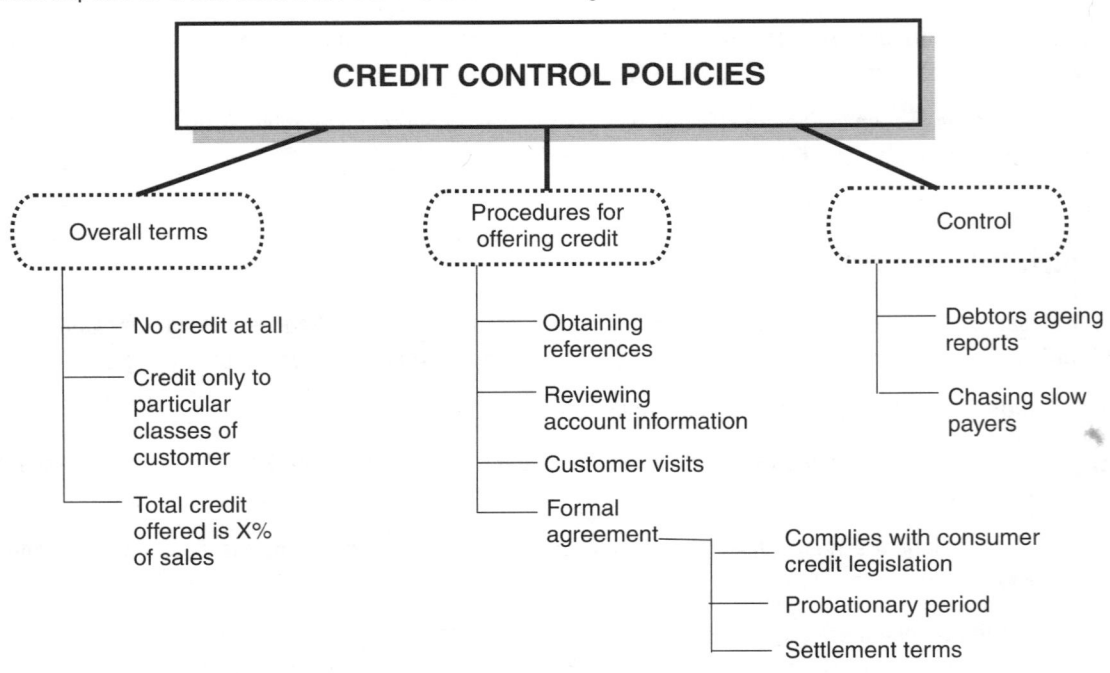

```
                        CREDIT CONTROL POLICIES
                       /           |            \
              Overall terms   Procedures for    Control
                              offering credit
                   |                |                |
           — No credit at all    — Obtaining      — Debtors ageing
                                   references       reports
           — Credit only to      — Reviewing      — Chasing slow
             particular            account           payers
             classes of            information
             customer            — Customer visits
           — Total credit        — Formal
             offered is X%         agreement — Complies with consumer
             of sales                           credit legislation
                                             — Probationary period
                                             — Settlement terms
```

3 Total credit

3.1 Setting total credit levels

Businesses have to establish an overall approach to credit control in the light of their firm's objectives for **profit**, **cash flow**, **asset use** and **reducing interest costs**.

Finding a **total level of credit** which can be offered is a matter of finding the least costly balance between enticing customers, whose use of credit entails considerable costs, and refusing opportunities for profitable sales.

For many customers, **delaying payment** is the **cheapest form of finance** available and there has been much publicity recently about the difficulties that delayed payments cause to small businesses. There is no easy answer to this problem.

3.2 Measuring total debtors

There are three methods of assessing how many days' sales are represented by debtors.

3.2.1 Debtors' turnover

The **days' sales in debtors' ratio (debtors' payment period)** can be taken from the financial statements. It represents the length of the credit period taken by customers.

$$\frac{\text{Total debtors} \times 365}{\text{Sales in 365 days}} = \text{days sales}$$

For example, in 20X4 Moonstar Ltd made sales of £700,000 and at 31 December 20X4, debtors stood at £90,000. The comparable figures for 20X3 were £600,000 (annual sales) and £70,000 (debtors at 31.12.X3).

	20X4		20X3	
Debtors represent	$\frac{£90,000 \times 365}{£700,000}$	= 47 days	$\frac{£70,000 \times 365}{£600,000}$	= 43 days

In 20X4, the company is taking longer to collect its debts.

3.2.2 Count-back method

Rather than annualising, this simply assumes that debtors represent the most recent sales.

Assume that at the end of March total debtors of Moony Ltd stood at £1m. Sales in March were £500,000; in February, £450,000 and in January £500,000.

	£
Total debtors at the end of March	1,000,000
Less March sales	500,000
	500,000
Less February sales	450,000
	50,000
Less January sales, unpaid portion	50,000
	–

We can calculate the days outstanding as follows.

	Days
March: entire turnover	31
February: entire turnover	28
January: $\frac{50,000}{500,000} \times 31$ days	3
	62 days

3.2.3 Partial month method

This analyses each month's sales by identifying the unpaid portion. These are then aggregated together. Assume that at the end of June, total debtors of Moony Ltd are £1.5m. Data related to the previous months are as follows.

PART B CREDIT CONTROL

	Sales (a) £	Unpaid (b) £	Days (c)	b/a × c Days
June	500,000	500,000	30	30.00
May	450,000	400,000	31	27.56
April	500,000	300,000	30	18.00
March	600,000	150,000	31	7.75
February	400,000	50,000	28	3.50
January	500,000	100,000	31	6.20
Before January	None	None	N/A	N/A
Total	2,950,000	1,500,000	N/A	93.01
		(ie Debtors)		

3.2.4 Which method is most useful?

- Financial analysts will be most interested to review the **annualised figure** for debtors calculated above. However, this will be of little practical interest to credit controllers.

- The **count-back method** also suffers from the oversimplified assumption that most debtors are recent.

- The **partial month method** not only provides an overall debtors ageing figure but, as importantly, it also enables analysis to be broken down by month.

3.3 Interest expense of extending credit

However the **days sales outstanding** (DSO) ratio is calculated, we can examine the effect of this on profitability and cash flow. The main cost of offering credit is the **interest expense**. How can we assess the effect on profit?

Example: Interest expense

Moonstar Ltd sells widgets for £1,000, which enables it to earn a profit, after all other expenses except interest, of £100 (ie a 10% margin). Moony Ltd buys a widget for £1,000 on 1 January 20X1. Moonstar relies on overdraft finance, which costs it 10% pa. What is the effect on profit if Moony does not pay:

(a) Until 31 December 20X1
(b) Until 30 June 20X1

Solution

(a) If Moony does not pay until 31 December 20X1, the effect on Moonstar's profits is:

	£
Net profit on sale of widget	100
Overdraft cost £1,000 × 10% pa	(100)
Actual profit after 12 months credit	Nil

In other words, the entire profit margin has been wiped out in 12 months.

(b) If Moony had paid after six months, the effect would be:

	£
Net profit	100
Overdraft cost £1,000 × 10% pa × $^6/_{12}$ months	(50)
	50

Half the profit has been wiped out. (*Tutorial note.* The interest cost might be worked out in a more complex way to give a more accurate figure.)

If the cost of borrowing had been 18%, then the profit would have been absorbed before seven months had elapsed. If the net profit was 5% and borrowing costs were 15%, the interest expense would exceed the net profit after four months.

Activity 8.1

Crisroe Ltd has an average level of debtors of £2m at any time, representing 60 days outstanding. (Their terms are thirty days.) The firm borrows money at 10% a year. The managing director is proud of the credit control: 'I only had to write off £20,000 in bad debts last year,' she says proudly. Is she right to be proud?

3.4 Other impacts on profitability

As we have seen the interest costs of debtors can significantly affect profitability. That said, if credit considerations are included in pricing calculations, extending credit can increase profitability if offering credit generates extra sales. The business should also consider other impacts on **working capital** of an increase in business, in particular the increased levels of **stock** and **amounts owing to creditors**.

To determine whether it would be profitable to extend the level of total credit, it is necessary to assess the following.

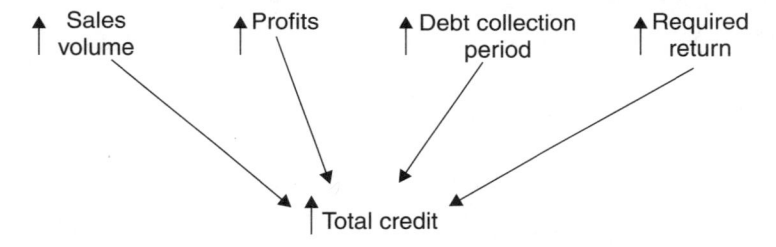

↑ Sales volume   ↑ Profits   ↑ Debt collection period   ↑ Required return
                          ↓
                    ↑ Total credit

Example: Total investment in debtors

Gallant Limited is considering a change of credit policy which will result in slowing down the average collection period from one to two months. The relaxation in credit standards is expected to produce an increase in sales in each year amounting to 25% of the current sales volume, with additional stocks of £100,000 and additional creditors of £20,000.

Sales price per unit	£10.00
Profit per unit (before interest)	£1.50
Current sales revenue per annum	£2.4 million

The required rate of return on investment is 20%.

Advise the company on whether or not it should extend the credit period offered to customers, in the following circumstances.

(a) If all customers take the longer credit of two months

(b) If existing customers do not change their payment habits, and only the new customers take a full two months' credit

Solution

The change in credit policy would be justifiable, in the context of this question, if the rate of return on the additional investment in working capital exceeds 20%.

Extra profit

Profit margin £1.50/£10 =	15%
Increase in sales revenue £2.4m × 25%	£0.6 million
Increase in profit (15% × £0.6m)	£90,000

The total sales revenue is now £3m (£2.4m + £0.6m)

(a) **Extra investment, if all debtors take two months credit**

	£
Average debtors after the sales increase (2/12 × £3 million)	500,000
Current average debtors (1/12 × £2.4 million)	200,000
Increase in debtors	300,000
Increase in stocks	100,000
	400,000
Increase in creditors	(20,000)
Net increase in 'working capital'	380,000

Return on extra investment $\dfrac{£90,000}{£380,000}$ = 23.7%

(b) **Extra investment, if only the new debtors take two months credit**

	£
Increase in debtors (2/12 × £0.6 million)	100,000
Increase in stocks	100,000
	200,000
Increase in creditors	(20,000)
Net increase in working capital investment	180,000

Return on extra investment $\dfrac{£90,000}{£180,000}$ = 50%

In both case (a) and case (b) the new credit policy appears to be worthwhile.

Activity 8.2

Sarhall Ltd is considering increasing the credit period that it gives to customers from one calendar month to one and a half calendar months in order to raise turnover from the present annual figure of £24 million representing 4m units per annum. The price of the product is £6 and it costs £5.40 to make. The increase in the credit period is likely to generate an extra 150,000 unit sales. Is this enough to justify the extra costs given that the company's required rate of return is 20%? Assume no changes to stock levels, as the company is increasing its operating efficiency. Assume that existing debtors will take advantage of the new terms.

3.5 Debtor quality and liquidity

One way in which a credit control department can minimise the risk of insolvent debtors is by maximising the **quality** of debtors. Debtor quality is determined by their **age** and **risk**.

Some **industries** have a higher level of risk than others, in other words, there is a higher probability that customers will fail to pay. Some markets are riskier than others. Selling goods to a country with possible payment difficulties is riskier than selling them in the home market.

3.6 Policing total credit

The total amount of credit offered, as well as individual accounts, should be policed to ensure that policy on total credit limits is maintained.

A **credit utilisation report** indicates the extent to which total limits are being utilised. An example is given below.

Credit utilisation report

Customer	Limit £'000	Utilisation £'000	%
Alpha	100	90	90
Beta	50	35	70
Gamma	35	21	60
Delta	250	125	50
	435	271	
		62.3%	

This might also contain other information, such as days' sales outstanding and so on.

Reviewed in aggregate, this can reveal the following.

- The **number** of **customers** who might **want more credit**
- The **extent** to which the **company is exposed** to debtors
- The **'tightness'** of the policy
- **Credit utilisation to total sales**

PART B CREDIT CONTROL

3.6.1 Analysing credit by industry

Credit utilisation can also be analysed by **industry** within country or by country within industry. It is also useful to relate credit utilisation to total sales.

Activity 8.3

What does the analysis below tell you about the company's exposure to the property industry?

Trade debtors' analysis as at 31 December

Industry	Current credit Utilisation £'000	% of total debtors %	Annual sales £million	As a % of total sales %
Property	9,480	25.0	146.0	19.2
Construction	7,640	20.2	140.1	18.4
Engineering	4,350	11.5	112.6	14.8
Electricals	4,000	10.6	83.7	11.0
Electricity	2,170	5.7	49.2	6.5
Transport	3,230	8.5	79.9	10.5
Chemicals, plastics	1,860	4.9	43.3	5.7
Motors, aircraft trades	5,170	13.6	105.8	13.9
	37,900	100.0	760.6	100.0

Activity 8.4

Your company is concerned about the effect of inflation, which currently stands at 6%, on its credit control policy. Outline the main points to consider, for discussion with your manager.

4 The credit control department

4.1 Role of the credit control department

The credit control function might only be a small section of a few people; on the other hand, it might be a large department.

Management need to decide how the credit control department fits into the rest of the organisation. This will be determined by the scope of its role. Possibilities include:

- If the credit controller is seen as little more than a **debt collector**, he or she will be part of the **accounts department**.

- The credit controller might report to a **sales manager** or the sales director, as credit control can be seen as an integral part of **marketing strategy**.
- In some companies, particularly in the US, the **credit manager** might report directly to the **managing director**.
- The credit manager might report directly to the **finance director**.

4.2 The credit cycle

The credit control function's jobs occupy a number of stages of:

- **Order cycle** (from customer order to invoice despatch)
- **Collection cycle** (from invoice despatch to the receipt of cash)

Together the order and collection cycle make up the **credit cycle.** The job of the credit control department can comprise all those activities within the dotted line below.

Stages in the Credit Cycle

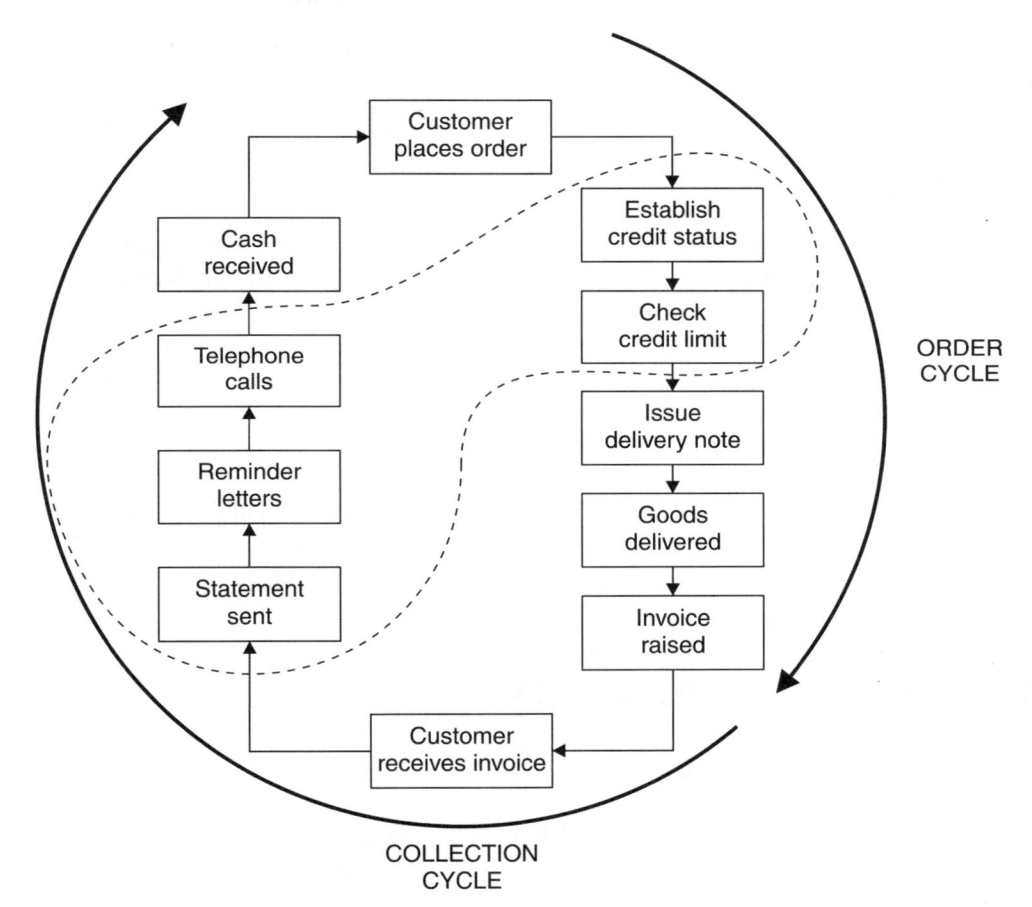

```
                    Customer
                  places order
                         |
                         v
        Cash         Establish
       received    credit status
          ^              |
          |              v
       Telephone       Check
         calls       credit limit        ORDER
          ^              |               CYCLE
          |              v
       Reminder        Issue
        letters    delivery note
          ^              |
          |              v
       Statement       Goods
         sent         delivered
          ^              |
          |              v
                       Invoice
                       raised
                         |
                         v
                    Customer
                 receives invoice

                  COLLECTION
                    CYCLE
```

4.2.1 Establish credit status

Credit status is set for new customers or customers who request a credit extension. (See Chapter 9)

4.2.2 Check credit limit

If the order is fairly routine, and there is no problem with credit status, then credit control staff examine records to see if the new order will cause the customer to exceed the credit limit. There are a number of possible responses, as follows.

- **Authorisation**. If the credit demanded is within the credit limit, and there are no reasons to suspect any problems, then the request will be authorised.
- **Referral**. It is possible that the credit demanded will exceed the limit offered in the agreement.

Referral	
Refusal	Credit limits are there to protect liquidity but business relationships could be damaged
Offer revised credit limit	If customer is solvent and a regular payer, therefore a low risk
Pay off existing balance	The customer can be asked to pay off some of what is owed before further credit is advanced.

4.2.3 The collection cycle

The credit control department has responsibility for the collection cycle, although the final payment is ultimately received by the accounts department. Collection involves reviewing overdue debts, and chasing them (see Chapters 10 and 11).

Activity 8.5

See if you can explain the likely effects of a company's credit control policy on the control of working capital in general.

5 Legal aspects of granting credit

5.1 Credit control and contracts

The credit controller's job often involves the law, especially when collecting debts. The sale of goods and/or services for cash is a type of contract. The credit controller's job is to ensure that the customer keeps his or her side of the contract.

5.2 What is a contract?

A **contract** is an agreement which legally binds the parties entering into the agreement. The essential elements to a contract are as follows.

- The parties intend to create **legal relations**.
- There is an **offer and acceptance**.
- It is a **bargain** for which something is offered for **consideration**.

5.3 Validity of a contract

The validity of a contract may be affected by any of the following factors.

5.3.1 Content

In general the parties may enter into a contract on whatever terms they choose. But it can only be enforced if it is sufficiently **complete** and **precise** in its terms. Some terms may be **implied** and some terms in the contract may be **overridden** by **statutory rules**.

5.3.2 Form

Some contracts (not all) must be made in a **particular form** or **supported** by **written evidence.**

5.3.3 Genuine consent

A contract may not be valid if one party has been **unduly influenced** into entering into it.

5.3.4 Legality

The courts will not enforce a contract which is **illegal** or **contrary to public policy**.

5.3.5 Capacity

Some persons have only **restricted capacity** to enter into contracts and are not bound by agreements made outside those limits.

5.4 Invalid contracts

A contract which does not satisfy the relevant tests may be either void, voidable or unenforceable.

Types of contract	
Void contract	No contract; parties not bound by it
Voidable contract	Contract which one party may avoid, that is terminate at his option. Rescission, cancelling the contract and restoring the parties to their pre-contract position, may be possible
Unenforceable contract	Valid contract, but if one party refuses to perform, other party cannot compel performance

5.5 Essential elements of a contract

5.5.1 Legal relations

The parties to a contract **intend to create legal relations** between themselves. In other words, the contract can be enforced or remedied by a court.

5.5.2 Offer

An **offer** is a **definite** promise to be bound on specific terms. It is not:

- The supply of information
- An invitation to negotiate
- An invitation to make an offer

An offer can expire:

- After a defined period of time
- If the person who has made the offer (offeror) withdraws it and makes this known
- If the person to whom the offer is made (offeree) rejects it
- If the offeree or offeror dies

5.5.3 Acceptance

Acceptance, on the other hand, is an **act** by the offeree to accept the offer. The fact that the offeror does not reject the offer does not guarantee acceptance. A request for information is not an acceptance.

Acceptance must be **unqualified agreement** to the terms of the offer. Acceptance which introduces any **new terms** is a **rejection and counter offer**.

Offer and acceptance mean that a binding contract is formed, so that **new terms** cannot be **introduced** into the contract unless both parties agree, and the **terms** of the **contract** appear from the **offer** and **acceptance**.

5.5.4 Consideration

Consideration is what a person must give in exchange for what has been promised to him. Normally, this would be the **price**. Consideration must have **some value** and be **sufficient**, that is, capable of being treated as consideration.

Consideration may take the form of an **act** or a **promise**. Anything which has already been done before a promise in return is given is **past consideration** which is generally insufficient to make the promise binding.

5.6 Mistake

Only in restricted circumstances does a mistake render a contract void. The mistake must be a mistake of **fact**; a mistake of **law** can never have this effect.

- If a **term of the contract** proves to be **untrue**, the party who has been misinformed may claim damages for breach of contract.
- If, however, the **untrue statement** is **not a contract term**, the person misled may be able to treat it as a misrepresentation, and **avoid the contract** or **recover damages.**

5.7 Misrepresentation

A misrepresentation has the following features.

- It is an untrue **representation of fact**. A statement of law, intention, opinion or mere 'sales talk' is not a representation.
- It is made by one party to the other **before** the contract is made.
- The party misled was **persuaded** by the **misrepresentation** to enter into the contract.

5.8 Breach of contract

A breach of contract is when one of the participants to an agreement does not carry out his or her side of the bargain. A party has a number of remedies when the other party is in breach of contract.

Remedies for breach of contract include:

- **Monetary damages** – compensation
- **Termination** – one party refusing to carry on with the contract
- **Quantum meruit** – payment for the part of the contract performed
- **Specific performance** – court order that one of the parties fulfil their obligations
- **Action for the price** – action to recover agreed price of contract
- **Injunction** – one party being required by the court to observe a negative restriction

Action for the price is generally the most important remedy for the credit controller.

Activity 8.6

Why do you think that action for the price is the most appropriate remedy for the credit controller?

5.9 Sale of goods

Contracts for the sale of goods and the offering of credit to customers have some special features. We will discuss them briefly, as they are relevant to the credit controller's job. Contracts for the sale of goods are governed by the Sale of Goods Acts 1893 and 1979.

Unless the contract specifies otherwise, the Acts hold the following.

- Where the goods are ready for delivery, title to the property **passes immediately even if payment is delayed**.
- Title only passes on goods sold by **'sale or return'** when the buyer approves of the goods (eg does not state that he or she rejects them).
- Where the seller imposes **conditions**, these conditions must be met before title passes.
- If goods are **measured** or **weighed**, title does not pass until this happens.
- If goods are **specially manufactured**, title passes when the goods are **specifically allocated** to the customer.

Activity 8.7

A friend of yours signs a contract with a publisher, in which he agrees to sell the manuscript of his novel for £1,000. The contract is signed on 1 July, and he hands over the manuscript. The publisher says he'll pay the £1,000 on 31 July. However, on 2 July your friend receives another offer, of £10,000, from another publisher. 'I haven't been paid, so I'll go and get my manuscript back,' he says. Can he?

5.10 Failure of buyer to pay

What if the buyer fails to pay? Unfortunately, the credit controller is rarely entitled to wade into the buyer's premises to reclaim the goods. However, a seller who has not been paid does retain certain rights.

- If the buyer is **insolvent** (see Chapter 11), then the goods can be **stopped in transit**.
- **Lien**. Any goods which have not been paid for can be retained by the seller at the seller's premises providing the buyer has not lawfully obtained possession.

- **Retention of title clauses** may be inserted in a contract stating that the unpaid seller can recover the goods, if they can be identified – although this is rarely enforceable in practice.

5.11 Consumer credit

Certain special restrictions relate to **consumer credit**, in other words, a credit agreement between a business and an individual. The Consumer Credit Act 1974 (CCA) regulates the provision of credit. 'Credit' includes:

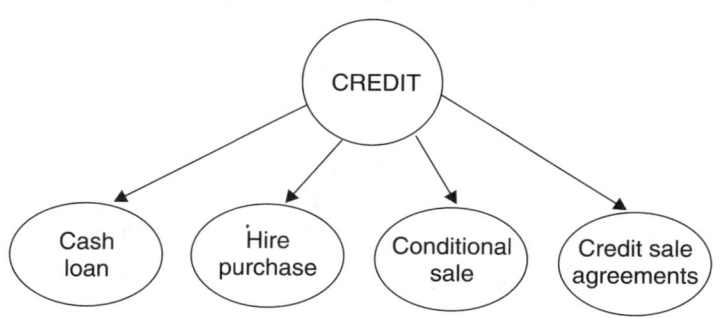

```
                    CREDIT
           /      |      |       \
      Cash     Hire   Conditional  Credit sale
      loan   purchase    sale      agreements
```

Building society mortgages and loans to limited companies are excluded.

The CCA aims to protect **individual debtors** who may be of limited financial experience and means, and may be vulnerable to the practices of 'loan sharks' and others.

The debtor is protected in a number of ways.

- The debtor can **withdraw** at any time, until the agreement is fully executed.
- The agreement must be in **writing**, must be **signed** by the **debtor** and must be legible and complete.
- The debtor has the **right to cancel** in certain cases, and must be notified of this. The debtor can cancel within five days of receiving notice.
- The creditor must include **all relevant information**.

6 Payment terms and settlement discounts

6.1 Credit terms

Credit terms are an **important aspect** of the **credit control policy**. As they are part of the contract between seller and customer, they should ideally be in writing.

They have to take into account the **expected profit** on the sale and the seller's **cash needs**. They also establish when **payment** is to be received, an important matter from the seller's point of view.

PART B CREDIT CONTROL

> **TERMS AND CONDITIONS OF SALE**
> - Nature of goods to be supplied
> - Price
> - Delivery
> - Date of payment
> - Frequency of payment
> - Discounts

The credit terms the seller offers depend on many factors.

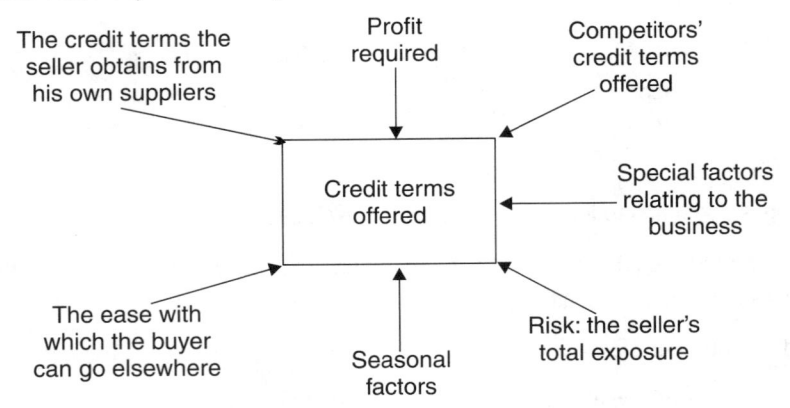

Factors affecting **Credit terms offered**:
- The credit terms the seller obtains from his own suppliers
- Profit required
- Competitors' credit terms offered
- Special factors relating to the business
- Risk: the seller's total exposure
- Seasonal factors
- The ease with which the buyer can go elsewhere

The terms must be **simple to understand** and easily enforceable. If the seller does not enforce his terms he is creating a precedent.

Payment terms	
Payment a specified number of days after delivery	Eg Net 10 (10 days)
Weekly credit	All supplies in week must be paid for by a specified date in next week
Half monthly credit	All supplies in one half of month must be paid for by specified date in next month
10th and 25th	Supplies in first half of month must be paid for by 25th, supplies in second half must be paid for by 10th of next month
Monthly credit	Payment for month's supplies must be paid by specified date in next month; if the payment date is 7th, it might be written Net 7 prox. Some monthly credit called Number MO; 2MO means payment must be in next month but one
Delivery	Certain payment terms geared to delivery - **CWO** Cash with order - **CIA** Cash in advance - **COD** Cash on delivery - **CND** Cash on next delivery

6.2 Methods of payment

Payment can be accepted in a variety of forms.

- Cash
- BACS
- Cheques
- Banker's draft
- Travellers' cheques or Eurocheques
- Postal orders
- Standing order
- Direct debit
- Credit card
- Debit card
- Bills of exchange
- Promissory notes

6.3 Settlement discounts

Some firms offer a settlement discount if **payment** is **received early**. Settlement discounts have a number of uses.

- If sensibly priced, they encourage customers to **pay earlier**, thereby avoiding some of the financing costs arising out of the granting of credit.
- The seller may be suffering from **cash flow problems**. If settlement discounts encourage earlier payment, they thus enable a company to maintain **liquidity**.
- Settlement discounts might **affect the volume of demand** if, as part of the overall credit terms offered, they encourage customers to buy.

To consider whether the offer of a discount for early payment is financially worthwhile you need to compare the **cost** of the discount with the **benefit** of a reduced investment in debtors.

Example: Settlement discounts

Julatkins Limited currently has sales of £3m, with an average collection period of two months. No discounts are given. The management of the company is undecided on whether to allow a discount on sales to its customers. In the event that a discount of 2% were allowed for payment within 30 days, the company estimates that the **average** collection period would be reduced to one month. The company normally requires a 25% return on its investments.

Advise the management whether or not to introduce the discount.

Solution

In this example the offer of a discount is not expected to increase sales demand. The advantage would be in the **reduction of the collection period**, and the resulting saving in the working capital investment required.

Our solution will value debtors at sales value.

PART B CREDIT CONTROL

(a) **Change in debtors**

	Debtors valued at sales price £
Current value of debtors (2/12 × £3m)	500,000
New value of debtors (1/12 × £3m)	250,000
Reduction in investment in debtors	250,000

(b) The cost of reducing debtors is the cost of the discounts, ie

2% × 50% × £3 million = £30,000

The cost is reduced by 50% as the average collection period is one month. This means that half the payments will qualify for a discount and half will not.

(c) The reduction in debtors of £250,000 would cost the company £30,000 per annum. If the company can earn 25% on its investments, the benefit is:

25% × £250,000 = £62,500

The discount policy would be worthwhile, since the benefit of £62,500 exceeds the cost of £30,000.

The percentage cost of an early settlement discount to the company giving it can be estimated by the formula:

$$\left[\frac{D}{(100-D)} \times \frac{365}{(N-S)} \right]\%$$

where:

(a) D is the discount offered (5% = 5, etc)
(b) N is the number of days credit offered net, for no discount
(c) S is the number of days credit allowed with the settlement discount

You should use this formula in the assessment which gives approximately the same result, if you find it quicker.

In the example above, the formula can be applied as follows.

$$\text{Cost of discount} = \frac{2}{(100-2)} \times \frac{365}{(60-30)}$$

$$= \frac{2}{98} \times \frac{365}{30}$$

$$= 24.8\%$$

Since 24.8% is less than the 25% by which the company judges investments, offering the discount is worthwhile.

Note that we **do not need to know how many customers** will take up the discount in order to calculate the approximate percentage cost (or 'opportunity cost') of granting the discount.

Activity 8.8

Crisroe grants credit terms of 60 days net to customers, but offers an early settlement discount of 2% for payment within seven days. What is the cost of the discount to Crisroe?

6.4 Late payment

Businesses may consider charging interest on overdue debts. However:

- **Charging for late payment** might be misinterpreted. The supplier might assume that charges for late payment give the customer the authority to pay late.

- A statutory **rate for interest** on overdue debts has not been established in the UK.

- Charging for payments relates only to the effect of the late payment on **profitability**, not on liquidity.

Activity 8.9

Thinking back to topics covered in earlier chapters, explain how good cash management may realise each of the following benefits.

(a) Better control of financial risk
(b) Opportunity for profit
(c) Strengthened balance sheet
(d) Increased confidence with customers, suppliers, banks and shareholders

Activity 8.10

Your company has been growing rapidly over the last two years and now wishes to introduce a more formal credit control policy. You are asked to give a brief presentation on the factors involved in setting up such a policy.

PART B   CREDIT CONTROL

Key learning points

- **Credit control** deals with a firm's management of its working capital. **Trade credit** is offered to business customers. **Consumer credit** is offered to household customers.

- Businesses must decide on the **level of total credit** they should offer based on likely **sales volume, profitability of sales, length of debt collection period, required rate of return**.

- **Total credit** can be measured in a variety of ways. Financial analysts use days sales in debtors, but as this is an annualised figure it gives no idea of the make-up of total debtors. Many firms need to consider the **cost of excess credit**.

- The **total investment in debtors** has to be considered in terms of its impact on the general investment in working capital.

- The **credit control department** is responsible for those stages in the credit cycle dealing with the offer of credit, and the collection of debts.

- A **sale of goods** is a type of contract. To be valid, a contract must result from the intention to create legal relations, must contain an offer and acceptance, and must be a 'bargain' for which consideration is offered.

- **Remedies for breach of contract** include damages, termination, action for the price, *quantum meruit*, specific performance.

- Sale of goods contracts are subject to special **legislation**. **Retention of title** clauses are rarely enforceable in practice.

- A firm must consider suitable **payment terms**. **Settlement discounts** can be offered, if they are cost effective and improve liquidity.

- The **Consumer Credit Act 1974** gives debtors who have entered consumer credit agreements a number of rights.

Quick quiz

1   You have found out the following details for your company's three biggest customers

	Credit limit £'000	Balance at 31 December 20X4 £'000	Credit sales during 20X4 £'000
Mary	50	30	500
Mungo	25	15	240
Midge	20	10	180

What is the credit utilisation for the three customers?

- A   6.0%
- B   10.3%
- C   19.3%
- D   57.9%

2   Which of the following are ways of measuring debtors ageing?

☐ Calculations of debtors from the financial statements

☐ The delivery method

☐ The count-back method

☐ The partial month method

3   What should you consider if you are extending the level of total credit?

4   What factors affect the validity of a contract?

5   The Sales of Goods Acts 1893 and 1979 assume the following rule about transfer of title:

Unless the contract specifies otherwise, title to the goods only passes when payment is made.

☐ True

☐ False

6   Goods and Chattels Ltd is considering increasing the period of credit allowed to customers from one calendar month to two months. Annual sales are currently £2.4m, and annual profits are £120,000. It is anticipated that allowing extended credit would increase sales by 20%, while margins would be unchanged. The company's required rate of return is 15%. What is the financial effect of the proposal?

- A   Reduction in profit of £102,000
- B   Reduction in profit of £42,000
- C   Increase in profit of £102,000
- D   Increase in profit of £14,000

7   What is meant by (a) Net 7; (b) 10th and 25th; (c) COD?

8   What is the percentage cost to a business of giving its customers a 1% discount in return for reducing the credit period they take from 60 to 20 days?

Answers to quick quiz

1. D $\dfrac{30+15+10}{50+25+20} = 57.9\%$

2. Calculation of debtors from the financial statements; the count-back method; the partial month method.

3. Possible increase in sales; profitability of extra sales achieved; increase in the average debt collection period; required rate of return on additional investment in debtors.

4. Content; form; genuineness of consent; legality; capacity.

5. False. Unless the contract specifies otherwise, title to the property passes immediately even if payment is delayed.

6. C Profit margin £0.12m/2.4m × 100% = 5%

		£
Existing debtors	£2.4m ÷ 12	200,000
New level of debtors	£2.4m × 1.2 ÷ 6	480,000
Increase in debtors		280,000
Additional financing cost	£280,000 × 15%	42,000
Additional revenue	£2.4m × 1.2 × 5%	144,000
Net increase in profit	£144,000 − £42,000	102,000

7. (a) Payment to be made within 7 days of delivery.

    (b) Supplies received from the 1st to the 15th of the month must be paid for by the 25th of that month; supplies received from the 16th up to the end of the month must be paid for by the 10th of the following month.

    (c) Cash to be paid on delivery.

8. $\text{Cost} = \left[\dfrac{1}{100-1} \times \dfrac{365}{60-20}\right]\%$

    = 9.22%

Activity checklist

This checklist shows which performance criteria, range statement or knowledge and understanding point is covered by each activity in this chapter. Tick off each activity as you complete it.

Activity

8.1	☐	This activity deals with Knowledge and Understanding 22: methods of analysing information on debtors; age analysis of debtors; average periods of credit given and received; incidence of bad and doubtful debts
8.2	☐	This activity deals with Knowledge and Understanding 22: methods of analysing information on debtors; age analysis of debtors; average periods of credit given and received; incidence of bad and doubtful debts
8.3	☐	This activity deals with Performance Criterion 15.3.B: identify and use internal and external sources of information to evaluate the current credit status of customers and potential customers
8.4	☐	This activity deals with Knowledge and Understanding 18: interpretation and use of credit control information
8.5	☐	This activity deals with Knowledge and Understanding 26: understanding that the accounting systems of an organisation are affected by its organisational structure, its administrative systems and procedures and the nature of its business transactions
8.6	☐	This activity deals with Knowledge and Understanding 6: legal issues: basic contract; terms and conditions of contracts relating to the granting of credit; data protection legislation and credit control information
8.7	☐	This activity deals with Knowledge and Understanding 6: legal issues: basic contract; terms and conditions of contracts relating to the granting of credit; data protection legislation and credit control information
8.8	☐	This activity deals with Performance Criterion 15.3.A: agree credit terms with customers in accordance with the organisation's policies
8.9	☐	This activity deals with Knowledge and Understanding 30: understanding that practice in this area will be determined by an organisation's credit control policies and procedures
8.10	☐	This activity deals with Performance Criterion 15.3.A: agree credit terms with customers in accordance with the organisation's policies

PART B　CREDIT CONTROL

chapter 9

Assessing creditworthiness

Contents

1 Introduction
2 Minimising the risk of default
3 Externally generated information: bank and trade references, and agencies
4 Internally generated information: financial and accounting analysis
5 Internally generated information: customer visits
6 Using credit control information
7 The Data Protection Act

Performance criteria

15.3.A Agree credit terms with customers in accordance with the organisation's policies
15.3.B Identify and use internal and external sources of information to evaluate the current credit status of customers and potential customers
15.3.C Open new accounts for those customers with an established credit status
15.3.D Ensure the reasons for refusing credit are discussed with customers in a tactful manner

Range statement

15.3.1 Internal information derived from: analysis of the accounts; colleagues in regular contact with current or potential customers or clients
15.3.2 External information derived from: credit rating agencies; supplier references; bank references

Knowledge and understanding

- Sources of credit status information
- External sources of information: banks, credit agencies and official publications
- Interpretation and use of credit control information
- Understanding that the accounting systems of an organisation are affected by its organisational structure, its administrative systems and procedures and the nature of its business transactions
- Understanding that recording and accounting practices may vary in different parts of the organisation
- Understanding that practice in this area will be determined by an organisation's credit control policies and procedures
- An understanding of the organisation's relevant policies and procedures

1 Introduction

This chapter covers a core topic in this unit, whether to grant credit to the customer who requests it.

One key skill is being able to use the information available to make an assessment of the customer's financial status. Hence you need to be able to recognise potential problems with **financial data, references** and other information sources within and outside your organisation. This will involve using some of the ratios you have learned about in financial accounting units.

You also need to **communicate** your decision to customers in an appropriate manner; this may mean writing to say that you will not be granting credit terms. Don't neglect the Data Protection aspects in the last section as these are highlighted in the guidance notes for this unit.

2 Minimising the risk of default

2.1 Credit risk of individual debtors

The previous chapter discussed the overall application of the firm's credit policy. In practice, a firm's credit control policy is applied to the risk posed by the **individual credit customer**.

A debtor who is **a low credit risk** is likely to be able to pay his or her debts when they fall due. Offering credit to a low risk debtor means that there is little chance that the creditor's profitability or liquidity will be threatened.

A debtor who is a **high credit risk** is more likely to be unable to pay, and so there is a greater threat to the company's liquidity and profitability.

However high risk debtors will not necessarily default. Many businesses make handsome profits from 'high risk' customers, by demanding **slightly higher** returns and by **managing** the debtors more carefully. Higher risk customers need not be shunned simply because they are higher risk.

Level of risk

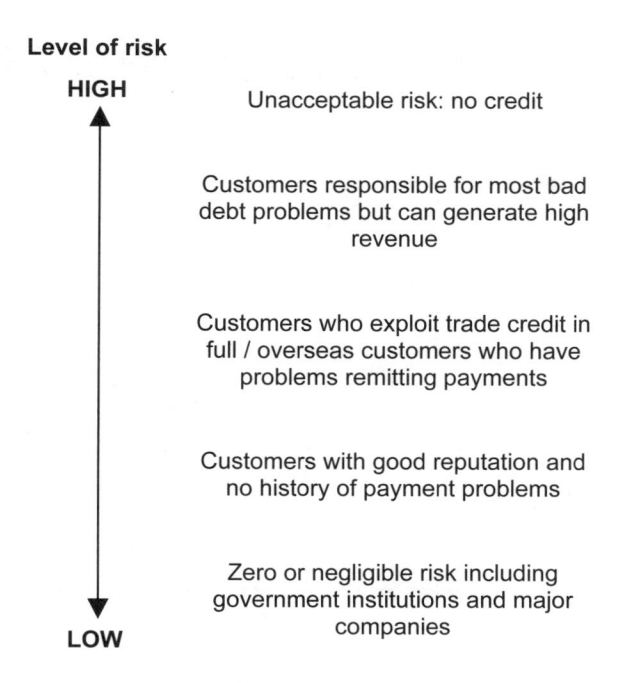

HIGH — Unacceptable risk: no credit

Customers responsible for most bad debt problems but can generate high revenue

Customers who exploit trade credit in full / overseas customers who have problems remitting payments

Customers with good reputation and no history of payment problems

Zero or negligible risk including government institutions and major companies

LOW

2.2 Credit assessments

Many large companies are able to employ specialist staff, to perform a detailed assessment of a client's **ability to pay**, and hence whether **credit** should be **granted**. Banks, whose business is lending money after all, have sophisticated techniques for assessing the risk of any borrower. The credit assessment businesses carry out will therefore vary.

- Some firms will simply **write to** the **debtor's bank** asking for a letter, or at best write to a credit reference agency.
- Some firms, especially if **lending** to a **large business**, are able to spend time examining the customer's accounts.

The circumstances of the creditor will be important.

- For a **multinational** company, a customer who requests £100 on credit will be relative 'small-fry'.
- If a customer requests £150 credit from his or her local **newsagent**, this is obviously much more material, simply because of the nature of the business.

Activity 9.1

Chapter 6 of this Text on whether to lend money discussed a bank's canons of lending, summarised as **CAMPARI**. These might be relevant to the credit controller. Can you remember what CAMPARI stood for?

PART B   CREDIT CONTROL

3 Externally generated information: bank and trade references, and agencies

> To: Britline Carriers PLC
> Sutton Lane, Liverpool
> LW6 9BC
> 0151 - 324 - 7345/6
>
> Please open a credit account in the name of:
> --
>
> Address --
>
> ---------------------------- Telephone ------------
>
> Below are supplied the names and addresses of referees of whom the customary trade enquiries may be made.
>
> I / We note your credit terms as set out in your Standard Conditions of Sale *and agree to pay in accordance therewith for any goods/services supplied by you. These terms are as follows.*
>
> | All accounts are strictly net and payable at the end of the month following the month of invoicing. |
>
> Expected maximum
> amount of credit
> required £ _ _ _ _ _   In total*
>   Weekly*
>   Monthly*
>
> Signature ----------------------
>
> (position) -----------------------
> (NB: If a partnership, all
>   partners should sign.)
>
> * delete non-applicable
>
> Our contact on accounts matters --
>
> Bankers
> Name of bank _ _ _ _ _ _ _ _ _ _ _ _ _ _ _   Full branch address
>   -------------------------
>   -------------------------
>
> Trade references
> (1) Name _ _ _ _ _ _ _ _ _ _ _ _ _ _ _   Address _ _ _ _ _ _ _ _ _ _ _ _ _ _
>   _ _ _ _ _ _ _ _ _ _ _ _ _ _
> (2) Name _ _ _ _ _ _ _ _ _ _ _ _ _ _ _   Address _ _ _ _ _ _ _ _ _ _ _ _ _ _
>   _ _ _ _ _ _ _ _ _ _ _ _ _ _

3.1 Use of references

Standard practice in the UK is often to invite the customer who is applying for credit to provide **references** (eg the customers bank, and other suppliers). Many suppliers have a standard form for prospective customers. An example of such a form is **shown above**. The supplier will send it to the customer who will fill it in.

3.2 Bank references

Bank references are useful. However banks are naturally cautious. The prospective customer is, after all, the bank's client. The bank has two 'duties of care'.

- **The customer.** The bank must not give an adverse opinion without justification. The bank cannot break confidentiality without the customer's consent.
- **The enquirer.** The bank can be considered **negligent**, and hence liable for damages, if the information it gives is misleading.

3.2.1 Contacting the bank

When writing to the bank it is necessary to be *precise* as to the credit you may be offering.

Wrong

'Do you consider X Ltd to be able to pay its debts?'

Right

'Do you consider X Ltd to be good for a trade credit of £1,000 per month on terms of 30 days?'

This gives the bank manager a reasonable idea as to the amount of money required, and the terms. The manager is more able to give an opinion.

3.2.2 Bank opinions

Typical bank opinions, in declining order of favour, are as follows.

	Opinion	Notes
Best	Undoubted.	No worries. The best opinion.
	Considered good for your figures.	Fine, but less favourable than 'undoubted'.
	Respectably constituted which should prove good for your figures.	'Should' suggests that the business is fine, but resources might be strained.
	Respectably constituted businesses whose resources would appear to be fully employed: we do not think they would undertake something they felt they could not fulfil.	This is not encouraging, as the bank makes no reference to the credit asked for.
Worst	Unable to speak for your figures.	This implies that the bank may consider the company potentially overstretched.

Other comments might qualify these statements, for example as follows.

- 'There are **charges registered**'. This normally implies that some of the business's assets are security for a debt (eg a bank loan).
- '**Considered** good for your **amount** if taken in a **series**.' This implies that the customer will be able to pay off the sum in instalments. Some clarification might also be needed.

3.3 Trade references

The bank reference can give certain basic assurances. For some customers, this might be all that is needed, especially if the reply from the bank suggests 'undoubted'. However, the supplier may want additional reassurance. The supplier obtains **trade references** from other businesses that the customer deals with.

When seeking trade references, businesses should **enclose** a **stamped addressed envelope**, and perhaps the enquiry should be couched as a questionnaire.

3.3.1 Problems with trade references

Businesses should take care when obtaining trade references.

- Some customers may name as trade references suppliers with whom they **deliberately maintain** an excellent payments record, simply in order to obtain good references.
- The **trade referee** should **offer similar terms** as the customer is requesting from the supplier.
- Even a **well known company** given as a referee should always be **followed up**. An unknown company's reference should be treated with more caution, in case of collusion.

3.4 Credit ratings

Credit ratings are formal opinions of the **creditworthiness** of an entity. They are used mainly by **investors** and **banks** to assess a company's creditworthiness.

Companies or entities are given **different grades** according to the security they offer. AAA, for example, is very secure. C might indicate default.

Credit ratings are only of **limited use** to trade creditors and credit controllers, but they **do** indicate certain basic facts about a company. A company with a low credit rating is having difficulty in its relationship with its **bankers**, and is likely to be a poor credit risk. However even if the credit rating is good, this may not help a trade creditor with little clout to obtain money rapidly.

BRITLINE CARRIERS PLC
Sutton Lane
Liverpool LW6 9BC
(0151-324 7345/6)

To: Credit controller
      A Big Company plc

Dear Sir,

We have recently received a request for credit from ....Ltd ('the firm'), a customer of ours, who gave yourselves as a reference. I would be most grateful if you could help me by answering the following questions, and returning them in the stamped addressed envelope provided.

1   For how long has the firm been trading with you?

                                                                    ..... Years   .....Months

2   Did the firm supply you with suitable trade and other references when it opened its account with you?

                                                                                       Yes/No

3   What are your normal credit terms for the firm?
    Amount: £.......

    Terms: Cash, weekly, monthly, other (please detail)

4   Does the firm make payments in accordance with your terms?

                                                                              Yes/No/Slow payer

5   Have you ever had to suspend credit facilities with the firm?

                                                                                       Yes/No

    If Yes, when?

Please give below or overleaf any more information which you consider relevant.

Yours faithfully,

3.5 Credit reporting agencies (credit bureaux)

Credit bureaux provide information about businesses so that their creditworthiness can be assessed by suppliers. Some offer background information about a client (eg copy of financial accounts). Others provide more up to date information and even offer a credit rating. Some specialise in a particular industrial or commercial sector.

Credit reporting agencies in the UK include **Experian** and **Dun & Bradstreet**.

Agency reports are useful to the credit controller to the extent that they are:

- A **summary** of some, but not all, of the information available
- One of **several sources of information** used to **cross-check** other information obtained, giving additional reassurance, especially where large credits are concerned

The **problems with agency reports** are as follows.

- **Up-to-date information** which would be **relevant** to the credit decision may not have reached its way on to the system (eg the collapse of a major customer).
- **Suppliers' references** may be **too old** to be relevant.
- Newly established concerns will not have much of a **track record** on which a judgement can be made.

Contents of typical agency report	
Legal data	Legal status is important, if there are restrictions on operations outlined in the company's statutory documents • Full name and registered address of the business • Names of directors, partners, proprietors • Authorised and issued share capital • Parent company, if part of a group • Secured charges • County Court judgements recorded
Commercial data	• Types of business • Location of offices, factories, branches etc • Main features of latest annual report • Details of latest annual report • Annual turnover • Balance sheet extracts
Credit data	• Bankers' opinions • Suppliers' opinions, if available • Possibly, the agency's own credit rating of the customer, and suggested credit limit for the customer • Possibly, the agency might keep records of credit offered by its members • Dun & Bradstreet offer a **'payment' profile service**. This contains information about **payment records** of companies

Activity 9.2

Crisroe Ltd has received a request for credit from Wilder Pharmaceuticals, a chain of shops, comprising 20 stores in the West Midlands. They are asking for a credit limit of £6,000 on 30 days terms. They supply a bank reference, and two trade references.

(a) The bank says: 'Respectably constituted, and should prove good for your figures'.

(b) The first trade reference features a £1,000 credit limit, payable in 60 days. There have been no problems with the account.

(c) The second trade reference is not a supplier at all but one of Wilder's customers. The customer's surname, Atkins, is the same as that of the managing director of Wilder Ltd.

Should Crisroe Ltd agree credit terms with Wilder as a result of this request?

3.6 Other sources of credit control information

A number of other sources of data about companies can be converted into useful credit control information.

3.6.1 The press

Listed companies produce **annual financial statements** and offer a half yearly report. The basics of these results, together with informed comment, is often published in papers such as the *Financial Times*.

3.6.2 Historical financial data

Extel became famous for Extel cards describing the basic financial data of a company, updated for important events such as recent results or rights issues. A **stockbroker** might conceivably offer an opinion. Some firms publish reviews for particular business sectors.

3.6.3 Companies Registry search

All companies have to **file certain financial information** with Companies House. However, small and medium sized companies can file accounts which omit certain information, such as the profit and loss account. A Companies House search can provide valuable evidence as to any secured lending.

3.6.4 County Court records

These could be inspected to see if the company has ever **defaulted** on a **debt**.

3.6.5 Analysing company accounts

We shall look at ratio analysis further in the next section of this chapter.

Activity 9.3

Explain how a credit rating agency can help in providing a credit assessment of a customer.

4 Internally generated information: financial and accounting analysis

4.1 Ratio analysis

A whole variety of **accounting ratios** can build up a broad picture of the customer. However you will be most interested in how much the accounts tell you about a business's ability to pay its debts on time.

A **problem with financial ratio analysis** is that historical information about profits, assets and liabilities is used as a definitive assessment of a **future cash flow position**, when it offers only an uncertain guide.

The analysis and interpretation of the profit and loss account and the balance sheet of a business can be done by:

- Calculating certain ratios
- Then using the ratios for **comparison** either **between one year** and the **next** for a particular business or **between one business** and **another**

For credit control purposes, the most relevant comparisons are between one year and the next, to identify trends or significantly better or worse results than before.

4.2 Profit margin

This is the **ratio of profit to sales**, and may also be called 'profit percentage'.

$$\frac{\text{Profit}}{\text{Sales}} = \frac{£20,000}{£100,000} = 20\%$$

This also means that its costs are 80% of sales. A high profit margin indicates that:

- *Either* costs are being kept well under control
- *And/or* sales prices are high

4.3 Net asset turnover

This is the ratio of **sales** in a year to the **amount of net assets (capital) employed**. For example, if a company has sales in 20X4 of £720,000 and has assets of £360,000, the net asset turnover will be:

$$\frac{\text{Sales}}{\text{Capital employed}} = \frac{£720,000}{£360,000} = 2 \text{ times.}$$

This means that for every £1 of assets employed, the company can generate sales turnover of £2 per annum.

To utilise assets more efficiently, managers should try to create a **higher volume of sales** for the **same assets** and so a higher asset turnover ratio.

4.4 Return on capital employed (ROCE)

This is the **amount of profit** as a percentage of **capital employed** (ie net assets).

For example:

$$\frac{\text{Profit}}{\text{Capital employed}} = \frac{£40,000}{£250,000} = 16\%$$

You should also realise the relation between **ROCE**, **profit margin** and **asset turnover**.

$$\underbrace{\frac{\text{Profit}}{\text{Capital employed}}}_{\text{ROCE}} = \underbrace{\frac{\text{Profit}}{\text{Sales}}}_{\text{Profit margin}} \times \underbrace{\frac{\text{Sales}}{\text{Capital employed}}}_{\text{Asset turnover}}$$

An increase in sales volume can offset a decrease in the profit margin, by increasing net asset turnover, while ROCE stays the same.

A business's profitability and return are not immediately relevant to whether a debt will be paid. However, they do indicate that, overall, the business is **healthy** and is able to **manage its operating cycle**.

4.5 Working capital

Working capital, as we have seen from Chapter 1, is the **difference between**:

- **Current assets** (mainly stocks, debtors and cash)
- **Current liabilities** (such as trade creditors and a bank overdraft)

Working capital is an indicator of liquidity. Firms can liquidate assets to pay debts.

If a company has more current liabilities than current assets, it has **negative** working capital. This means that to some extent, **current liabilities** (eg you, the supplier) are helping to finance the **fixed assets** of the business. However, a business must be able to pay its bills on time. This means that to have negative working capital could be financially unsound and dangerous.

4.6 Stock turnover period

A **stock turnover period** is the length of time an item of **stock** is **held in stores** before it can be used.

Stock turnover periods can be calculated separately for raw materials stocks, work in progress, finished goods etc.

Stock turnover periods are calculated as:

$$\frac{\text{Average stock held}}{\text{Cost of goods sold}} \times 12 \text{ months}$$

Although it is strictly better to use average values, it is more common to use the value of **closing** stocks shown in a balance sheet – at one point in time – to estimate the turnover period.

4.7 Debtors turnover period

The **debtors turnover period**, or **debt collection period**, is the **average length of the credit period** taken by customers. It is the time between the **sale** of an item and the **receipt of cash** for the sale from the customer.

The debt collection period is calculated as:

$$\frac{\text{Average debtors}}{\text{Annual credit sales}} \times 12 \text{ months}$$

For example, if a company sells goods for £1,200,000 per annum in regular monthly quantities, and if debtors in the balance sheet are £150,000, the debt collection period is:

$$\frac{£150,000}{£1,200,000} \times 12 \text{ months} = 1.5 \text{ months}$$

In other words, debtors will pay for goods 1½ months, on average, after the time of sale.

4.8 Creditors turnover period

The **creditors turnover period**, or period of credit taken from suppliers, is the length of time between the **purchase of materials** and the **payment to suppliers**. The period of credit taken from suppliers is calculated as:

$$\frac{\text{Average trade creditors}}{\text{Total purchases in one year}} \times 12 \text{ months}$$

For example, if a company sells goods for £600,000 and makes a gross profit of 40% on sales, and if the amount of trade creditors in the balance sheet is £30,000, the period of credit taken from the suppliers is:

$$\frac{£30,000}{(60\% \text{ of } £600,000)} \times 12 \text{ months} = 1 \text{ month}$$

In other words, suppliers are paid in the month following the purchase of goods. To a credit controller assessing whether a customer deserves credit, this is a very important ratio.

Activity 9.4

Curtis Ltd is a customer of Sarhall Ltd. Curtis's 20X4 accounts show the following.

	£
Sales	360,000
Cost of goods sold	180,000
Stocks	30,000
Debtors	75,000
Trade creditors	45,000

Calculate the length of the operating cycle.

4.9 Implications of turnover periods

If the stock turnover period gets longer or if the debt collection period gets longer, the total amount of stocks or of debtors will increase. Similarly, if the period of credit taken from the suppliers gets longer, the amount of creditors will become bigger.

From the supplier's viewpoint, both of these developments are important as they suggest **growing liquidity problems** in the potential debtor.

The supplier will also be interested in other aspects of the firm's current assets.

- Does the customer have **high cash balances**? If yes, the customer hoards cash, but has no problem paying in principle: not so much 'can't pay' as 'won't pay', perhaps.

- Do the accounts show any **borrowing** and bank arrangements the debtor has? The debtor could borrow substantial funds at short notice and repay creditors with these.

4.10 Current ratio

The **current ratio** is commonly used to indicate **liquidity**.

$$\frac{\text{Current assets}}{\text{Current liabilities}}$$

A 'prudent' current ratio is sometimes said to be **2:1**. In other words, current assets should be twice the size of current liabilities.

In practice, many businesses operate with a much lower current ratio. In these cases, the best way to judge their liquidity would be to look at the **current ratio** at **different dates** over a period of time. If the trend is towards a lower current ratio, we would judge that the liquidity position is getting steadily worse.

There are also certain complications that you need to consider when calculating the current ratio.

PART B   CREDIT CONTROL

4.10.1 Bank overdrafts

Bank overdrafts are **technically repayable on demand**, and therefore must be classified as **current liabilities**. However, many companies have semi-permanent overdrafts, and the likelihood of their having to be repaid in the near future is remote.

4.10.2 Are the year-end figures typical of the year as a whole?

You need to take particular care when assessing seasonal businesses. For example, many large retail companies choose an accounting year end soon after the January sales. Their balance sheets show a higher level of cash and lower levels of stock and creditors than would be usual at any other time in the year.

4.11 Quick ratio

The quick ratio is the ratio of current assets **excluding stocks** to current liabilities. The quick ratio is also known as the **liquidity ratio** and as the **acid test ratio**.

The **quick ratio** is used when we take the view that stocks take a long time to get ready for sale, and then there may be some delay in getting them sold, so that stocks are not particularly liquid assets.

A 'prudent' quick ratio is **1 : 1**. In practice, many businesses have a lower quick ratio. Again the best way of judging a firm's liquidity would be to look at the trend in the quick ratio over a period of time.

However, no one ratio can be used in isolation, as the activity below will demonstrate.

Activity 9.5

Gallant Ltd is a customer of Crisroe Ltd. Gallant's liquidity has declined significantly over the last 12 months. The following financial information is provided:

	Year to 31 December 20X2 £	20X3 £
Sales	573,000	643,000
Cost of goods sold	420,000	460,000
Cash/(overdraft)	5,000	(10,000)
Debtors	97,100	121,500
Creditors	23,900	32,500
Stocks	121,400	189,300

All purchases and sales were made on credit.

Tasks

(a) Analyse the above information, which should include calculations of the operating cycle (the time lag between making payment to suppliers and collecting cash from customers) for 20X2 and 20X3.

(b) Discuss the implications of the changes which have occurred between 20X2 and 20X3.

Notes

(a) Assume a 365 day year for the purpose of your calculations and assume that all transactions take place at an even rate.

(b) All calculations are to be made to the nearest day.

4.12 Gearing

Companies are financed by different types of capital. Each type expects a **return** in the form of **interest** or **dividend**.

Gearing is a method of comparing how much of the long-term capital of a business is provided by:

- **Equity** (ordinary shares and reserves)
- **Prior charge capital holders** (loan creditors, preference shareholders entitled to interest or dividends before ordinary shareholders can receive their dividends)

The two most usual methods of measuring gearing are:

$$\frac{\text{Prior charge capital (long-term loans and preference shares)}}{\text{Equity (ordinary shares plus reserves)}} \times 100\%$$

- A business is **low-geared** if gearing is less than 100%.
- It is **neutrally-geared** if gearing is exactly 100%.
- It is **high-geared** if gearing is more than 100%.

$$\frac{\text{Prior charge capital (long-term loans and preference shares)}}{\text{Total long-term capital}} \times 100\%$$

- A business is now low-geared if gearing is less than 50%.
- It is neutrally-geared if gearing is exactly 50%.
- It is high-geared if it exceeds 50%.

Low gearing means that there is **more equity finance** in the business than there is prior charge capital. High gearing means the opposite – prior charge capital exceeds the amount of equity.

4.13 Importance of gearing

Gearing can be important when a company wants to **raise extra capital.** If its gearing is already too high, the business might find that it is difficult to raise a loan.

Gearing is important from the credit control viewpoint because **trade debts** generally take **lower priority** in a company's planning than interest payments on other forms of debt. If a company becomes insolvent, secured loans are repaid first.

4.14 Interest cover

Interest cover is a measure of financial risk which is designed to show the risks in terms of profit rather than in terms of capital values. It shows the number of times that **interest payments** are **'covered' by profits.** It is of particular interest to a bank making lending decisions.

$$\text{Interest cover} = \frac{\text{Profit before interest and tax}}{\text{Interest}}$$

As a general guide, an **interest cover** of **less than three times** is considered low, indicating that profitability is too low given the gearing of the company.

4.15 Debt ratio

For the analysis of a potential customer for credit, another useful financial risk ratio is the **debt ratio**. This measures the percentage amount of the **company's total assets** (fixed and current) that are being **financed by credit** of one sort or another.

$$\frac{\text{Total creditors (due for payment either within one year or after more than one year)}}{\text{Net fixed assets} + \text{total current assets}}$$

Trends in this ratio over time can be monitored. A higher ratio indicates a **higher financial risk**. A ratio in excess of **50%** indicates a high level of total borrowing, but there is no 'ideal' maximum debt ratio within which companies should try to operate.

Example: Debt ratios

Julatkins Ltd has the following debt ratios.

	At 31 December Year 1	At 31 December Year 2
$\dfrac{\text{Creditors (short and long-term)}}{\text{Assets (fixed and current)}}$	$\dfrac{(20{,}446 + 2{,}931)}{(13{,}848 + 17{,}763)} = 74.0\%$	$\dfrac{(21{,}874 + 2{,}041)}{(3{,}782 + 23{,}020)} = 89.2\%$

Do these indicate liquidity problems?

Solution

The debt ratio was high in Year 1 at 74%. It worsened to 89% at the end of Year 2. This indicates that creditors are financing too much of the company's business. This company is clearly a high credit risk. Any request by its purchasing department for even more trade credit or for extra bank loans ought to be met with (at the very least) a strong reluctance, and probably a flat refusal.

Activity 9.6

You are given summarised information about two of Sarhall's customers that are in the same line of business.

Balance sheets at 30 June

	A			B		
	£'000	£'000	£'000	£'000	£'000	£'000
Land			80			260
Buildings		120			200	
Less depreciation		40			–	
			80			200
Plant		90			150	
Less depreciation		70			40	
			20			110
			180			570
Stocks		80			100	
Debtors		100			90	
Bank		–			10	
		180			200	
Creditors	110			120		
Bank	50			–		
		160			120	
			20			80
			200			650
Capital brought forward			100			300
Profit for year (after interest)			30			100
			130			400
Less drawings			30			40
			100			360
Land revaluation			–			160
Loan (10% pa)			100			130
			200			650
Sales			1,000			3,000
Cost of sales			400			2,000

Task

Produce a table of six ratios calculated for both businesses.

Activity 9.7

Write notes for a report briefly outlining the strengths and weaknesses of the two businesses in the previous activity. Include comment on any major areas where the simple use of the figures could be misleading.

4.16 Cash flow and credit risk

A creditor should focus its attention on how strong the company's cash flows appear to be. We can use the classification outlined in Chapter 1.

Item	Comment
Net operational cash flow − Priority payments	Should be positive
= Cash for discretionary spending − Investment spending	Should normally be positive
= Cash after investment spending	If negative, the company must obtain money from non-trading sources, perhaps by borrowing

Activity 9.8

What data would you look for in the financial statements of a new customer who asks for credit?

5 Internally generated information: customer visits

5.1 Purpose of visits

In addition to the accounting analysis described above, visits to the client can fill information gaps. Visits have two purposes.

- Any **specific queries** arising from the credit **reference data** can be discussed.
- The credit controller can get a **feel for the business** and those running it.

5.2 Evidence from visits

The sales manager might accompany the credit manager. The credit manager should take a look around the business, and needs to speak to people at a suitable level, perhaps the financial controller.

Feature	Yes/No
Premises: do they look **adequate to support the operations** of the business?	
Are visitors **treated courteously**? (If a person is rudely or inefficiently dealt with on a company's own premises, this does not bode well for the company's normal client management.)	
Do the **accounts department** and purchase ledger department appear **well run**, with properly kept files of invoices, reports etc and a suitable system for recording transactions? If not, invoices and reminders go missing, and payment is delayed as a result of this lack of organisation.	
Does the **sales ledger** appear **efficiently run**: in other words, is the business able to secure payment from its own customers?	
What **payment system** does the company use (eg BACS)?	
Is the overall impression, deriving from the factory and office, that the business is **prospering**?	
Is there an obvious build up of **obsolete or slow moving stock**? (This would indicate a problem with sales.)	

6 Using credit control information

6.1 Granting credit

Having obtained information about the new customer, we are now able to decide whether to grant credit. First of all, a new customer will be offered a set **level of credit**, on appropriate terms. The customer's request may be granted, but provisionally, subject to a formal review at a later date.

Your organisation may not wish to **grant the customer's request** in its entirety. For example, assume a potential customer wanted a credit limit of £1,000 and 30 days. As a preliminary, the supplier might offer:

- £500 repayable within 30 days or
- £1,000 repayable within 15 days

Only after the customer has established a suitable payments record would this be increased.

6.2 Refusing credit

With some customers, the risk of granting credit is too great for the volume of extra sales that may result. Perhaps the available information indicates the customer may be in **financial difficulties**. There may not be enough information available to make an assessment of a customer that is a new business.

If you are informing an applicant that their request for credit has been turned down, you need to do so **tactfully**. The customer may be prepared to pay cash for now, and you want to avoid if possible losing this business. Maybe in the future a further application for credit will be successful, if more information becomes available.

An example letter refusing credit is shown below.

BRITLINE CARRIERS PLC
Sutton Lane, Liverpool LW6 9BC
Telephone: 0151 – 324 7345/6

Directors:
D Smith (Managing)
P Patel
C Wilkes

Registered office:
Sutton Lane Liverpool LW6 9BC
Reg. No 34567
Reg. in England

Ref: NC/nn TO 16

21 June 20X0

The Purchasing Manager
New Products & Services Ltd
Sea Road
SOUTHPORT LW20 9PP

Dear Ms Overton

Credit application

Thank you for your application to open credit facilities with us. We have considered your application carefully against our prescribed criteria for potential credit customers. As a result of this exercise, we are sorry to inform you that we do not feel able to offer credit facilities to yourselves at this time.

We would emphasise that we do not have a negative view of your company, but we lack sufficient information to be able to take a decision to grant you credit. After you have traded for a while, you may be able to supply us with additional information. When this occurs, we would encourage you to make a further application.

In the meantime if you are willing to trade with us on a cash basis, we would be happy to supply you.

Thank you again for the interest you have expressed in our company and we look forward to hearing from you.

Yours sincerely,

P Benbow, Receivables Officer
Credit Control Department (extension 916)

Enc

Activity 9.9

Listed below are some sources of information that you may use as evidence that credit should be refused.

- An adverse reference from the bank
- An adverse reference from a supplier

- An adverse report from a credit reference agency
- Legal evidence (County court records)
- Adverse press comment
- Poor figures in the company's accounts

If you have refused the customer credit using one or more of these sources, what kind of positive evidence might cause you to change your mind, and how much hope would you give the customer that credit might eventually be granted?

6.3 Monitoring credit

The **payment record** must be **monitored** continually. This depends on successful sales ledger administration.

- **Invoices** must be **posted** at the right time.
- **Receipts** should be **posted** when they arrive, and **allocated** specifically to the **invoices** to which they relate.
- Any **queries** (eg customers debiting their own credit balance with a debit note as 'notification' to the supplier) need to be dealt with quickly.
- Orders should **always** be **vetted against credit limits.** This indicates the importance of prompt updating, as above.
- A **customer history analysis** can show sales on a rolling twelve-month basis, amounts owed and sales outstanding at each month end. It monitors trends and debtor ageing.

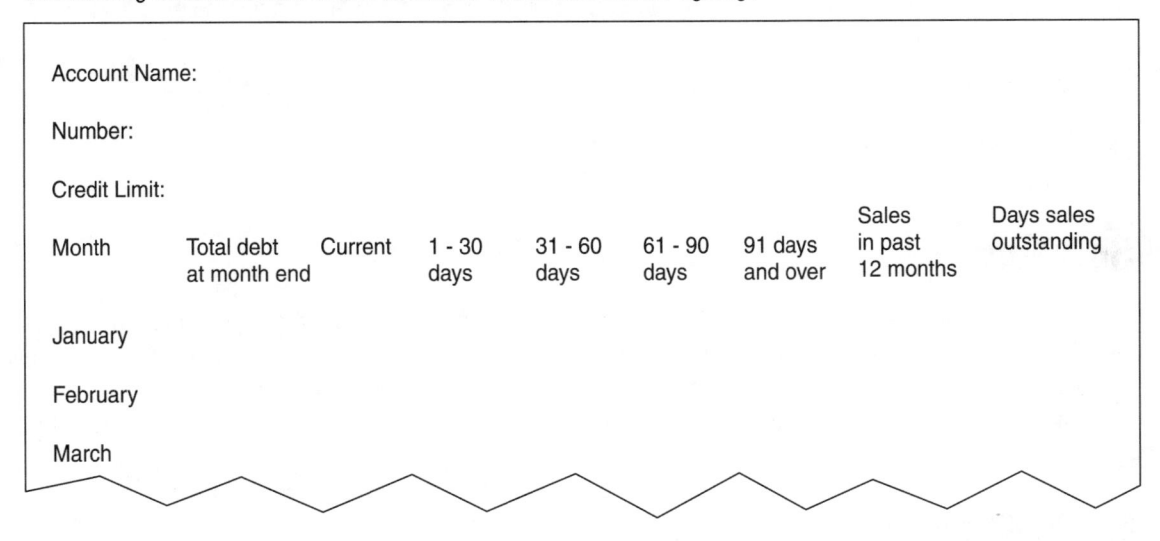

Account Name:							
Number:							
Credit Limit:							
Month	Total debt at month end	Current	1 - 30 days	31 - 60 days	61 - 90 days	91 days and over	Sales in past 12 months	Days sales outstanding
January								
February								
March								

With this information it should be possible to develop in-house credit ratings.

6.4 In-house credit ratings

A system of **in-house credit ratings** simplifies credit monitoring. For example, your employer could have five credit-risk categories for its customers.

You could use these credit categories or ratings to decide either **individual credit limits** for customers within that category or the **frequency of the credit review**. You may have guidelines that would help you make decisions.

Over time, you would **assess** the **payment habits** of a customer, and **amend** the **customer's credit rating** (and credit limits). Any deterioration in a customer's payment record could raise concerns about the customer's creditworthiness.

Example: Categorisation of debtors

Sarhall categorises its credit customers into the following four groups:

1. Prompt payers
2. Those who pay within 30 days of the due date
3. Those who pay between 30 and 60 days of the due date
4. Those who pay over 60 days late

The recent payment record of a regular customer is as follows.

Invoice number	Date of invoice	Date payable	Payment received	Days overdue
3257	7 March	7 April	28 April	21
3816	26 June	26 July	1 September	37
3942	19 July	19 August	1 September	13
4185	3 September	3 October	5 November	33
				104

Average days overdue = 26 days (104 ÷ 4)

Into which payment category would you put the customer?

Solution

The customer would be rated in credit category 2 by the company. A review of the payment record suggests that the customer delays payment until around the end of the month following the due date. This is quite typical business practice, and although the customer is not a good payer, there is a definite payment pattern that suggests that the customer is an **average credit risk**.

6.5 Credit taken ratio

A **credit taken ratio** can be used to monitor the credit limits of customers. This compares the amount currently owed by a customer with the annual sales turnover in his account. We examined this for whole industries in Chapter 8.

Example: Credit taken ratio

Sarhall has two debtors, Curtis and Thomas. Each customer owes £20,000. Annual sales to Curtis are about £200,000, and annual sales to Thomas are about £100,000. What is the credit taken ratio for each customer, and what are the implications of the ratios?

Solution

The credit taken ratio is 10% for Curtis (20,000 ÷ 200,000 × 100%) and 20% for Thomas. Thomas could be regarded as a higher credit risk. The company might wish to keep the credit-taken ratio for customers below a certain limit. If this limit were 20%, a request from Thomas for further credit would be refused until the outstanding debts are settled. The company would be willing, however, to consider a request from Curtis for more credit.

6.6 Credit reviews

Credit control staff should **examine** a **customer's payment record** and the **debtors aged analysis** should be examined regularly, as a matter of course. They should bring breaches of the credit limit, or attempted breaches of it, to the attention of the credit controller. The credit controller will not have the time to examine *each* customer's account thoroughly every month.

The credit controller's efforts will be expended on those thought to be **higher risk**, or where there are other special factors (a debt that has gone bad).

Rating		Payment record	Financial indicators	Frequency of credit reviews	Credit limit (as % of customer's annual purchases)
A	Very high risk	Accounts overdue by 60 + days	Low profits Poor liquidity Highly indebted		Cash only (payment with order)
B	High risk	Accounts overdue by 30 – 60 days	Deteriorating profitability, liquidity, or gearing. High credit taken ratio	Monthly	Reduce to 10% of annual purchases
C	Average risk	Accounts overdue up to 30 days	Stable position	Quarterly	15% of annual purchases
D	Below average risk	Accounts paid on time	Stable or improving position	Six-monthly	25% of annual purchases
E	Low risk	Accounts paid early Public sector customers	Strong financial position, or public sector ownership	Annually	For negotiation with the customer

Activity 9.10

Suppose that you work for an accountancy firm, and you have been asked to advise a manufacturing company client on guidelines for a credit control system. Make brief notes for a presentation to the client on possible guidelines, covering the following points:

(a) Categorisation of debtor risk
(b) Assessment of individual customers' risk categorisation
(c) Procedures to check that the customer has received goods and an invoice

7 The Data Protection Act

7.1 Data protection rules

The growth of information technology and the concern for civil freedoms and individual privacy has meant that legislation has been passed restricting the use of computer-held data. In the UK the current legislation is the **Data Protection Act 1998**. This Act is an attempt to protect the **individual**. The terms of the Act cover data about individuals – **not data about corporate bodies**.

7.2 Key points of the Data Protection Act 1998

- **Data users** and computer bureaux have had to **register** under the Act with the **Data Protection Registrar**, and can only **hold** and **use data** for registered purposes.

- The legislation covers **paper-based** and **computer systems.**

- **Processing of personal data** is **forbidden** unless the subject has granted permission, or in certain other circumstances such as legal obligations or public interest.

- **Individuals** (data subjects) have certain **legal rights**. These include the right to see the data held, the right to know why data is being processed, the right to **compensation for loss** or **unauthorised disclosure** of **inaccurate** data, and the right to **compensation** for, or **correction** of, inaccurate data.

- Data holders cannot process **sensitive data** (racial, political, religious, health, sexual) about the data subject unless express consent has been obtained.

- **Data holders** must adhere to the **data protection principles**.

Key learning points

- **Credit risk** is the possibility that a **debt** will **go bad**. High risk customers can be profitable, but need to be managed carefully.

- **Data about potential debtors** can be obtained from a number of sources.

- Banks owe a **duty of care** to their customers and to the enquirer: their assessments of a debtor's credit status are likely to be precisely worded.

- **Trade references** are useful, but should not be used uncritically.

- **Credit reference agencies** supply a variety of legal and business information thereby saving time for the enquirer. An agency might give its own suggested rating.

- Some companies are able to employ **credit analysts** to examine a firm's **financial accounts**. As these are historical statements, they are no guide to a debtor's **future creditworthiness**.

- However, **ratio analysis** can give some idea of trends and highlight areas for further investigation.

- The **current ratio** is the ratio of current assets to liabilities. The **quick ratio** measures liquidity more precisely.

- The **creditors payment period** indicates the average length of time a company takes to pay its debts. Together with **debtors turnover** and **stock turnover** this gives some idea as to the operations cycle.

- **Gearing ratios** indicate to trade creditors a debtor's overall borrowing: trade creditors are normally unsecured.

- **Visits** to the customer's premises can provide useful information.

- As well as using the information obtained to decide whether to **grant credit**, credit control departments should **monitor debtors** by using **credit ratings** and **details of credit taken.**

- The **Data Protection Act** makes certain restrictions about the use of data about individual customers and the use of personal data.

Quick quiz

1. Give an example of grading customers by risk.

2. Which of the following are a bank's duties of care in giving credit reference information?

    ☐ Not to give an adverse opinion on a customer without justification

    ☐ Not to give an undoubted opinion

    ☐ Not to give an opinion unless the person asking for an opinion is a customer of the bank

    ☐ Not to give misleading information to an enquirer

3. What should you bear in mind when following up trade references?

4. What might a report from a credit reference agency typically contain?

5. What is the problem with using published financial accounts for credit control information?

6. The .... is the ratio of current assets to current liabilities.

7. The .... is the ratio of total creditors to net fixed assets plus total current assets.

8. The Data Protection Act applies to data held about limited companies as well as individuals.

    ☐ True

    ☐ False

9. When analysing the accounts of a potential credit customer, which of the following ratios would be the least relevant?

    A   Gearing
    B   Interest cover
    C   Debt ratio
    D   Gross profit margin

10. Place the following opinions on potential customers in order, starting with the most favourable.

    A   Considered good for your figures
    B   Undoubted
    C   Unable to speak for your figures
    D   Respectably constituted business which should prove good for your figures.

Answers to quick quiz

1. Risks might be classified as: zero or negligible risk; ordinary risk; potential slow payers; high risk; unacceptable risk.

2. Not to give an adverse opinion on a customer without justification; not to give misleading information to an enquirer.

3. Suppliers may maintain an untypically good payment record with those they nominate as referees; referees who are not well known businesses should be treated with caution; the referee should ideally be on similar terms as those applied for by the customer.

4. Legal, commercial and credit information

5. Historical information is an unreliable guide for the future.

6. The **current ratio** is the ratio of current assets to current liabilities.

7. The **debt ratio** is the ratio of total creditors to net fixed assets plus total current assets.

8. False. It covers data about individuals only.

9. D Gross profit margin.

10. B, A, D, C.

PART B CREDIT CONTROL

Activity checklist

This checklist shows which performance criteria, range statement or knowledge and understanding point is covered by each activity in this chapter. Tick off each activity as you complete it.

Activity

9.1	☐	This activity deals with Performance Criterion 15.3.C: open new accounts for customers with an established credit status
9.2	☐	This activity deals with Performance Criterion 15.3.A: agree credit terms with customers in accordance with the organisation's policies
9.3	☐	This activity deals with Performance Criterion 15.3.B: identify and use internal and external sources of information to evaluate the current credit status of customers and potential customers
9.4	☐	This activity deals with Performance Criterion 15.3.B: identify and use internal and external sources of information to evaluate the current credit status of customers and potential customers
9.5	☐	This activity deals with Performance Criterion 15.3.B: identify and use internal and external sources of information to evaluate the current credit status of customers and potential customers
9.6	☐	This activity deals with Performance Criterion 15.3.B: identify and use internal and external sources of information to evaluate the current credit status of customers and potential customers
9.7	☐	This activity deals with Performance Criterion 15.3.B: identify and use internal and external sources of information to evaluate the current credit status of customers and potential customers
9.8	☐	This activity deals with Performance Criterion 15.3.B: identify and use internal and external sources of information to evaluate the current credit status of customers and potential customers
9.9	☐	This activity deals with Performance Criterion 15.3.D: ensure the reasons for refusing credit are discussed with customers in a tactful manner
9.10	☐	This activity deals with Knowledge and Understanding 26: understanding that the accounting systems of an organisation are affected by its organisational structure, its administrative systems and procedures and the nature of its business transactions

chapter 10

Managing debtors

Contents

1. Introduction
2. Maintaining information on debtors
3. Collecting debts
4. Default insurance, factoring and invoice discounting
5. Debt collection from difficult customers

Performance criteria

15.4.A Monitor information relating to the current state of debtors' accounts regularly and take appropriate action

15.4.C Ensure discussions and negotiations with debtors are conducted courteously and achieve the desired outcome

15.4.D Use debt recovery methods appropriate to the circumstances of individual cases and in accordance with the organisation's procedures

Range statement

15.4.1 Information on debtors: age analysis of debtors; average periods of credit given and received; incidence of bad and doubtful debts

15.4.2 Appropriate action: information and recommendations for action passed to appropriate individual within own organisation; debtor contacted and arrangement made for recovery of the debt

Knowledge and understanding

- Sources of credit status information
- External sources of information: banks, credit agencies and official publications
- Legal and administrative procedures for the collection of debts
- Interpretation and use of credit control information
- Methods of collection
- Factoring arrangements
- Debt insurance
- Evaluation of different collection methods
- Understanding that the accounting systems of an organisation are affected by its organisational structure, its administrative systems and procedures and the nature of its business transactions
- Understanding that recording and accounting practices may vary in different parts of the organisation
- Understanding that practice in this area will be determined by an organisation's credit control policies and procedures
- An understanding of the organisation's relevant policies and procedures

1 Introduction

The management of debtors is a very practical topic, providing a good test of your business awareness.

In this chapter we examine how specific accounts are **managed**, and how you should decide what credit control action is required. You may also be asked to take action, such as drafting a reminder letter to an overdue debtor.

A further key decision in debtor management is whether to involve third parties in **factoring** or **discounting** arrangements. Again you will be expected to make judgements about which type of arrangement is appropriate.

The **aged debtor analysis** is an important means of tracking outstanding balances, and you need to feel comfortable using it.

2 Maintaining information on debtors

2.1 Managing information

We have already seen that the credit controller should obtain information from a variety of sources to decide whether or not to grant credit and what the credit level should be. The credit controller's job does not end there, however. After all, a customer's **creditworthiness** may **change over time** and the credit controller needs to keep track of the position.

2.2 Aged debtors listing

The aged debtors listing is one of the principal ways in which credit controllers monitor debtors.

An age analysis of debtors can be prepared manually or, more easily, by computer.

An **aged debtors listing** will probably look very much like the schedule illustrated below. The analysis splits up the total balance on the account of each customer across different columns according to the **dates of the transactions** which make up the total balance.

Thus, the amount of an invoice which was raised 14 days ago will form part of the figure in the column headed 'up to 30 days', while an invoice which was raised 36 days ago will form part of the figure in the column headed 'up to 60 days'. (In the schedule below, 'up to 60 days' is used as shorthand for 'more than 30 days but less than 60 days'.)

SARHALL LIMITED
AGE ANALYSIS OF DEBTORS AS AT 31.1.X2

Account number	Customer name	Balance	Up to 30 days	Up to 60 days	Up to 90 days	Over 90 days
B004	Brilliant Ltd	804.95	649.90	121.00	0.00	34.05
E008	Easimat Ltd	272.10	192.90	72.40	6.80	0.00
H002	Hampstead Ltd	1,818.42	0.00	0.00	724.24	1,094.18
M024	Martlesham Ltd	284.45	192.21	92.24	0.00	0.00
N030	Nyfen Ltd	1,217.54	1,008.24	124.50	0.00	84.80
T002	Todmorden College	914.50	842.00	0.00	72.50	0.00
T004	Tricorn Ltd	94.80	0.00	0.00	0.00	94.80
V010	Volux Ltd	997.06	413.66	342.15	241.25	0.00
Y020	Yardsley Smith & Co	341.77	321.17	20.60	0.00	0.00
Totals		6,745.59	3,620.08	772.89	1,044.79	1,307.83
Percentage		100%	53.6%	11.5%	15.5%	19.4%

2.3 Using the aged debtors' analysis

You can use the aged debtors' analysis to help decide what action to take about older debts. Going down each column in turn starting from the column furthest to the right and working across, we can see that there are some **rather old debts** which ought to be investigated. Perhaps some older invoices are still in dispute. Perhaps some debtors are known to be in financial difficulties.

Various amendments can help make the aged debtors' analysis easier to use.

- A report can be printed in which **overdue accounts** are seen first: this highlights attention on these items.

- Reports can also give details for individuals of **sales revenue** and **days sales outstanding**.(see below)

- The details given for individuals can also be **aggregated** by class of customer, for example by region, type of customer or industry sector.

PART B CREDIT CONTROL

Account number	Customer name	Balance	Up to 30 days	Up to 60 days	Up to 90 days	Over 90 days	Sales revenue in last 12 months	Days sales outstanding
B004	Brilliant Ltd	804.95	649.90	121.00	0.00	34.05	6,789.00	43

We can see from the age analysis of Sarhall's Ltd's debtors given earlier that the relatively high proportion of debts over 90 days (19.4%) is largely due to the debts of Hampstead Ltd. Other customers with debts of this age are Brilliant Ltd, Nyfen Ltd and Tricorn Ltd.

Activity 10.1

Extracts from the aged debtors analysis for Crisroe Ltd as at 31 January are set out below.

Name	Code	Total owing	0-30 days	30-60 days	60-90 days	>90 days
		£	£	£	£	£
Collyers Ltd	C041	6,000		6,000 Inv. 5784		
Hurst and Sons	H036	14,000	3,000 Inv 6012	4,000 Inv 5761	5,000 Inv 5005	2,000 Inv 4253
WM Mercers	M018	12,000	5,000 Inv 6123	1,000 Inv 5399 3,000 Inv 5691	3,000 Inv 4984	
St Leonards & Co	S008	8,000		2,000 Inv 5757	4,000 Inv 5098	2,000 Inv 4554
Total		40,000	8,000	16,000	12,000	4,000
Percentage Nearest whole %		100%	20%	40%	30%	10%

The following transactions relating to these customers took place in February.

Collyers Ltd Paid Invoice 5784. Invoice 6455 £8,000 issued.

Hurst and Sons Paid Invoices 5005 and 5761. Invoices 4253 and 6012 remain unpaid. Invoice 6667 £7,000 issued.

WM Mercers Paid Invoices 4984 and 5399. Invoices 5691 and 6123 remain unpaid.

St Leonards & Co All invoices remain unpaid.

Task

Prepare an aged debtors analysis for these debtors as at 28 February.

2.4 Other ratios

Additional ratios which might be useful in debtor management, in addition to days' sales outstanding, are as follows.

2.4.1 Overdues as a percentage of total debt

For example, assume that Sarhall Limited offers credit on 30 day terms. Brilliant Ltd's debt could be analysed as:

$$\frac{£121.00 + £34.05}{£804.95} = 19.3\% \text{ overdue}$$

2.4.2 Disputed debts

If debts are disputed, it is helpful to see what proportion these are of the total debtors and the total overdue. If, of Sarhall's total debtors of £6,745.59, an amount of £973.06 related to disputed items, the ratio of disputed debts to total outstanding would be:

$$\frac{£973.06}{£6,745.59} = 14.4\%$$

As a percentage of total items *over* 30 days old:

$$\frac{£973.06}{£6,745.59 - £3,620.08} = 31\%$$

An increasing disputes ratio can indicate:

- Invoicing problems
- Operational problems

2.5 Debtors' ageing and liquidity

The credit controller will also be interested in the **total percentage figure** calculated at the bottom of each column.

- Why might a credit controller be worried by an increase in the ageing?
- If the credit controller knows the customers are going to pay, should it matter?

Think back to your work on **cash forecasting**. Any reduction in the inflow caused by an overall increase in the debtors period affects the company's **ability to pay its debts** and increases its use of **overdraft finance:** unauthorised overdrafts carry a hefty fee as well as interest.

PART B CREDIT CONTROL

Example: Breed Ltd

The cash flow forecast of Breed Ltd for January to March 20X5 is as follows.

	January £	February £	March £
Receipts from debtors	1,500	1,000	1,400
Payments	(1,200)	(1,300)	(900)
Surplus/deficit for the month	300	(300)	500
Cash at bank/(overdraft) brought forward	(400)	(100)	(400)
Cash at bank/(overdraft) carried forward	(100)	(400)	100

At the end of March, there is a forecast surplus of £100. Assume that all customers take exactly one month credit (ie January cash receipts reflect December sales). Breed Ltd has an arranged overdraft facility of £700, which it seems to be well within. The facility is reviewed at the end of each period, and excess borrowing over £700 costs 10% of the amount over that limit.

Let us now assume that customers suddenly take longer to pay. There are no bad debts, but customers now pay two months after the sale. In other words, December invoices sales are paid for in February, and so on. Show how this affects the company's cashflow.

Solution

	January £	February £	March £
Receipts from debtors		1,500	1,000
Payments	(1,200)	(1,300)	(900)
Bank charges*		(90)	(79)
Surplus/(deficit)	(1,200)	110	21
Cash at bank/(overdraft) brought forward	(400)	(1,600)	(1,490)
Cash at bank/(overdraft) carried forward	(1,600)	(1,490)	(1,469)

* Bank charges in February are £1 for every £10 over the overdraft limit at the end of January and so on.

What this example shows is the dramatic impact that fluctuations in the debtors ageing, even a one-off change, can have on a firm's cash position.

- From working comfortably within the agreed overdraft, the firm has found itself carrying a **long-term overdraft** which is quite expensive.
- The firm's **own creditworthiness** is likely to suffer.
- The firm **pays more in overdraft fees and interest**.

2.6 Problems with individual customers

The credit controller should try and avoid situations when a customer starts to delay payment. He or she should review information from:

- Sales staff regarding how the company is doing
- The press for any stories relevant to the company

- Competitors
- The trade 'grapevine'

These can supply early warning signals.

2.7 Refusing credit

If, however, there is a persistent problem, the credit controller might have to insist on a **refusal of additional credit**.

- **Sales staff**, who will possibly receive less commission as a result of lower sales, are likely to **resent** a refusal of credit.
- However, if there is a possibility of default, the loss of a **potential** sale is surely less severe than the failure of **actual** money to arrive.

3 Collecting debts

3.1 Debt collection

```
Customer orders
      ↓
Check credit limits
      ↓
Deliver goods with
  delivery notes
      ↓
  Raise invoices
      ↓
Send statement of
outstanding invoices
      ↓
Pursue unpaid invoices
      ↓
  Receive cash
```

3.1.1 Issuing invoices and receiving payments

Having agreed credit terms with a customer, a business should issue an invoice and expect to receive payment when it is due. The sales ledger staff are responsible for **issuing invoices** and **receiving payments**. They should ensure that:

- The **customer** is **fully aware** of the **terms**.
- The **invoice** is **correctly drawn up**.
- They are **aware** of any **potential quirks** in the customer's system.

3.1.2 Pursuing slow payers

Credit control staff will be responsible for **chasing late payers**. Alternatively specialist debt collection staff might pursue debts, under the supervision of the credit manager. In the case of very late payers, an **external debt collection agency** might be employed.

Procedures for pursuing overdue debts must be established, for example:

- **Issuing reminders or final demands**
- **Chasing payment by telephone**
- **Making a personal approach** for payment from the credit manager or a salesman
- **Notifying the debt collection** section about what debts are overdue so that further credit will not be given to the customer until he has paid the due amounts
- Handing over the task of debt collection to a **specialist debt collection section**
- **Instituting legal action** to recover a debt
- **Hiring an external debt collection agency** to collect the debt

3.2 Sales paperwork

Sales **paperwork** should be dealt with promptly and accurately.

- **Send out invoices immediately** after delivery of goods.
- **Carry out checks** to **ensure** that **invoices are accurate**.
- **Investigate queries and complaints** and, if appropriate, issue credit notes **promptly**.
- **Issue monthly statements early if practical** so that all items on the statement might then be included in customers' monthly settlements of bills.

3.3 Customer awareness of terms

Any business can increase its chances of getting paid by ensuring, at various stages, that **the customer has no right to plead ignorance** of the due date, or that the seller attaches no importance to it.

- Credit control should **discuss payment dates** and **terms** during the initial negotiations as payment terms can be costed into pricing calculations.
- When the **order** is **confirmed in writing**, **payment terms** should **appear clearly,** and not be left to the small print.
- When a **customer account** is **set up**, the credit agreement should contain a clause where a customer **acknowledges agreement** to the supplier's terms and conditions.
- The invoice should **state clearly** the **payment terms**.
- Payment terms should also be **prominently displayed** on the monthly statement.

3.4 Proper invoicing

Slip-ups in invoicing by a supplier might **create delays in payment** by a customer. The internal controls in the customer's procedures for paying the debt might prevent the debt from being paid because of the discrepancies or faults.

Activity 10.2

What details should sales ledger staff check when they are checking invoices for discrepancies or faults?

3.5 Knowledge of customer payment systems

Credit control staff should know how customers want to pay.

- Some customers have an **invoice run** on a **monthly basis**. There is a cut-off point after which data cannot be input to the system. Delays might be caused by a backlog.
- Other customers, regardless of their actual obligations, **ration the amount** paid out per month.
- Some customers will only pay when sent a **reminder** or when specifically asked by suppliers.
- Other customers will not pay until **threatened** with legal action.

3.6 Statements and reminders

Invoices are usually followed by a **monthly statement** to customers which will:

- List the new invoices during the month
- Indicate the cash received
- Indicate the outstanding balance due
- Analyse the debts by age
- Serve as a reminder to the customer about payment

PART B CREDIT CONTROL

STATEMENT OF ACCOUNT

Pickett (Handling Equipment) Limited
Unit 7, Western Industrial Estate
Dunford DN2 7RJ

Tel: (01990) 72101   Fax: (01990) 72980   VAT Reg No 982 721 349

Accounts Department
Finstar Ltd
67 Laker Avenue
Dunford DN4 5PS

Date: 31 May 20X2

A/c No: F023

Date	Details	Debit £ p	Credit £ p	Balance £ p
30/4/X2	Balance brought forward from previous statement ①			492 22
3/5/X2	Invoice no. 34207 ②	129 40		621 62
4/5/X2	Invoice no. 34242 ②	22 72		644 34
5/5/X2	Payment received - thank you ④		412 17	232 17
17/5/X2	Invoice no. 34327 ②	394 95		627 12
18/5/X2	Credit note no. 00192 ③		64 40	562 72
21/5/X2	Invoice no. 34392 ②	392 78		955 50
28/5/X2	Credit note no. 00199 ③		107 64	847 86
	Amount now due		⑤ £	847 86

Terms: 30 days net, 1% discount for payment in 7 days. E & OE ⑥

Registered office: 4 Arkwright Road, London E16 4PQ   Registered in England No 2182417

Key

1. Balance brought forward
2. New invoices sent out
3. Credit notes sent out
4. Payments received
5. Balance now outstanding
6. Terms

Instead of statements, a business might issue **reminder notices** to slow payers, such as the one below.

BRITLINE CARRIERS PLC
Sutton Lane, Liverpool LW6 9BC
Telephone: 0151 – 324 7345/6

Directors:
D Smith (Managing)
P Patel
C Wilkes

Registered office:
Sutton Lane Liverpool LW6 9BC
Reg. No 34567
Reg. in England

Ref: NC/nn TO 16

21 June 20X0

Accounts Department
Tradewell Office Products & Services Ltd
Easy St
MANCHESTER M12 7SL

Dear Sir

OVERDUE ACCOUNT: 33521

Further to the statement sent to you on 16 May 20-- it appears that your account for April 20-- totalling £1,402.70 remains outstanding. Please find enclosed a copy statement.

The terms of credit extended to your company were agreed as 30 days from receipt of statement.

Please settle the above account by return of post.

Yours faithfully,

P Benbow, Receivables Officer
Credit Control Department (extension 916)

Enc

3.7 'Key account' customers

In most businesses, major **'key account' customers** will receive special treatment in the sales effort. A more personal approach will be also given to managing the debts in these cases. The salesman or a debt collection officer (perhaps the credit manager himself) may make an approach to the customer to request payment.

3.8 Reconciliation and 'on account' payments

A problem you might encounter is a customer who pays a round sum to cover a variety of invoices. The round sum may be a **payment 'on account'**: in other words, the customer might not state to which invoices the payment refers. This might occur because the customer is having liquidity problems. Unallocated payments on account should be **investigated**.

3.9 Customer queries

Many problems with debtors do not arise out of insolvency or liquidity, but for **operational reasons**.

- Invoices might be disputed.
- Goods may be returned if they do not accord with the specified order.

Many customer queries are not the responsibility of the credit control department. However, any customer query should be investigated, before the firm starts instituting its bad debt procedures. **Courtesy** should be maintained at all times. It might also help to do a **reconciliation** of items in the debtor's and the creditor's accounting records.

4 Default insurance, factoring and invoice discounting

4.1 Default insurance

Companies might be able to obtain **default insurance** against certain approved debts going bad, through a specialist insurance firm.

When a company arranges credit insurance, it must submit **specific proposals** for credit to the insurance company, stating:

- The **name** of **each customer** to which it wants to give credit
- The **amount of credit** it wants to give.

The insurance company will accept, amend or refuse these proposals, depending on its assessment of each of these customers.

Default insurance is normally available for only up to about **75%** of a company's potential bad debt loss. The remaining **25%** of any bad debt costs are **borne** by the company itself. This is to ensure that the company does not become slack with its credit control and debt collection procedures.

4.2 Domestic credit insurance

Credit insurance for **domestic** (ie not export) businesses is available from a number of sources. However most insurance companies will spend a considerable effort in examining a company's books and systems before they will accept any of the risks.

There are several types of credit insurance on offer.

4.2.1 'Whole turnover' policies

Whole turnover policies can be used in two ways.

- They can cover the firm's **entire sales ledger**, although, normally speaking, the actual amount paid out will rarely be more than 80% of the total loss for any specific claim.

- Alternatively, the client can **select a proportion of its debtors** and insure these for their entire amount. In other words, 80% (say) of each debt is insured or the entire amount of the debts incurred, say, by perhaps 80% of the customers.

Premiums on a whole turnover policy are usually **1%** of the **insured sales**.

Activity 10.3

Crisroe Ltd has a whole turnover policy for its debts. The policy is underwritten by Moon Assurance plc and is on a whole turnover basis, whereby 80% of the sales ledger is covered. In the first quarter of 20X4, the company made total sales of £4m and, at the end of the quarter, debtors for credit sales stood at £1.4m. Crisroe has traded with Gilyates Ltd, for whom the underwriters approved a credit limit of £1,700. At the end of the quarter, Gilyates had outstanding debts of £2,100. Gilyates turns into a 'bad debtor' when the company's buildings are completely destroyed by fire.

Crisroe writes to Moon claiming for the bad debt. How much will Crisroe be entitled to as compensation?

4.2.2 Annual aggregate: excess of loss

Under an **annual aggregate excess of loss policy**, the insurer pays 100% of debts above an agreed limit. This is similar to motor insurers requiring that the first amount (eg £50) of a loss is the responsibility of the insured.

4.2.3 Specific account policies

Insurance can be purchased to cover a **specific debtor account** in the event of some contingency. For example, a policy might depend on the debtor being formally declared insolvent.

4.3 Export credit insurance

The credit risks which an **exporter** must consider come under two headings.

(a) **Buyer risks (commercial risks)**. These are similar to those risks encountered in domestic sales, except that the credit period on export sales is often longer. Also, suing someone overseas is often a longer and more expensive process than suing a domestic customer.

PART B CREDIT CONTROL

(b) **Country risks (market or political risks).** These include not only risks in the buyer's country, but also obstacles in the UK (eg cancellation of an export licence) or in a third country through which payment must be made.

Cover for short-term business (eg up to 180 days) is provided by private-sector insurers, such as Gerling NCM Credit Insurance. Gerling NCM offers:

(a) An **international guarantee** offering cover of around 95% in respect of various buyer and country risks
(b) A **domestic policy**

The Government's **Export Credits Guarantee Department (ECGD)** provides longer term help to UK firms in the following main ways.

(a) ECGD issues **guarantees to banks**. Against the strength of this security, the bank provides, usually at favourable interest rates, finance to support the export contract.

(b) ECGD offers **specific guarantees** to exporters who want to finance sales either out of their own funds or by way of ordinary borrowings.

4.4 Factoring

Factoring is an arrangement to have debts collected by a factor company which advances a proportion of the money it is due to collect.

4.4.1 Why factors are used

Some businesses might have difficulties in financing the amounts owed by customers (debtors). There are two main reasons for this.

(a) If a **business's sales** are rising **rapidly**, its total debtors will rise quickly. The business, although making profits, might be in trouble as it has too many debtors and not enough cash.

(b) If a business grants **long credit** to its customers, it might run into cash flow difficulties for much the same reason.

4.4.2 Services provided by factors

Factors are organisations that offer their clients a financing service to overcome these problems. They are prepared to advance cash to the client against the **security** of the **client's debtors**. The business will assign its debtors to the factor and will typically ask for an advance of funds against the debts which the factor has purchased, up to 80% of the value of the debts.

For example, if a business makes credit sales of £100,000 per month, the factor might be willing to advance up to 80% of the invoice value (here £80,000) in return for a **commission charge**. **Interest** will be charged on the amount of funds advanced. The balance of the money will be paid to the business when the customers have paid the factor, or after an agreed period.

The main aspects of **factoring** are:

(a) **Administration** of the **client's invoicing, sales accounting** and **debt collection** service

(b) **Credit protection** for the **client's debts**, where the factor takes over the risk of loss from bad debts and '**insures**' the client against such losses. The factor usually purchases these debts '**without recourse**' to the client, which means that if the client's debtors do not pay what they owe, the factor will not ask for his money back from the client

(c) **Making payments** to the client in **advance of collecting the debts**

4.4.3 Advantages of factoring

The appeal of factor financing to **growing firms** is that factors might advance money when a bank is reluctant to consider granting a larger overdraft. Advances from a factor are therefore particularly useful for companies needing more and more cash to expand their business quickly, by purchasing more stocks and allowing more credit sales.

Other **benefits of factoring** for a business customer include:

- The business can **pay** its **suppliers promptly**, and so be able to take advantage of any early payment discounts that are available.
- The business can **maintain optimum stock levels,** because the business will have enough cash to pay for the stocks it needs.
- The business can **finance growth through** sales rather than by injecting fresh external capital.
- The business gets **finance linked** to its **volume of sales**. In contrast, overdraft limits tend to be determined by historical balance sheets.
- The managers of the business do **not** have to **spend their time** on the problems of **slow paying debtors**.
- The business does **not incur** the **costs** of **running** its own **sales ledger department**.

4.4.4 Disadvantages of factoring

An important **disadvantage of factoring** is that debtors will be making payments direct to the factor, which is likely to present a **negative picture of the business**.

4.5 Invoice discounting

Invoice discounting is the **purchase** (by the provider of the discounting service) **of trade debts** at a discount. Invoice discounting enables the business from which the debts are purchased to raise working capital.

Invoice discounting is related to factoring. Many factors will provide an invoice discounting service.

The invoice discounter does **not** take over the administration of the client's sales ledger, and the arrangement is purely for the **advance of cash**. A business should only want to have invoices discounted when it has a temporary cash shortage, and so invoice discounting tends to consist of 'one-off' deals.

Confidential invoice discounting is an arrangement where a debt is confidentially assigned to the factor, and the client's customer will only become aware of the arrangement if he does not pay his debt to the client.

Activity 10.4

The Managing Director, the Chief Accountant and the Chief Internal Auditor were meeting to discuss problems over debt collection recently identified in Crisroe Ltd. One point made strongly by the Chief Internal Auditor was that his staff should be involved in much more than the routine verification tasks normally undertaken. It is, therefore, agreed that the internal audit section should look at the problem and consider the possibility of using the services of a factor to take over some, or all, of the work of the credit control section.

Task

Outline the matters that should be considered before a decision is taken to use the services of a factor.

5 Debt collection from difficult customers

5.1 Identification of slow payers

Businesses need to identify those customers whose payment records leave something to be desired.

- The **largest outstanding balances** and the **accounts** with **most arrears can be examined first**. This focuses attention on value.
- A list can also be prepared of '**live accounts**' which have not received payments in the preceding month.

5.2 Methods of chasing slow payers

If neither the invoice nor the statement elicit any response the business has a number of alternative techniques. These include the following.

- **Letters**: cheap but not very effective
- **Telephoning**: expensive, but fairly effective
- **E-mail:** cheap and significantly more effective than letters
- **Fax transmission**: medium cost, medium effectiveness
- **Personal visit**: very expensive, but very effective

Each of these methods is appropriate to different circumstances. Broadly speaking, the higher the value of the debt the more personal should be the intervention.

Lower value ⎯⎯⎯⎯⎯⎯⎯⎯⎯⎯⎯⎯⎯→ Higher value

Letter → E-mail → Fax → Telephone ⎯→ Personal visit

A **customer record card** can be used to keep track as to how the collection process is going.

Account no Account name Address						Telephone Fax Contact name Extension		
Date and time	Phone	Letter		Spoke to	Date promised		Amount promised	Details

Such a card can be prepared from a daily telephone log of all calls.

5.3 Letters

Here is a checklist you can consult for the contents of any letter.

Letter checklist	
Address the letter to a **named individual** (or job title at the very least)	
Indicate your **job title** and **telephone extension**	
Sign the **letter personally**	
Display the **amount overdue** prominently	
Ask for **payment by return of post**	
Copy the letter to the person responsible for ordering the supplies in the first place. (This can mean additional pressure on the accounts department.)	
Be specific about any **further action** to be taken	
Do not make threats you are not prepared to implement	

Customers might soon learn your collection procedures, so it helps to vary the content and timing of letters.

The first reminder should be like the one you saw earlier in this chapter.

5.4 Final demands

If the **first reminder** fails to elicit an appropriate response, the firm may:

- Issue a **second reminder**, then a **third reminder**
- Issue a **final demand**, after which legal action is taken

PART B CREDIT CONTROL

Given that the customer has already received and ignored an invoice, a statement and a reminder, there may seem to be little point in adding a second, gently worded reminder letter. However your organisation may wish to **increase the pressure gradually**, as legal action may unnecessarily antagonise an important customer.

Examples of final demands are given **below**.

(a)

BRITLINE CARRIERS PLC
Sutton Lane, Liverpool LW6 9BC
Telephone: 0151 – 324 7345/6

Directors:
D Smith (Managing)
P Patel
C Wilkes

Registered office:
Sutton Lane Liverpool LW6 9BC
Reg. No 34567
Reg. in England

Ref: NC/nn TO 16

21 July 20X0

Chief Accountant
Tradewell Office Products & Services Ltd
Easy St
MANCHESTER M12 7SL

FINAL DEMAND

Dear Mr X

Re: OVERDUE AMOUNT: £1,402.70 (Account 33521)

We regret to note that you have not replied to our previous reminder of 21 June when we requested payment of the above overdue amount.

Your account will now be transferred to A & B Ltd for collection, with any additional costs chargeable to you. Immediate payment of the full amount by return can avoid this distasteful action.

Yours faithfully

S Earland
Chief Credit Controller (Extension 600)

(b)

> **BRITLINE CARRIERS PLC**
> Sutton Lane, Liverpool LW6 9BC
> Telephone: 0151 – 324 7345/6
>
> Directors:
> D Smith (Managing)
> P Patel
> C Wilkes
>
> Registered office:
> Sutton Lane Liverpool LW6 9BC
> Reg. No 34567
> Reg. in England
>
> Ref: NC/nn TO 16
> Financial Director
> Tradewell Office Products & Services Ltd
> Easy St
> MANCHESTER M12 7SL
>
> 21 July 20X0
>
> FINAL DEMAND
>
> Dear Mr X
>
> Re: OVERDUE AMOUNT: £1,402.70 (Account 33521)
>
> We regret to note that you have not replied to our previous reminder of 21 June when we requested payment of the above overdue amount.
>
> We would advise you that should the debt remain unpaid within seven days we will immediately place your account with the County Court. Full payment by return will avoid the need for this distasteful action.
>
> Yours faithfully
>
> C Wilkes
> Financial Director

The debtor may **only have paid** part of the bill. This can be used as an excuse to demand payment of the rest. Short payment could mean any number of things:

- Invoices not input to the sales ledger system before a cheque run
- Deduction of a disputed amount
- Agreement with sales staff
- Deliberate under-payment

A valued customer might be **goaded into action** perhaps if the supplier threatens to refuse to sell any more goods on credit until the debt is cleared. This is less serious than legal action, but still significant.

In the end a final demand should be **final.** If the customer fails to pay, the matter should be put into the hands of a third party such as a solicitor or debt collector.

Activity 10.5

You are employed in the office of Sarhall Ltd of Gemmill House, Black Street, London E23 4AR. One of the company's customers is a Mr Trapnel. He owes £750 for the supply of Elbow Grease, and this amount has been outstanding for some time. You have already sent an invoice (reference X123), a statement (on 3 June 20X8) for this amount and a first reminder letter (on 14 July). The invoice date was 1 June and was payable by 30 June.

Draft a letter to Mr Trapnel, reminding him of the debt, and saying that you might have to consider taking him to court. Mr Trapnel's address is 20, Camel Street, London N1 4PR. Today's date is 21 August. Sarhall Ltd's terms are that payment should be received 30 days after the invoice date and Mr Trapnel was aware of this when he was offered credit.

5.5 Telephone

The **telephone** provides greater nuisance value than a letter, and the **greater immediacy** can encourage a response. However telephone calls may be more expensive than letters and the telephone may take up more of your time. There may also be problems of getting through to the right person.

Some useful hints for collecting by telephone are outlined below.

(a) **Be prepared**. Have all relevant information to hand so you do not have to call back, or hunt through files.

(b) During the call, **keep calm**, make notes. Most importantly, guide, if you can, the conversation towards a suitable **close**, where the customer repeats back what is agreed, how much is to be paid, and the timing of payment.

5.5.1 Dealing with excuses

A successful collector will know how to deal with the variety of excuses or evasions he or she might be faced with.

Excuses	
Customer denies receiving the invoice	Offer to **fax** a copy immediately, and ask the customer to confirm there and then that payment will be authorised
The cheque is in the post	Ask for the **cheque number**, the **date** it was **posted** and the address to which it was sent. Other questions include requests to stop the cheque and post a new one (eg if incorrectly addressed)
The cheque has been drawn up, but the chief accountant has yet to sign it	Ask to speak directly to the chief accountant, ask for the cheque number, when it was passed for payment etc
The computer is run on a monthly basis	Ask if a manual cheque can be raised. This is perfectly possible for most firms
The chief accountant is ill, on holiday	Ask if there are any other signatories. There must be some
We have a problem with our cash flow	**Immediately** try to find out whether this is a genuine problem (eg impending insolvency) or just an excuse

5.5.2 Dealing with switchboard operators

The **switchboard operator** is often the gatekeeper to the organisation as a whole. If the switchboard operator has obviously been given instructions to stall calls to the purchase ledger, then you know there are problems. If the switchboard operator refuses to put you through, you can ask to speak to other people.

5.5.3 Dealing with decision-makers

Once you have reached the **decision-maker** you need to **put your case firmly and politely.**

- **Approach the decision-maker** (surname etc) and ensure this is the right person with whom to deal.
- Do **not be too informal**, as this might imply a lack of professionalism.
- The call should be timed for when the debtor is at his or her **most vulnerable** – at the beginning of the working day, for example.
- Ensure beforehand that the **customer** has **not been offered a special arrangement.**
- Ensure that the **customer agrees** the **amount** and **timing** of the payment.
- There is **no need** to be **apologetic;** the credit controller is merely exercising a right to receive payment.

The following '**Ten Commandments**' are suggested by Pauline Malandine (in *Credit Management Handbook,* edited by Burt Edwards).

- Be **courteous**
- Be **businesslike**
- **Remember** that 'your chasing call is not only the end of one sales chain but the start of another'
- Be **co-operative**
- Be **urgent**
- Be **prompt**
- Be **tactful**
- Be **repetitive** (ie keep mentioning the sum required)
- Be **prepared**
- Be **persistent**

> **Mnemonic**
> the CURB PaPeR TaPe Co

5.6 E-mail

E-mail is **used increasingly** as a method of demanding payment. It can give a sense of **urgency** and can also be used frequently without excessive time being needed by the sender. E-mail messages cannot be diverted by the recipient as easily as telephone messages can be.

5.7 Fax transmission

A **fax** can be used to demand payment as a supplement to a phone call, or to give a sense of 'urgency'. Fax can also **inconvenience** the customer slightly: fax paper costs money, and your (repeated) requests may prevent other faxes coming through.

5.8 Personal visits

Personal visits are time-consuming.

- They should **never** be made **without an appointment**.
- They should only be made to **important customers** who are worth the effort.
- Any **agreement** should be quickly **confirmed in writing**.

5.9 Personnel issues

As a rule of thumb, the **older** the debt, and the **more problems** with collecting it, the **more senior** should be the company official sending the letters, and the more senior should be the proposed recipient.

Activity 10.6

What collection techniques would you recommend for the following debtors, assuming you have offered 30 days credit?

(a) A customer with a good payment record is a week late.
(b) A major customer is two months late, and already an invoice, a statement and a reminder have been sent.

Key learning points

- When managing **debtors**, the **creditworthiness** of customers needs to be assessed. The risks and costs of a customer defaulting will need to be balanced against the profitability of the business provided by that customer.

- For control purposes, **debtors** are generally analysed by age of debt in an **aged debtor analysis**. The analysis can **highlight overdue debts**, and can highlight **customer** and **account types**.

- There should be efficiently organised procedures for ensuring that **overdue debts** and **slow payers** are dealt with effectively.

- The earlier debtors pay, the better. **Early payment** can be encouraged by **good administration** and by **discount policies**. The risk that some debtors will never pay can be partly guarded against by insurance.

- **Credit insurance** can be obtained against some bad debts. However, the insurers will rarely insure an entire debt portfolio as they are unwilling to bear the entire risk. Also credit control procedures should be of a suitable standard to avoid any unnecessary exposure.

- **Factoring** is **collection of debts** by a **factor company** which advances a proportion of the money. Factoring can provide finance linked to the volume of sales, and may offer **administration** and **credit protection**.

- **Invoice discounting** is the sale of debts for a **discount** in **return for cash.**

- Some customers are **reluctant** to pay. The debt collector should keep a record of every communication. A **staged process** of reminders and demands, culminating in debt collection or legal action, is necessary.

PART B   CREDIT CONTROL

Quick quiz

1   Which of the following would be the last document issued to a customer in the order processing and debt collection cycle?

    A   Statement
    B   Reminder
    C   Advice note
    D   Invoice

2   How might the creditworthiness of a potential new customer be checked?

3   What is a debtors age analysis?

4   In what order would a company normally undertake the following actions to collect debt?

    A   Hiring an external debt collection agency to collect the debt
    B   Notifying the debt collection department
    C   Sending a reminder
    D   Instituting legal action to recover the debts

5   Which of the following would not normally be shown on a monthly statement to customers?

    A   The outstanding balance due
    B   The ageing of the balance due
    C   The invoices issued to the customer during the accounting year
    D   The cash received during the last month

6   Whole turnover policies can be bought for a selection of debtors, not the entire sales ledger.

    ☐ True

    ☐ False

7   What services do factors provide?

8   What is invoice discounting?

9   Draft guidelines for writing letters to slow payers.

Answers to quick quiz

1   B   The normal sequence is advice note, invoice, statement, reminder.

2   References; credit ratings agency; annual report and accounts; visits to customer.

3   A listing of the balances on debtors' accounts, showing, usually in bands, how long debts have been due.

4   C   Sending a reminder
    B   Notifying the debt collection department
    D   Instituting legal action to recover the debt
    A   Hiring an external debt collection agency to recover the debt

5   C Only the new invoices issued during the last month and the outstanding invoices (possibly) are likely to be shown.

6   True. A whole turnover policy need not cover all of a company's debtors.

7   Debtor administration; credit protection; advance payments.

8   The purchase of a selection of invoices at a discount.

9   (a) Address to a named individual.
    (b) State sender's job title.
    (c) Sender to sign personally.
    (d) Show amount overdue prominently.
    (e) Ask for payment by return of post.
    (f) If a letter is stated as final (prior to third party involvement), then it should be treated as such.
    (g) Be specific about the further action to be taken.
    (h) Vary the content and timing of letters.

Activity checklist

This checklist shows which performance criteria, range statement or knowledge and understanding point is covered by each activity in this chapter. Tick off each activity as you complete it.

Activity

Activity		Description
10.1	☐	This activity deals with Performance Criterion 15.4.A: monitor information relating to the current state of debtors' accounts regularly and take appropriate action
10.2	☐	This activity deals with Knowledge and Understanding 30: understanding that practice in this area will be determined by an organisation's credit control policies and procedures
10.3	☐	This activity deals with Performance Criterion 15.4.D: use debt recovery methods appropriate to the circumstances of individual cases and in accordance with the organisation's procedures
10.4	☐	This activity deals with Performance Criterion 15.4.D: use debt recovery methods appropriate to the circumstances of individual cases and in accordance with the organisation's procedures
10.5	☐	This activity deals with Performance Criterion 15.4.C: ensure discussions and negotiations with debtors are conducted courteously and achieve the desired outcome
10.6	☐	This activity deals with Performance Criterion 15.4.C: ensure discussions and negotiations with debtors are conducted courteously and achieve the desired outcome

PART B CREDIT CONTROL

chapter 11

Remedies for bad debts

Contents

1 Introduction
2 Bad and doubtful debts
3 Third party involvement and going to court
4 Bankruptcy: an outline
5 Insolvency: an outline
6 Provisions and write-offs

Performance criteria

15.4.A Monitor information relating to the current state of debtors' accounts regularly and take appropriate action

15.4.B Send information regarding significant outstanding accounts and potential bad debts promptly to relevant individuals within the organisation

15.4.C Ensure discussions and negotiations with debtors are conducted courteously and achieve the desired outcome

15.4.D Use debt recovery methods appropriate to the circumstances of individual cases and in accordance with the organisation's procedures

15.4.E Base recommendations to write off bad and doubtful debts on a realistic assessment of all known factors

Range statement

15.4.1 Information on debtors; age analysis of debtors; average periods of credit given and received; incidence of bad and doubtful debts

15.4.2 Appropriate action: information and recommendations for action passed to appropriate individual within own organisation; debtor contacted and arrangement made for recovery of the debt

PART B CREDIT CONTROL

Knowledge and understanding

- Legal and administrative procedures for the collection of debts
- The effect of bankruptcy and insolvency on organisations
- Methods of analysing information on debtors: age analysis of debtors; average periods of credit given and received; incidence of bad and doubtful debts
- Understanding that the accounting systems of an organisation are affected by its organisational structure, its administrative systems and procedures and the nature of its business transactions
- Understanding that recording and accounting practices may vary in different parts of the organisation
- Understanding that practice in this area will be determined by an organisation's credit control policies and procedures
- An understanding of the organisation's relevant policies and procedures

1 Introduction

The most significant topics in this chapter are recognising when a debtor account is running into trouble, and deciding whether to provide against a debt as a **doubtful** or **bad debt**.

You can use various methods to recover at least part of the debt. An important aspect of this chapter is the costs and benefits of these methods and you need to be able to recommend the most appropriate method.

You need to have an understanding of the bankruptcy and insolvency legislation to determine whether a debt should be written off.

2 Bad and doubtful debts

2.1 Problem of bad and doubtful debts

Even the best-run credit control system cannot ensure that a business which is offered credit **is never** exposed to the risk of bad and doubtful debts, which increase the cost of offering credit.

(a) A **doubtful debt** is a debt where there is some uncertainty as to whether it will be paid: the key feature is **uncertainty**. The debtor might still pay up but this is not guaranteed.

(b) A **bad debt**, on the other hand, is a debt which will not be paid.

Doubtful debts and bad debts **reduce profits**.

(a) A **provision** may have to be made **against doubtful debtors** in the accounts, either against specific debtors or as a percentage of total debtors, based on past experience.

(b) Even if the doubtful debt is eventually paid in full, there will be **expenses** due to the effect on cash flow (especially if the debt is large) and expenses of debt recovery procedures.

(c) The **expense** of **'chasing' some small debtors** to the extent, for example, of taking them to court may well exceed the debt itself. It might be **better** just to write them off.

(d) Bad debts, which will never be recovered, can be **written off against profits**. Bad debts relating to a specific customer are allowable for tax purposes, although general provisions are not.

2.2 Warning signs

We have dealt with establishing credit risk in an earlier chapter. Circumstances change, however. The risk that a particular debtor may not pay may increase for any number of reasons which could not have been foreseen at the time credit was granted.

2.2.1 Warning signs – personal customers

Warning signs of 'bad debts' relating to debts incurred by personal customers might include the following.

- Any **sudden or unexpected change** in payment patterns
- Requests for **credit extension**
- Notice of **court action** for **personal bankruptcy**
- **Refusal to communicate** or reply to correspondence and/or phone calls

Activity 11.1

Jot down as many factors as you can think of which would increase the risk of a debt from a personal customer going 'bad'.

2.2.2 Warning signs-business customers

With **business customers**, a debt can become doubtful or go 'bad' for any number of reasons. We give some examples below.

- The **sudden loss of a major customer**, hurting your customer's own cash flow
- The **failure of your customer's own customers** to pay on time
- **Disaster**, such as a fire
- **Industrial action**
- **Sudden changes in overdraft terms**, affecting liquidity

Sudden problems may not be easily predicted. However, a business can become a bad debtor owing to a 'creeping' insolvency, a trend in poor cash management.

Activity 11.2

Working in credit control means that you must look out for signs of impending problems with your business customers. Give examples of the signs that you might spot that you would need to report to the credit control manager.

2.3 Warning signs in financial statements

A business's **annual financial statements** can give warning signs of difficulties, such as poor or declining ratios. The problem is that when a company is having difficulties, financial statements are at their least reliable.

- The **accounts** might be **late**.
- There might be pressure on auditors to **sanction imprudent accounting policies**.
- Some of the accounting ratios calculated may be contradictory. For example, there may be an **increase in sales** when the company is **overtrading** and running out of cash.
- Financial statements need only be **published annually**, and so might be **out of date for** the credit controller's purposes.

Z-scoring is an example of a technique used to analyse financial statements. Z-scores are based on a 'solvency model' which uses certain ratios. These ratios are combined into a single equation to give the company a Z-score. The higher the score, the safer the company. A declining score indicates increasing riskiness.

2.4 A-scores

A-scoring is more subjective, but it takes account of the limitations of financial statements by using other evidence to assess a company.

A-scores	
Defects	<ul><li>The company is dominated by a single individual</li><li>The posts of Chairman and Chief Executive are combined</li><li>Other directors do not have much of a say</li><li>The Board of Directors does not contain a broad spectrum of expertise</li><li>The Finance Director is weak</li><li>There are few professional managers below Board level</li><li>The company has poor accounting systems</li><li>The company is not responsive to change in certain key areas</li></ul>
Mistakes	<ul><li>The company borrows too much and suffers sudden misfortune</li><li>The company expands faster than it really can afford to (overtrading)</li><li>The company depends on the success of a big project</li></ul>

11: REMEDIES FOR BAD DEBTS

A-scores	
Symptoms	• Financial ratios, Z-scores etc are in decline • Sudden changes of accounting policies • Non-financial signs (eg fall in market share)

2.5 Warning signs revealed in internal review

Most credit controllers do not have time to look for information and perform regular analyses on most of their customers. Often first signs that a debt is going bad will come from a company's **own sales ledger**, through a **review of the aged debtors' listing** or **late payments**. A suggested procedure is as follows.

- The company should **maintain a list of customers** to which the firm is most exposed.
- Any **unusual** or **delayed transactions** should be **followed up more closely**.

This information needs to be conveyed to the appropriate personnel.

Activity 11.3

You have just been given the aged debtors listing, which no-one has looked at for ages. The account for one of your customers, who is not normally a slow payer, shows some peculiarities.

	Current	30+	Days 60+	90+	Total
Amount outstanding	1,000	–	–	400	1,400

You investigate further and find out that the customer always pays within the 30 day period and has paid all recent invoices, so the £400 outstanding seems rather odd.

What should you do?

3 Third party involvement and going to court

3.1 Need for legal action

Beyond a certain point the creditor has no alternative but to threaten **legal action**. If this does not produce a suitable result, the creditor has to take one of a variety of measures to collect the debt.

3.2 Debt collection agencies

Debt collection agencies (alternatively called 'credit collection agencies') are the most effective way of pursuing debts. Some debt collection agencies offer a variety of credit control services, including running the credit control department in its entirety.

Most debt collection agencies are happy to be **paid by results**. Some agencies require an **advance subscription** to be paid for their services, or require clients to submit a 'coupon' for each case submitted. Most, however, receive a straight percentage of debts recovered.

Any collection agency will employ suitable techniques, depending on the client.

- Some collect on a letter and telephone basis. This is often the case where the client has passed on a large number of **consumer debts**.
- Others, especially for more difficult cases, collect **'on the doorstep'**.
- Collectors sometimes negotiate a **payment plan** with individual debtors.

Debt collection agencies are considered to be **normal business services,** and the use of a collection agency is unlikely to result in the end of a commercial relationship.

Activity 11.4

You are considering employing the services of a debt collection agency. List the main considerations in this decision.

3.3 Specialist solicitors

Employing a solicitor is seen as being more serious than employing a debt collector.

When instructing a solicitor to sue, an appropriate letter should be sent *in brief*. You should let the solicitor know the following.

- Whether **goods**, **services**, **materials** or any combination of them were **supplied**
- The **date(s)** when the **liability arose** (Generally speaking this will be the date when the goods/services/materials were supplied. The invoice date should also be provided for reference.)
- The debtor's **legal status**
- General **background** information (eg if the debtor has raised any complaints, whether or not these were genuine, and how they were resolved)
- **Copy invoice** agreeing with the amount claimed

3.4 Going to court

Before going to the expense and trouble of going to court, a business must be sure of its case, and should therefore do the following.

- Be sure that the debtor is a genuine **debtor** rather than a dissatisfied customer: if the latter, the customer's complaints should be examined and dealt with if possible.
- Check **who** the **debtor is** (individual, firm, limited company).
- Ensure the **name is correct**. Individuals' full names should be used. For unincorporated businesses, a form of words such as 'Joe Bloggs trading as Bloggs Enterprises' is preferable. A limited company should be sued in the name in which it is registered at Companies' House.
- Before suing, it is advisable to check the **original credit information**. Is the customer likely to have sufficient assets?

3.4.1 Which court?

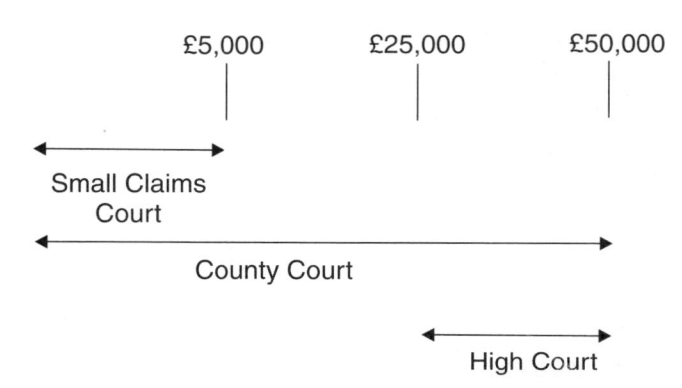

```
              £5,000      £25,000     £50,000
                 |           |           |
        <----------------->
          Small Claims
             Court
        <--------------------------------->
                   County Court
                             <--------------->
                                 High Court
```

The decision as to whether the action shall go to the High Court or the County Court depends on:

- The type of transaction
- Any public interest issues
- The legal and factual complexity of the case
- The speed at which the case can be tried

3.5 Court procedures

Once the court has received the necessary paperwork, it will issue a default **summons**.

- If the **debtor** does nothing (ie does not reply to the summons) judgement goes against him. That is why the writ requires an **acknowledgement of service**.
- The debtor can admit the claim: in other words the debtor **accepts** the amounts owing.
- If the debtor admits the claim, the debtor may offer to pay by **instalments**. The creditor can accept this; if not the court will fix a suitable means of payment.

A **pre-trial review** is a preliminary review of the case, conducted by the registrar to ensure that all the relevant material is available.

On the day fixed for the **trial**, the creditors will have to bring evidence to prove the claim and to defend against any counterclaim the debtor might bring. If the defendant does not appear, the judgement may well go against him.

3.6 Enforcement

The county court judgement must be enforced, which may need to be achieved by one of the following methods.

Enforcement of judgements	
Warrant of execution	The court bailiff seizes and sells debtor's goods; however debtor may remove the assets
Attachment of earnings	Weekly amount deducted from debtor's earnings
Garnishee order	Person owing money to the debtor pays it to the creditor
Bankruptcy petition	See Section 4
Administrative order	Debtor makes regular payments into court
Charging order	Property charged cannot be sold by debtor. Can be sold for creditor's benefit if debt not settled within six months

3.7 Sale of goods

The Sale of Goods Acts provides certain remedies for creditors, providing the contract is drawn up in the right way.

- **Lien.** A seller who is unpaid and who still has possession of the goods can hold on to them.
- **Retention of title.** Some contracts specify that the supplier retains title to the goods until the supplier has been paid.

3.8 Commercial arbitration

Arbitration is an alternative to litigation in commercial disputes. An **arbitration agreement** allows differences to be submitted to a third party for settlement by that party.

- The parties to the agreement must submit to being **examined on oath** by the **arbitrator** and must produce all relevant documents which may be called for.
- The award made by the arbitrator can be considered **final and binding** on the parties.
- The arbitrator can normally offer **specific performance** of a contract, as a remedy.

3.8.1 Advantages of arbitration

- The proceedings are **less formal**, more flexible, quicker and cheaper than litigation.
- The parties can **select** an **arbitrator** in whom they have confidence (eg an expert).
- The **arbitrator** is likely to be **familiar** with the commercial activities of the parties.
- The hearing is most often in **private**, so avoiding publicity.
- The **atmosphere** of arbitration is **more friendly** than a court action. This is important if the parties are intending to continue their commercial dealings with each other.

3.8.2 Disadvantages of arbitration

- Plaintiff and defendant in a court action must observe **time limits** preparing their cases, and so arbitration may provide more scope for deliberate time-wasting by a defendant.
- A judge has power to grant **interim relief** to the parties or curtail proceedings by means of a summary judgement. An arbitrator's powers are **less extensive**.
- Arbitrators may be **unqualified** in legal matters, and hence their decision may be **subjective.**

3.9 Negotiated settlements

Most commercial disputes do not make it to court. Apart from cases covered by arbitration procedures, negotiations between the parties may be conducted at any time. They may even occur during trial.

3.9.1 Payment into court

A defendant may make a payment into court of a sum **less than the full amount** claimed by the plaintiff. The plaintiff must then decide **whether to accept** the amount paid in, or to **press on** with his **case** in the hope of eventually being awarded a greater amount.

Continuing the action at this stage **carries risks** for the plaintiff. Not only may the eventual judgement be for less than the amount paid in (indeed, he may even lose the case), but he may also have to **pay** the **defendant's costs** incurred after the payment into court was made.

3.9.2 Without prejudice offer

Instead of paying money into court, the defendant may make a **without prejudice offer**. If the offer is accepted it **becomes binding** on **both parties**. If it is not accepted, the court must **not** be informed of it. This is to prevent the judge from forming an unfavourable view of the defendant.

3.9.3 Open offers

Open offers differ from 'without prejudice' offers in that they may be brought to the **notice of the court**. Their advantage over 'without prejudice' offers is that, like payments into court, they place the plaintiff under the risk of having to pay the defendant's subsequent costs if the offer is refused.

Activity 11.5

Why, as a credit controller, might you be reluctant to go to arbitration, assuming there is no dispute about the goods and services supplied?

4 Bankruptcy: an outline

4.1 Bankruptcy and insolvency procedures

Sometimes the only course available to a creditor or group of creditors is to use bankruptcy and insolvency legislation to obtain payment or, perhaps at best, part-payment.

The procedures dealing with an **individual's bankruptcy** on the one hand and a **limited company's insolvency** on the other differ significantly.

4.2 Voluntary arrangements

A **voluntary arrangement** enables an individual to make binding agreements with creditors, minimising official involvement.

A voluntary arrangement can either be an **alternative** to bankruptcy, before it gets started, or a way of **ending a situation** of bankruptcy, so that the voluntary arrangement takes over from the bankruptcy proceedings.

4.3 Bankruptcy petition

Three weeks before creditors petition a court for a bankruptcy order, they must issue a **statutory demand**. The debtor might offer a **settlement**. The court will refuse to declare the debtor bankrupt if the creditor 'unreasonably' refuses. Otherwise the court will issue a bankruptcy order once the **petition** is received.

- For the petition to be granted, the debt must be at least **£750**, and **unsecured**.
- The petition will be dismissed if the **statutory demand** has been **complied** with, or there is **reasonable prospect** of paying the debt.

- A supervisor of a voluntary arrangement can petition for bankruptcy if the debtor has not **complied** with **obligations,** or if the debtor supplied false information.
- The **debtor** can **petition for bankruptcy** in certain cases.

The consequences of the petition are as follows.

- With a few exceptions, if the debtor **pays money** to **creditors** or **disposes of property**, such **transactions** are **void**.
- Any other **legal proceedings** relating to the debts or the debtor's property are **held in abeyance**.
- An interim receiver is appointed to **protect the estate** (eg by selling goods that will diminish in value).

4.4 The process of bankruptcy

Once the petition is granted, the **official receiver** takes custody and control of the bankrupt's property, until a creditors' meeting, when a **trustee in bankruptcy** is appointed. The trustee has a number of powers, similar to those that the debtor had over his or her own property, before being made bankrupt. The trustee realises the debtor's assets and makes a distribution to creditors.

Once the bankruptcy order is made, the debtor is termed an **undischarged bankrupt**. The debtor is **deprived** of the **ownership** of his or her property, and is subject to certain other restrictions and requirements such as the need to keep records.

4.5 The creditors' position

Creditors should **submit** a **written claim** to the trustee, detailing how the debt is made up. The creditor may also need to substantiate any claim with documentary evidence. Creditors will be sent a form on which details can be given.

Different groups of creditors have different claims and are ranked in order. Claims are paid to creditors in rank order, as follows.

- **Fees** paid by an apprentice or articled clerk relating to an unexpired period of training
- **Preferential creditors.** These include employees and pension scheme contributions
- **Ordinary creditors** (all others)

4.6 Discharge

Bankruptcy as a legal state is ended by **discharge**. Discharge releases the bankrupt from his bankruptcy debts, although secured creditors may realise their security.

PART B   CREDIT CONTROL

Activity 11.6

You receive information that one of your customers, a sole trader, has successfully petitioned the court to make himself bankrupt. He cannot pay his debts as they fall due. He owes your company the sum of £1,000 for raw materials which he has used up. You learn that the bank has a fixed charge.

(a) Briefly outline the main stages of bankruptcy procedure.

(b) Along with other trade creditors, you hope to get a substantial amount of the £1,000 back. You learn, however, that the customer has bank debts of £40,000. His house is worth £40,000. How optimistic are you of recovery?

5 Insolvency: an outline

5.1 Company insolvency

A company is **insolvent** when it cannot pay its debts as they fall due. The term **'unable to pay its debts'** is defined in s 123 of the Insolvency Act 1986 as follows.

- A creditor (owed over £750) has served on the company, a **written demand** requiring the company to pay the sum and the company has, for three weeks, failed to do so.
- A **court order** in favour of a creditor of the company is returned **unsatisfied** in whole or in part.
- It is demonstrated to the satisfaction of the court that the company is **unable** to **pay its debts** as they fall due.
- It is proved to the satisfaction of the court that the **value of** the company's **assets** is **less than** the amount of its **liabilities**.

5.2 The creditors' position

The company's creditors will want to recover their money from the insolvent company in some way. There are a number of possible options.

- Liquidation
- Receivership or administrative receivership
- Administration
- Voluntary arrangement

5.3 Compulsory liquidation

In a **liquidation,** the company is dissolved, the **assets** are **realised**, debts are paid out of the proceeds and any **surplus amounts** are returned to shareholders.

Compulsory winding up or liquidation is carried out by a **liquidator**, on behalf of the shareholders and/or creditors of the firm. Generally speaking, a compulsory winding up occurs because a company is **unable** to **pay its debts**, or the court considers it **'just and equitable'**.

Once the liquidation order has been made, the assets of the company remain the company's assets, but **under the liquidator's control**.

The liquidator's job is to ensure that the **creditors are paid**. The liquidator is under *no* obligation to carry on the business, although the liquidator may do so if this is the most effective way of satisfying creditors.

Once the liquidator's work is done, the **company** can be **wound up**.

5.4 Voluntary liquidation

A **voluntary winding up** or **liquidation** occurs when shareholders and/or creditors decide to do so. Creditors have the decisive role, however, as they have prior claim over the company's assets, to the extent that their debts are not paid.

5.5 Proof of debts

The liquidator will require satisfactory evidence that a creditor's claim is properly admissible as a liability. This is done (where necessary) by a formal procedure for **proof of debts.**

5.6 Order of application of assets in liquidation

The **order of application of assets in liquidation** is as follows.

- **Secured creditors** who have **fixed charges** are entitled to be paid out of their **security** so far as it suffices.
- The **costs of winding up** are paid next. They rank before floating charges.
- **Preferential unsecured debts** are paid next, principally employees.
- **Debts secured by floating charges** come next in order.
- **Unsecured non-preferential debts** come next (eg trade).
- **Deferred debts** (eg unpaid dividends to shareholders) come last in order.

5.7 Alternatives to liquidation

We have seen that winding up a company is a fairly drastic step. What then are the alternatives to full-blown liquidation when a company is insolvent to some degree?

5.7.1 Administrative receivership

A company's secured creditors, in preference to presenting a winding up petition, may appoint a **receiver** (under a fixed charge) or an **administrative receiver** (under a floating charge).

PART B CREDIT CONTROL

The function of a receiver is to **manage** or to **realise the assets** which are the security, in order to pay out of those assets the amount due to the secured creditors whom he represents. If he is able to discharge these debts he vacates the office of receiver and the **directors resume full control**.

This may well result in the secured **creditor receiving payment.** However it can often result in a **healthy company** being destroyed for the sake of the secured creditors.

New legislation which is shortly to come into force abolishes administrative receivership for debentures dated after the legislation is implemented.

5.7.2 Administration

If a company is not yet in liquidation, the company, its directors, or any of its creditors, may present a petition to the court to make an **administration order** in respect of the company. The order puts an insolvency practitioner in control of the company **with a defined programme**, and meanwhile insulates it from pressure by creditors.

The **administration order** provides for the **unsecured creditor** an alternative to **suing for the debt** in the courts or petitioning for winding up. For the **secured creditor**, it provides an **alternative to both these solutions** and to putting in a receiver.

An important effect of an administration order is that it results in a **freezing of collection of debts** by the creditors. This provides the administrator with a **breathing space**, not available to a receiver, in which to try to save the company, or achieve a better result for all the creditors.

5.7.3 Voluntary arrangements

The insolvency of a company may of itself **increase its debts** and/or **reduce its resources**. An insolvent company may **default on its commercial contracts**, or it may **dismiss its employees** who are then entitled to redundancy payments. Hence creditors may want to accept a compromise with the company, particularly if there is a prospect of selling off the company's business as a going concern or pulling it back into solvency.

A voluntary arrangement is either a **composition** (part payment) in satisfaction of a company's debts or a **scheme of arrangement** of its affairs. A scheme of arrangement might, for example, be an agreed postponement or rescheduling of payment of debts pending reorganisation or sale of the business.

6 Provisions and write-offs

6.1 Accounting treatment of bad debts

In many liquidations, receiverships and administrations, the creditors are unlikely to receive in full the amount they are owed. Thus this debt will be considered bad or doubtful.

There are two alternatives to dealing with bad and doubtful debts in the accounts and accounting records.

- They can be **written off completely**.

- They can be **provided against**. The debtor balance remains in the sales ledger control account and sales ledger, but a counterbalance credit is set up to provide against them.

6.2 Double entry for bad debts

The double entry for **writing off a bad debt** is as follows:

Debit: Profit and loss account
Credit: Sales ledger control account

with the amount of the debt written off. The records in the sales ledger (memorandum accounts) would also be cancelled.

Example: Writing off of bad debts

Crisroe Ltd has a sales ledger totalling £100,000. (There are no reconciling items between this total and the balance on the sales ledger control account.) One of its debtors collapses and the management of Crisroe Ltd are convinced that the debtor's £15,000 debt cannot be recovered and they therefore resolve to write it off. What is the double entry for writing off the bad debt?

Solution

(a) The double entry is:

	£'000	£'000
Dr Bad and doubtful debt expense (profit and loss)	15	
Cr Sales ledger control account (balance sheet)		15

The balance on the sales ledger control account is now £85,000

(b) There would also be an entry to the sales ledger to that effect, which would also reduce its total by £15,000, to equal £85,000.

6.3 Double entry for provision

As an alternative, the company might prefer to **set up a provision**. In other words, the company's management cannot be *sure* that no money is available.

The firm sets up a new balance sheet account for the provision for bad and doubtful debts.

Debit: Bad and doubtful debt expense (P & L)
Credit: Provision for bad and doubtful debts (balance sheet)

The sales ledger control account will continue to show the **gross figure**, as will the sales ledger. But for financial reporting purposes, the figure for debtors will be the total on the sales ledger control account *less* the provision.

In financial reporting terms, the result is similar: profit has been reduced by the amount of the bad or doubtful debt, but the way in which it is done is different.

- **Setting up** a **provision is prudent**; but there is still the possibility that the debt will be recovered.
- Part of a debt can be **provided against**.
- The **continued existence** of the debt in the sales ledger is perhaps a **spur** to collect it; if it were written off it would be forgotten.

Example: Provision for doubtful debts

Crisroe Ltd is now providing against the £15,000 debt.

Solution

		£'000	£'000
Dr	Bad and doubtful debt expense (profit and loss)	15	
Cr	Provision for bad and doubtful debts		15

No entry would be made in the sales ledger.

However, to calculate the figure for debtors in the balance sheet:

	£'000
Sales ledger control account	100
Provision for bad and doubtful debts	(15)
	85

6.4 Writing off a doubtful debt

Sometimes, the doubtful debt will have to be **written off**. The profit and loss account has already been debited, so there is no extra expense. The double entry is:

Debit: Provision for bad and doubtful debts
Credit: Sales ledger control account

The sales ledger entry is also amended to account for the write off.

6.5 Deciding whether to provide

You should only make **provisions and write offs** after consideration of all suitable factors. It is too easy to be hasty, and a slight delay in receiving payment is no excuse for writing off the debt. Factors to be considered are:

- **Success of attempts to collect the debt**
- **Expense of pursuing the debt** (which may well be more than the debt is worth)

- **Likelihood of insolvency** proceedings and communication from liquidators, receivers or administrators as to the collectability of the debt.

Activity 11.7

Can you give some examples of debts that should be provided against?

6.6 Monitoring bad debts: bad debts/sales ratios

The credit controller should monitor the overall level of bad debts suffered by a business. The following report format might be adopted.

	Jan	Feb	March	April
Sales	£1,000	£2,000	£1,000	£4,000
Bad debts recognised	£20	£50	-	£10
% of sales	2%	2½%	-	0.25%
Bad debts originated	£50	£30	£40	?
% of sales	5%	1.5%	4%	N/A

(a) **Bad debts recognised** refers to the time when the debt went bad.
(b) **Bad debts originated** refers to the date when the sale was initially made.

The report **records the bad debt expense** in the correct period, and **monitors the effectiveness** of credit control in certain months. An **increasing ratio** of **bad debts** to **sales** implies a deteriorating quality of credit control, unless it results from a policy to sell to higher risk customers.

The bad debts ratio can be calculated on either of the following bases:

$$\text{Bad debts ratio} = \frac{\text{Bad debts}}{\text{Turnover on credit}} \times 100\%$$

$$\text{Bad debts ratio} = \frac{\text{Bad debts}}{\text{Total debtors}} \times 100\%$$

Activity 11.8

Briefly describe the alternatives to putting a company into liquidation.

PART B CREDIT CONTROL

Activity 11.9

Crisroe Ltd suffers from a high level of bad debts and a provision for doubtful debts of 3% of outstanding debtors is made at the end of each year.

Information for 20X7, 20X8 and 20X9 is as follows.

	Year to 31 December		
	20X7 £	20X8 £	20X9 £
Outstanding debtors at 31 December	44,000	55,000	47,000
Bad debts written off during year	7,000	10,000	8,000

Tasks

(a) State the amount to be shown in the profit and loss account for bad debts and provision for doubtful debts for the years ended 31 December 20X7, 20X8 and 20X9.

(b) State the value of debtors which would be shown in the balance sheet as at 31 December in each of these years.

(This Activity revises your bookkeeping knowledge and also reinforces the need for sound credit control.)

Key learning points

- A **debt** can go **bad** for a variety of reasons. It might have been **'high risk'** in the first place. **Unforeseen circumstances** can arise, although for both business and personal customers, it is often possible to detect **warning signs** of impending disaster. Existing customers might take longer to pay.

- There are some sophisticated **scoring systems** available for analysing companies, which input data from financial accounts and other data into a model.

- **Debt collection agencies** collect debts for a commission.

- If it comes to **court**, a county court may issue a default summons. The judgement may be enforced in a variety of ways, including bailiffs, garnishee orders, or insolvency proceedings.

- **Bankruptcy** is where an individual's property is sold for the creditors' benefit. **Insolvency** is when the assets of a company are taken over by a third party appointed by creditors. The company is run until the debts are paid, or may be wound up.

- Decisions by credit controllers on whether to provide for or write off debts will depend on the **success of attempts** to **collect the debt**, the **expense** of **pursuing** the debt, and the likelihood of **insolvency**.

PART B CREDIT CONTROL

Quick quiz

1. What factors should govern a firm's decision whether to write off a debt?

2. What is a bad debt?

3. A court action to settle a dispute over an amount of £12,000 in the UK will be heard in:

    A   The Small Claims Court
    B   The County Court
    C   The High Court
    D   Chancery Division

4. List three methods of enforcing a County Court judgement.

5. Which of the following is **not** a route that a creditor might choose to follow as a means of recovering money from an insolvent company?

    A   Administrative receivership
    B   Liquidation
    C   Arbitration
    D   Administration

6. Bad debts ratio = $\dfrac{\text{............................}}{\text{............................}} \times 100\%$

7. Bad debts ratio can also = $\dfrac{\text{............................}}{\text{............................}} \times 100\%$

8. Janet has made a provision of £100 in her accounting records against a debt owed to her by John, one of her customers. She reads in the local paper that John has just been declared bankrupt and that his creditors will not receive what they are owed. What is the double entry that Janet should make in her books?

    A   Debit: Provision for bad and doubtful debts £100
        Credit: Bad and doubtful debts expense £100

    B   Debit: Provision for bad and doubtful debts £100
        Credit: Sales ledger control account £100

    C   Debit: Bad and doubtful debts expense account £100
        Credit: Provision for bad and doubtful debts £100

    D   Debit: Bad and doubtful debts expense account £100
        Credit: Sales ledger control account £100

Answers to quick quiz

1. Success in attempts to collect the debt; the expense of pursuing the debt; the likelihood of insolvency proceedings.

2. A debt which will not be paid.

3. B   The County Court

4. Any three of:

   (a) Warrant of execution
   (b) Attachment of earnings
   (c) Garnishee order
   (d) Petition for bankruptcy
   (e) Administrative order
   (f) Charging order

5. C   Arbitration is an alternative to litigation in commercial disputes. It is not a means of debt recovery in the event of insolvency.

6. Bad debts ratio = $\dfrac{\text{Bad debts}}{\text{Turnover on credit}} \times 100\%$

7. Bad debts ratio can also = $\dfrac{\text{Bad debts}}{\text{Total debtors}} \times 100\%$

8. B   Debit: Provision for bad and doubtful debts £100
        Credit: Sales ledger control account £100

PART B CREDIT CONTROL

Activity checklist

This checklist shows which performance criteria, range statement or knowledge and understanding point is covered by each activity in this chapter. Tick off each activity as you complete it.

Activity

11.1	☐	This activity deals with Performance Criterion 15.4.A: monitor information relating to the current state of debtors' accounts regularly and take appropriate action.
11.2	☐	This activity deals with Performance Criterion 15.4.B: send information regarding significant outstanding accounts and potential bad debts promptly to relevant individuals within the organisation
11.3	☐	This activity deals with Performance Criterion 15.4.C: ensure discussions and negotiations with debtors are conducted courteously and achieve the desired outcome
11.4	☐	This activity deals with Performance Criterion 15.4.D: use debt recovery methods appropriate to the circumstances of individual cases and in accordance with the organisation's procedures
11.5	☐	This activity deals with Performance Criterion 15.4.D: use debt recovery methods appropriate to the circumstances of individual cases and in accordance with the organisation's procedures
11.6	☐	This activity deals with Knowledge and Understanding 11: the effect of bankruptcy and insolvency on organisations
11.7	☐	This activity deals with Performance Criterion 15.4.E: base recommendations to write off bad and doubtful debts on a realistic assessment of all known factors
11.8	☐	This activity deals with Knowledge and Understanding 11: the effect of bankruptcy and insolvency on organisations
11.9	☐	This activity deals with Knowledge and Understanding 22: methods of analysing information on debtors: age analysis of debtors; average periods of credit given and received; incidence of bad and doubtful debts

Answers to Activities

Answers to activities

Chapter 1

Answer 1.1

The tractor is a **fixed asset investment**. It doesn't matter how it was financed: it is not working capital in the sense we have discussed it here.

Answer 1.2

(a) **Items in the cash cycle**

   (i) Stocks held for use in the production process or resale
   (ii) Taking time to pay suppliers
   (iii) Receiving cash from sales

(b) A supermarket receives cash (or cash equivalents such as cheques, credit card or debit card payments) at the time of sale, and probably does not pay its suppliers until some time after this.

(c) False.

Answer 1.3

	Months
Raw material stock turnover period	1.5
Less: credit taken from suppliers	(1.0)
Finished goods stock turnover period	2.0
Debtors' payment period	3.0
Operating cycle	5.5

Answer 1.4

(a) **A regular revenue receipt**
Examples might include cash sales, investment income (bank interest or dividends).

(b) **An exceptional payment**
Examples might include costs of closing redundant capacity.

ANSWERS TO ACTIVITIES

(c) **A capital payment**
Examples might include purchase of fixed assets or the purchase of a new business.

(d) **An annual disbursement**
Examples might include payments to the Inland Revenue, a final dividend to shareholders, a bonus to the directors.

Answer 1.5

A cash flow statement is an important part of a company's accounts because it shows details of figures, **actual cash flows**, that **cannot be manipulated** by companies. Creative accounting techniques can affect the balance sheet and profit and loss accounts, but they do not normally affect the cash flow statement.

Answer 1.6

The principal reasons why profit will not equal cash flow are as follows.

(a) The '**matching concept**' means that costs and revenues do not equal payments and receipts. Revenue is recognised in the profit statement when goods are sold, and any revenue not received is recorded as a debtor. Similarly, costs are incurred when a resource is acquired or subsequently used, not when it happens to be paid for.

(b) Some items appearing in the profit statement do not affect cash flow. For example, depreciation is a '**non-cash' deduction** in arriving at profit.

(c) Similarly, items may affect cash flow but not profit. **Capital expenditure** (apart from depreciation) and stock level adjustments are prime examples.

Answer 1.7

	Profit £	Operational cash flow £
Sales	200,000	200,000
Opening debtors (∴ received in year)		15,000
Closing debtors (outstanding at year end)		(24,000)
Cash in		191,000
Cost of sales	170,000	170,000
Closing stock (bought, but not used, in year)		21,000
Opening stock (used, but not bought, in year)		(12,000)
Purchases in year		179,000
Opening creditors (∴ paid in year)		11,000
Closing creditors (outstanding at year end)		(14,000)
Cash out		176,000
Profit/operational cash flow	30,000	15,000

Answer 1.8

The three issues underlying the management of cash and the control of credit are as follows.

(a) **Profitability** relates to maintaining a surplus of income over expenditure, for example obtaining the best return on an investment. However, some cash management activities incur costs (eg interest payments, discount allowed) which are incurred as expenses necessary in the course of business: a discount may be offered to secure a sale, for example. These costs should be minimised.

(b) **Liquidity** refers to a business's ability to pay its debts as they fall due. A firm must have access to cash in order to pay its creditors. A failure of liquidity can lead to insolvency, in which case the firm will go out of business.

(c) **Safety** involves minimising the risk that, for example, a debt will not be collected, cash will be stolen, or that an 'investment' will turn out to be worthless.

All are equally important, but in different ways and over different timescales. As the example of Barings showed, unacceptable risk (a safety issue) can lead to insolvency. In the long term, a failure to be profitable can lead to collapse.

Chapter 2

Answer 2.1

Your list might have included some of the following.

(a) A **change in the general economic environment**. An economic recession will cause a slump in trade.

(b) A **new product**, launched by a competitor. This may take business away from the company's traditional and established product lines.

(c) **New cost-saving product technology** may force the company to invest in the new technology to remain competitive.

(d) **Moves by competitors** (for example a price reduction or a sales promotion) have to be countered by the company.

(e) **Changes in consumer preferences** may result in a fall in demand.

(f) The government takes action against **certain trade practices** or against trade with a country with which the company has dealings.

(g) **Strikes or other industrial action** may damage the business.

(h) **Natural disasters**, such as floods or fire damage, may curtail the company's activities.

ANSWERS TO ACTIVITIES

Answer 2.2

Purchases = Cost of sales − Opening stock + Closing stock

= £40,000 − £5,000 + £6,000

= £41,000

Payments to suppliers = Purchases + Opening creditors − Closing creditors

= £41,000 + £10,000 − £12,000

= £39,000

Answer 2.3

August receipts will be as follows:

	£
Cash: 20% August sales	16,000
Credit: 48% July sales	57,600
31% June sales	31,000
Total	104,600

Answer 2.4

The **opening cash balance** at 1 October will consist of Tony's initial £15,000 less the £8,000 spent on fixed assets purchased in September, ie the opening balance is £7,000. Cash receipts from credit customers arise two months after the relevant sales.

Payments to suppliers are a little more tricky. We are told that cost of sales is 100/150 × sales. Thus for October cost of sales is 100/150 × £3,000 = £2,000. These goods will be purchased in October but not paid for until November. Similar calculations can be made for later months. The initial stock of £5,000 is purchased in September and consequently paid for in October.

The cash budget can now be constructed.

CASH BUDGET FOR THE SIX MONTHS ENDING 31 MARCH 20X7

	October £	November £	December £	January £	February £	March £
Receipts						
Debtors			3,000	6,000	6,000	10,500
Payments						
Suppliers	5,000	2,000	4,000	4,000	7,000	7,000
Running expenses	1,600	1,600	1,600	1,600	1,600	1,600
Drawings	1,000	1,000	1,000	1,000	1,000	1,000
	7,600	4,600	6,600	6,600	9,600	9,600
Net cash flow	(7,600)	(4,600)	(3,600)	(600)	(3,600)	900
Opening balance	7,000	(600)	(5,200)	(8,800)	(9,400)	(13,000)
Closing balance	(600)	(5,200)	(8,800)	(9,400)	(13,000)	(12,100)

Answer 2.5

(a)

	January £'000	February £'000	March £'000	April £'000	May £'000	June £'000
Sales revenue						
Cash (40%)	44	52	56	60	64	72
Credit (60%, 2 months)	48	60	66	78	84	90
	92	112	122	138	148	162
Purchases	60	80	90	110	130	140
Wages						
75%	12	15	18	21	24	27
25%	3	4	5	6	7	8
Overheads	10	15	15	15	20	20
Dividends			20			
Capital expenditure			30			40
	85	114	178	152	181	235
Net cash flow	7	(2)	(56)	(14)	(33)	(73)
b/f	15	22	20	(36)	(50)	(83)
c/f	22	20	(36)	(50)	(83)	(156)

(b) The overdraft arrangements are quite inadequate to service the cash needs of the business over the six-month period. If the figures are realistic then action should be taken now to avoid difficulties in the near future. The following are possible courses of action.

(i) **Activities** could be **curtailed**.

(ii) **Other sources of cash** could be explored, for example a long-term loan to finance the capital expenditure and a factoring arrangement to provide cash due from debtors more quickly.

(iii) Efforts to increase the **speed of debt collection** could be made.

(iv) **Payments to creditors** could be delayed.

(v) The **dividend payments** could be **postponed** (the figures indicate that this is a small company, possibly owner-managed).

(vi) Staff might be persuaded to work at a **lower rate** in return for, say, an annual bonus or a profit-sharing agreement.

(vii) **Extra staff might** be taken on to reduce the amount of overtime paid.

(viii) The **stockholding policy** should be reviewed; it may be possible to meet demand from current production and minimise cash tied up in stocks.

Answer 2.6

Kim O'Hara would be best served by a **cleared funds forecast**, Creighton plc by a cash book based forecast.

Answer 2.7

Cash forecasts

Cash flow based forecasts are forecasts of the amount and timing of cash receipts and payments. **Balance sheet based** forecasts are a prediction of the amount of cash that will be needed on a particular date: they are not estimates of individual inflows and outflows.

The main advantage of a **cash forecast** is it can help ensure that **sufficient funds** will be **available** when they are needed to sustain the activities of an enterprise. It demonstrates clearly how much cash will be required, when it will be required and how long it will be required for.

Balance sheet forecasts

The main advantage of a **balance sheet** forecast is that it can be used as a **longer-term estimate**, to assess the scale of funding requirements or cash surpluses the company expects over time.

A **balance sheet forecast** can act as a check on the **realism of cash flow based forecasts**. The estimated balance sheet should be roughly consistent with the net change in the cash budget, after allowing for approximations in the balance sheet forecast assumptions.

Chapter 3

Answer 3.1

(a) The seasonal variation for the 15 days using the **additive** model are as follows:

		Actual	Trend	Seasonal variation
Week 1	Monday	560	648.90	– 88.90
	Tuesday	840	651.84	+ 188.16
	Wednesday	728	654.78	+ 73.22
	Thursday	658	657.72	+ 0.28
	Friday	434	660.66	– 226.66
Week 2	Monday	574	663.60	– 89.60
	Tuesday	875	666.54	+ 208.46
	Wednesday	770	669.48	+ 100.52
	Thursday	679	672.42	+ 6.58
	Friday	448	675.36	– 227.36
Week 3	Monday	588	678.30	– 90.30
	Tuesday	910	681.24	+ 228.76
	Wednesday	812	684.18	+ 127.82
	Thursday	700	687.12	+ 12.88
	Friday	462	690.06	– 228.06

Average variations

	Monday	Tuesday	Wednesday	Thursday	Friday	
Week 1	−88.90	+188.16	+73.22	+0.28	−226.66	
Week 2	−89.60	+208.46	+100.52	+6.58	−227.36	
Week 3	−90.30	+228.76	+127.82	+12.88	−228.06	
Total	−268.80	+625.38	+301.56	+19.74	−682.06	
Average	−89.60	+208.46	+100.52	+6.58	−227.36	1.40
Adjustment to reduce variation to 0	+0.28	+0.28	+0.28	+0.28	+0.28	+1.40
Adjusted average	−89.32	+208.74	+100.80	+6.86	−227.08	0

(b) The seasonal variation for the 15 days using the **multiplicative** model are as follows:

		Actual	Trend	Seasonal percentage
Week 1	Monday	560	648.90	86.3
	Tuesday	840	651.84	128.9
	Wednesday	728	654.78	111.2
	Thursday	658	657.72	100.0
	Friday	434	660.66	65.7
Week 2	Monday	574	663.60	86.5
	Tuesday	875	666.54	131.3
	Wednesday	770	669.48	115.0
	Thursday	679	672.42	101.0
	Friday	448	675.36	66.3
Week 3	Monday	588	678.30	86.7
	Tuesday	910	681.24	133.6
	Wednesday	812	684.18	118.7
	Thursday	700	687.12	101.9
	Friday	462	690.06	67.0

Average variations

	Monday	Tuesday	Wednesday	Thursday	Friday	
Week 1	86.3	128.9	111.2	100.0	65.7	
Week 2	86.5	131.3	115.0	101.0	66.3	
Week 3	86.7	133.6	118.7	101.9	67.0	
Total	259.5	393.8	344.9	302.9	199.0	
Average	86.5	131.3	115.0	101.0	66.3	500.1
Adjustment to reduce variation to 500		0.1				0.1
Adjusted average	86.5	131.2	115.0	101.0	66.3	500

ANSWERS TO ACTIVITIES

Answer 3.2

(a)

Year	Quarter	Sales (A)	Moving total of 4 quarters sales	Centred total	Moving average (÷8) (B)	Variation (A − B)
20X2	1	200				
	2	110				
			870			
	3	320		1,754	219	+101
			884			
	4	240		1,776	222	+18
			892			
20X3	1	214		1,798	225	−11
			906			
	2	118		1,832	229	−111
			926			
	3	334		1,858	232	+102
			932			
	4	260		1,870	234	+26
			938			
20X4	1	220		1,882	235	−15
			944			
	2	124		1,906	238	−114
			962			
	3	340				
	4	278				

(b)

Year	Quarter	1	2	3	4	Total
20X2				+101	+18	
20X3		−11	−111	+102	+26	
20X4		−15	−114			
		−26	−225	+203	+44	−4
Unadjusted average		−13.0	−112.5	+101.5	+22.0	−2
Adjustment (4 ÷ 2)		+0.5	+0.5	+0.5	+0.5	+2
Adjusted average seasonal variations		−12.5	−112.0	+102.0	+22.5	0

(c) **Step 1**

Average increase in trend line value $= \dfrac{238 - 219}{7}$

$= 2.7$ units

Step 2

Trend line values in third quarter $= 238 + (5 \times 2.7)$

$= 251.5$ units

Step 3

Predicted sales = Trend line value + seasonal variation

$= 251.5 + 102$

$= 353.5$, say 354 units

Answer 3.3

(a) (i) The index suggests prices will increase by 3.5% and so produces a budget of £200,000 × 1.035 = £207,000.

    (ii) The budget in (i) assumes that quantities consumed remain the same. If quantities increase by 10% the budget will be £207,000 × 110% = £227,700.

(b) The budget estimates could be in error for a number of reasons.

    (i) The **estimates** of quantities and prices for next quarter could be **inaccurate**.

    (ii) The **current budget** (of £200,000) may **not be a suitable basis** on which to base the next quarter's budget. It may have been incorrectly set or next period's workload may not reflect that of the current period.

    (iii) The maintenance department may have a **budget limit** imposed on it.

    (iv) The **weightings** on which the index is made may go out of date.

Answer 3.4

Using the spreadsheet model, the answers to these questions can be obtained simply and quickly, using the editing facility in the program.

(a) To test the consequences of slower payments by debtors, it would merely be necessary to **alter the contents** of cells B25, B26 and B27 in our example from 0.6, 0.4 and 0 to 0.4, 0.5 and 0.1 respectively, and then to run the model again.

(b) Similarly, the consequences for cash flow of slower sales growth of only ½% per month can be tested by **altering the value** of Cell B23 in our example from 1.0125 to 1.005.

Chapter 4

Answer 4.1

A bank's policy towards its customers is likely to be influenced by the following factors:

- Its need to satisfy its own shareholders
- Government monetary policy (the level of interest rates and so on)
- Its own creditworthiness (ie how cheaply it can borrow money)
- The general economic climate

Answer 4.2

(a) **Time deposits** are deposit accounts which bear interest but cannot be withdrawn by cheque. Some notice of withdrawal of funds (above a certain amount possibly) is required, unless the investor is prepared to suffer loss of interest.

(b) Banks are required to have **balances with the Bank of England** to meet their debts and also to meet 'cash ratio' regulations, which require them to keep a certain percentage of their deposits in their Bank of England account.

(c) **Bills** are IOUs which require one party to pay another a certain sum sometime in the future.

Answer 4.3

The answer is (a). Item (b) is not an asset of the bank – it is a liability (a sum of money owed by the bank to its customers). It might be tempting to choose item (c), if you think about the large number of High Street sites owned by the retail banks, but in fact the value of this asset is dwarfed by the financial assets of the banks.

Answer 4.4

Deposits

The greater part of the money supply consists of **bank and building society deposits**. Levels of deposits will be determined in part by the level of bank and building society lending.

Effect on money supply

This ability of banks to 'create' credit affects the **overall money supply**. Growth in the money supply may be undesirable because it may lead to inflation. Bank borrowing by individuals is often used to finance current consumption out of future income, and excessive bank lending may fuel aggregate demand leading to inflationary pressures and to increased imports. For such reasons, a government may seek to reduce growth in levels of bank lending.

Government intervention

If the government finances a budget deficit by **sales of gilts** to the banking sector, it may try to offset the impact of monetary growth by curbs on credit.

Political views about different forms of **economic policy intervention** can also be important. Some governments may be unwilling to impose controls, preferring market forces to take their course. One method of seeking to subdue bank lending is to **conduct policies** which keep the cost of credit – the interest rate – relatively high. Such a policy seeks to **inhibit the demand for credit** by the operation of the market forces in the lending sector, although the policy often involves careful government intervention through the management of interest rates. Other methods include imposing reserve asset ratios on banks, requirements on banks to lodge special deposits at the Bank of England, and 'lending ceilings' on banks.

Answer 4.5

The **cost of overdraft** interest **will fall**. Furniture is often brought on credit, and so people may buy more furniture on the cheaper credit available. Lower interest rates mean cheaper mortgages and so people will be encouraged to move to larger houses and more first time buyers will enter the market. More house sales mean that more people will want to buy new furniture. The store's sales should hopefully increase.

Chapter 5

Answer 5.1

Examples include:

- (a) **Maintaining** the **value of any security** which is pledged to secure a loan
- (b) **Informing the bank** as to the **progress of the business**, especially its demands for cash (Forecasts of expected future cash flow are often required for credit to be advanced.)
- (c) **Only using the overdraft for appropriate financial needs** and within authorised limits

Answer 5.2

There are four recognised exceptions where a bank may disclose information about its customer's affairs.

- (a) **Where the bank is required by law to disclose**
- (b) **Where there is a public duty to disclose**
- (c) **Where the interest of the bank requires disclosure**: for example, when the bank sues a customer to recover what he owes
- (d) **Where the customer has given express or implied consent**: for example, by inviting a third party to apply to the bank for a 'banker's reference' or when a business customer sends an employee to collect a bank statement

Answer 5.3

Examples of payments frequently made by direct debit include:

- Mortgage and other loan repayments
- Insurance and personal pension premiums
- Minimum amounts due to credit card issuers
- Subscriptions to large clubs and associations
- Utilities (gas, electricity, telephone)
- Equipment rental and maintenance

Answer 5.4

Bank customers can be broadly **divided into personal customers and business customers**. Within this broad division are several sub-groups: for example in the business sector there are small businesses and large corporates.

Investment opportunities

Business customers can operate a **high interest instant access account** with rates linked to money market rates and with the interest paid gross. If they have surplus funds for 3 months or more they may want certificates of deposit (CDs) which they can turn into cash if they need to at a later date.

Money transmission

Customers want to be able to pay money in, move their money around, withdraw money and make payments. **Efficient money transmission** is very important to businesses and they will make use of all the regular payment services plus one or two specific products. A firm may use the BACS facilities to make large payments such as wages and salaries. Businesses will make more extensive use of CHAPS and those retail businesses accepting credit cards will need the merchant services provided by the bank to facilitate payments.

Lending

The third group of products used is **lending products**, including overdrafts, budget accounts, loans, mortgages and credit cards.

Businesses naturally need finance and this may be provided through **commercial loans, overdrafts and mortgages**. The merchant banking division would be able to offer leasing and hire purchase too.

Foreign trade

Firms involved in **foreign trade** would be interested in **foreign services**. Payments can be made overseas using SWIFT, currencies exchanged, finance provided in foreign currency, and bills of exchange discounted, collected or negotiated.

Chapter 6

Answer 6.1

Banks will prefer security that is easy to realise because:

(a) The costs of **realising the security** will be **low**.

(b) The security's value is unlikely to deteriorate (through a change in market prices, obsolescence or decay) between the date the **customer defaults** and the **date the security is realised**.

(c) The bank will minimise loss of income from interest on the loan or overdraft.

ANSWERS TO ACTIVITIES

Answer 6.2

The banker will pour himself a glass of CAMPARI, as it were, and say no. The managing director can pledge no security, and the purpose of the loan is not for business reasons. Furthermore, Crisroe Ltd's ability to repay looks increasingly in doubt.

Answer 6.3

On the face of it, nearly everything is wrong with this banking proposition from the bank's viewpoint.

- (a) The purpose of the advance is **speculative**.
- (b) The borrower would be putting in **no capital at all**, and so the entire risk would be the bank's.
- (c) The **repayment terms** – no capital repayment until the end of the term – are far from ideal!
- (d) The **5 year term** of the loan is rather long for personal lending (although not unacceptably long).
- (e) There is **no security**.
- (f) The **interest rate** offered is **poor**.

It is hard to see any case at all for agreeing to the advance. Yet this example is based on an actual situation in practice, where the banker agreed to the customer's proposition. His overriding considerations were the **character** and the **connection** of the borrower. The customer appeared to have considerable personal integrity, business experience and financial acumen; and a refusal to lend to the director of a major national company which had various accounts with the bank seemed to be inviting unnecessary bad will for the bank.

Answer 6.4

Although the directors might believe that they are asking the bank to help with financing their current assets, they are really asking for **assistance** with the **purchase of a fixed asset**. The bank lending would leave the total current assets of the company unchanged, but will increase the current liabilities.

Consequently, bank borrowing on overdraft to buy a fixed asset would reduce the working capital of Crisroe Limited from £60,000 to £10,000. In contrast, borrowing £50,000 to finance extra current assets would increase current assets from £120,000 to £170,000, and with current liabilities going from £60,000 to £110,000, total working capital would remain unchanged at £60,000 and liquidity would arguably still be adequate.

Answer 6.5

A **loan** is for a **fixed amount, repayable in a certain period**. A customer's demand for overdraft credit is much more volatile; the bank has to keep the facility open, even though it is not being used all the time.

Answer 6.6

Advantages of an overdraft

- (a) The customer **only pays interest when he is overdrawn**.

ANSWERS TO ACTIVITIES

(b) The bank has the flexibility to **review** the customer's overdraft facility periodically, and perhaps agree to additional facilities, or insist on a reduction in the facility.

(c) An overdraft can do the same job as a **medium-term loan**: a facility can simply be renewed every time it comes up for review.

(d) Being short-term debt, an overdraft will not affect the calculation of a company's **gearing**.

Bear in mind, however, that overdrafts are normally **repayable on demand**.

Advantages of a loan

(a) Both the customer and the bank **know exactly** what the repayments of the loan will be and how much interest is payable, and when. This makes planning (budgeting) simpler.

(b) The customer does not have to worry about the bank deciding to reduce or **withdraw** an overdraft facility before he is in a position to repay what is owed. There is an element of 'security' or 'peace of mind' in being able to arrange a loan for an agreed term.

(c) Medium-term loans normally carry a **facility letter** setting out the precise terms of the agreement.

Appropriateness of each means of finance

(a) In most cases, when a customer wants finance to help with **'day to day' trading** and cash flow needs, an overdraft would be the appropriate method of financing. The customer should not be short of cash all the time, and should expect to be in credit on some days, but in need of an overdraft on others.

(b) When a customer wants to borrow from a bank for **only a short period of time**, even for the purchase of a major fixed asset such as an item of plant or machinery, an overdraft facility might be **more suitable** than a loan. This is because the customer will stop paying interest as soon as his account goes into credit.

(c) When a customer wants to borrow from a bank, but cannot see his way to repaying the bank except over the course of a few years, the **medium-term nature** of the financing is best catered for by the provision of a loan rather than an overdraft facility.

Answer 6.7

The **advantages of leasing** are as follows.

(a) Leasing **reduces the amount of capital** needed to operate the company, as compared with purchasing the asset which requires a capital outlay. Hire purchase also normally requires a **down payment** to be made at the start of the contract.

(b) When the asset is being used to generate additional business, the use of a lease allows **costs and revenues** to be **matched** as the income from the use of the asset can be applied to pay the lease premiums.

(c) Lease finance can be arranged relatively **cheaply, quickly and easily**.

(d) Cash budgeting is **made easier** since the timing and amount of the premiums are **known at the outset**.

Chapter 7

Answer 7.1

The attributes that an asset must possess in order to be considered liquid are as follows.

(a) The **asset** must be **capable** of **being transformed** into a means of making payments quickly. Payments are made with notes and coin or by drawing on deposits in bank current accounts. There are degrees of liquidity, depending on the speed with which the asset can be transformed into cash or a current account deposit. The most liquid assets are cash itself and a current account deposit; time deposits with seven days' notice of withdrawal are slightly less liquid; and longer term deposits are less liquid still.

(b) The asset must also be **convertible** into a **means of payment** in a short time without the loss of (nominal) value. For example, if an asset with a nominal value of £100 can be turned into cash immediately (perhaps by selling it) but would realise only, say, £98, there would have been a loss of capital value of £2.

If the asset can be **transformed** without the **loss of capital value**, but at the expense of foregoing some interest on the asset, the asset would still be considered liquid.

Answer 7.2

Surplus cash flows will be **earned** by a **company** that is trading profitably and does not have high capital expenditures or other outlays to use up the cash inflows. Four possible reasons for a cash surplus are:

(a) **Higher income from sales**, due to an increase in sales turnover
(b) **Lower costs**, due perhaps to a cost-cutting exercise or improved productivity
(c) **Lower capital expenditure**, perhaps because of an absence of profitable new investment opportunities
(d) **Income from selling off parts** of the business

The board of directors might keep the surplus in **liquid form**:

(a) To **benefit from high interest rates** that might be available from bank deposits, when returns on re-investment in the company appear to be lower
(b) To have **cash available should a strategic opportunity arise**, perhaps for the takeover of another company in which cash consideration might be needed
(c) To **buy back shares** from shareholders
(d) To **pay an increased dividend** to shareholders at some time in the future

Answer 7.3

A commercial bank operates with a widely varied pattern of interest rates for the following reasons.

(a) Banks will **lend money at a lower rate of interest** to **lower-risk customers**. This is apparent in short-term lending, where very low interest rates are charged on lending in the interbank market to leading banks, whereas higher interest rates are charged on similar short-term lending to even large and well-established companies. Higher interest rates will also be charged on personal loans to customers in a higher risk category.

(b) Interest rates **vary** with the **duration** of the loan or deposit. Saving schemes requiring some notice of withdrawal will attract a higher yield than an ordinary deposit account. With an ordinary current account, where customers can withdraw funds on demand, often no interest at all is paid.

(c) Banks' interest rates **vary** with the **size of loans and deposits**. Generally, a lower interest rate will be charged for larger 'wholesale' loans and a higher interest rate offered for larger 'wholesale' deposits.

(d) The **need to make a profit** on re-lending is clearly evident in the banks' rate of interest. For example, retail loans to customers will be at an interest rate higher than the bank's base rate, whereas low or nil interest is paid on current accounts, and the rate paid on deposit accounts is less than the bank's base rate.

(e) A **substantial proportion** of a bank's business is conducted in **foreign currencies**. The interest rate in which a bank deals, in the eurocurrency markets, will vary according to the currency, and the general level of interest rates in that country.

Answer 7.4

$$\text{West Sussex CAR} = \left(\left(1+\frac{0.06}{2}\right)^2 - 1\right) \times 100\%$$

$$= 6.09\%$$

$$\text{East Sussex CAR} = \left(\left(1+\frac{0.059}{4}\right)^4 - 1\right) \times 100\%$$

$$= 6.03\%$$

West Sussex offers the highest rate of interest

Answer 7.5

$$\text{Interest yield} = \frac{\text{Coupon rate}}{\text{Market price}} \times 100\% = \frac{9}{134.1742} \times 100\% = 6.71\%$$

Answer 7.6

	£
Purchase consideration	
£5,000 @ £111.5064 per £100	5,575.32
Accrued interest: 56 days at 13¾% (£5,000 × 0.1375 × 56/365)	105.48
Broker's commission on consideration	
0.8% on £5,575.32	44.60
Total purchase cost	5,725.40

Answer 7.7

Return from gilts

All of the index-linked stocks offer a **small real return** (around 2% – 3%) depending on the stock. This is achieved by providing that both interest payments and the redemption value are index-linked. The index used is the **Retail Prices Index**. Many commentators have criticised this index as not being sufficiently representative of the rates of inflation suffered by the sort of investors likely to buy the stock. For example, pensioners spend a far higher proportion of their income on food than the 'average family' on which the index is based.

Advantages for investor

For the investor who is prepared to take a reasonably long-term view, index-linked gilts represent a certain way of **'beating inflation'**. As with all low coupon gilts, index-linked stocks are likely to be attractive to higher rate taxpayers who prefer capital gains to income, given that capital gains on gilts are exempt from capital gains tax.

Answer 7.8

(a) An **investment in the ordinary shares** of UK quoted companies carries the risk that income and capital may drop or even be lost altogether. The risk will be affected by such factors as:

   (i) The general economic and political climate

   (ii) The profitability of the industry in which the company operates

   (iii) The degree of competition within the industry

   (iv) The management of the company

   (v) Its level of gearing

   (vi) The spread of shareholdings and the effect this has on the market in the company's shares and hence their market valuation

   To a large extent, an **investor** should be able to **minimise his risk** by efficient diversification. The risk associated with political and economic conditions will affect all securities to a greater or lesser extent. The effects on income and capital can, however, be minimised by active portfolio management.

(b) Capital placed in a **bank deposit account** has a **low risk** that the bank will default. Nevertheless there are other risks involved. The **interest rate** on the account is **variable** and may fall after the investment has been made. The effect of this can be reduced by switching into a fixed rate investment if it seems likely that market interest rates will fall.

   As with all cash investments, there is a risk that the buying power of the capital will be significantly **eroded by inflation**. Although the relatively good return which an Investment Account produces will help to compensate him for the effects of inflation, any investor who believes that the rate of inflation may rise above the interest rate should consider shifting his portfolio into equities, which over time often resist inflation rather better.

(c) The **risk of default** on British Government stocks is **negligible**. In this case, there is no risk of the interest rate falling, although the income may not keep up with inflation. There is, however, a **risk of loss of capital** both in **money terms** (because gilt prices may fall), and in **real terms** (as any increase in value to

ANSWERS TO ACTIVITIES

redemption or earlier sale may not compensate for the fall in the value of money). An investor can protect himself against **temporary falls in value** by buying only gilts which he expects to be able to hold until redemption. Some degree of protection against the risks of inflation can be obtained in the manner already outlined.

Answer 7.9

(a) The finance department should keep **records** of all the company's bank accounts. **Cheques** for the account should be kept under lock and key, and signature rights on cheques restricted to selected senior personnel. An **up-to-date list of signatories** should be maintained by the finance department and the bank.

(b) **Share certificates** should be held in **secure accommodation**, and the company should keep a register of all the investments it holds.

Chapter 8

Answer 8.1

At the moment, Crisroe Ltd is paying 10% × £1m (ie $^{30}/_{60}$ days × £2m) = £100,000 in interest caused by customers taking the extra month to pay.

Answer 8.2

The existing value of debtors is:

$$\frac{£24m}{12\,months} = £2m$$

If sales increased by 150,000 units, the value of debtors would be:

$$1½ \times \frac{£24m + (150,000 \times £6)}{12\,months} = £3,112,500.$$

The debtors have to be financed somehow, and the additional £1,112,500 will cost £1,112,500 × 20% = £222,500 in financing costs.

The profit on the extra sales is: 150,000 units × (£6 – £5.40) = £90,000

The new credit policy is not worthwhile, mainly because existing customers would also take advantage of it.

Answer 8.3

An industry analysis of credit exposure shows in this case that over 45% of the company's trade debtors (about £17 million) are in the **property and construction industries**.

The size of the exposure to property and construction could seem excessive, in view of the cyclical nature of these industries, the current economic outlook, and the comparatively slow payment rate from these customers. (These industries account for only 37.6% of annual sales, but 45.2% of trade debtors.)

Directors should decide whether the company should be willing to accumulate trade debtors in these sectors, in order to sustain sales, or whether the credit risk would be too high.

Answer 8.4

Inflation **increases** the **importance of credit control**, because the cost of the investment in debtors, in real terms, is higher. If a company grants credit of £100,000 for 3 months, and the rate of inflation is 6% per annum, the value in 'today's money' of the eventual receipts in 3 months' time would be about 1½% less – ie about £1,500 less. If the rate of inflation went up to, say, 12%, the value of the same receipts in 3 months' time would be about £3,000 less. In other words, the cost of granting credit increases as the rate of inflation gets higher. Also, with higher inflation, customers have an increased incentive to pay late.

Answer 8.5

Working capital includes **stock, debtors, creditors and cash**. The effect of credit policy on working capital is that if more credit is granted, there will be a slowdown in the inflow of cash (unless the extension of credit also results in an increase in sales). Discounts for early payment would also affect cash flows. Similarly, tightening up on credit and so granting less credit will result in a speeding up of cash inflows, provided that there is no reduction in sales as a consequence of the restriction of credit.

The total amount of working capital should be **kept under control** because the investment in working capital must be financed, and so excessive debtors are unnecessarily costly and would reduce the organisation's return on capital employed.

Credit policy is therefore significant both from the point of view of **liquidity** (cash flow) and the **management of finance** (investment).

Answer 8.6

Action for the price

Action for the price is most relevant to the credit controller because it means simply trying to obtain payment from the customer.

Other remedies

Given that the credit controller is trying already to obtain money from the customer, the imposition of a further debt of **damages** may not help. **Terminating** the contract may be expensive and be less desirable than carrying out the contract, and insisting the customer keeps their side of the bargain. **Quantum meruit** is of some relevance to credit controllers dealing with construction contracts. **Specific performance** is more a remedy for the customer to enforce on the person or business carrying out the work.

Answer 8.7

No. The fact he would have got a better offer is irrelevant.

Answer 8.8

Crisroe is offering customers the option of paying £98 after seven days per £100 invoiced, or payment in full after 60 days.

Using the formula, the approximate cost of the discount to Crisroe is calculated as:

$$\left[\frac{2}{(100-2)} \times \frac{365}{(60-7)}\right]\% = 14.1\%, \text{ ie } 14\% \text{ approx}$$

The discount is only worthwhile financially if Crisroe can save interest costs of 14% per annum or more, so that by obtaining £98 on day seven instead of £100 on day 60, more than £2 in interest costs could be saved in the time between day 7 and day 60.

Answer 8.9

(a) **Better control of financial risk** is given by determining and maintaining the proper level of cash within a company in accordance with the organisation's financial procedures and within defined authorisation limits.

(b) **Opportunities for profit** are available by reducing to a minimum the opportunity cost associated with maintaining cash balances in excess of the company's operating needs. Earnings (or surpluses) are improved by freeing up surplus cash for investment purposes while reducing interest charges through minimising borrowing.

(c) **The balance sheet** can be strengthened by reducing or eliminating cash balances in excess of target balances and putting surplus cash to work by investing it (eg in the overnight money market); by reducing or eliminating cash borrowing and keeping interest costs as low as possible.

(d) **Increased confidence can be given to customers, suppliers, banks and shareholders** by having access to funds to disburse to suppliers (creditors), banks (interest, fees and principal payments) and shareholders (dividends) when due. Confidence is also given by providing good instructions to customers (debtors) to enable the organisation to convert receipts into usable bank deposits.

Answer 8.10

The factors involved in establishing a credit control policy are as follows.

(a) A **total credit policy must be decided**, whereby the organisation decides how much credit it can and should allow to debtors in total. Debtors should not be excessive in relation to total sales turnover, and the cost of financing debtors should also be considered. The debtor policy that is established will include maximum periods for payment.

(b) A **credit policy** must be set for **deciding credit terms** for individual customers. This will include establishing a system of credit rating, and procedures for deciding the maximum credit limit and terms for the payment period.

(c) The purpose of allowing credit is to **boost sales demand**. Management must consider how 'generous' credit terms should be to encourage sales, whilst at the same time avoiding excessive increases in bad debts, and problems with chasing payment from slow payers.

(d) Granting credit will inevitably mean that problems will arise with **slow payers** and **bad debts**. Procedures must be established for collecting debts from slow payers and writing off bad debts.

(e) **Discounts** might be offered for **early payment of debts**. A decision should be taken as to how much discount, if any, should be offered to encourage early payment, thereby reducing the volume of debtors.

Chapter 9

Answer 9.1

Character of the customer
Ability to borrow and repay
Margin of profit
Purpose of the borrowing
Amount of the borrowing
Repayment terms
Insurance against the possibility of non-payment

Answer 9.2

The bank reference is hardly damning, but it is not an overwhelming endorsement either: Wilder *should* prove to be a good customer. Therefore the **quality of the trade reference** is more important. The first reference, while indicating no problems, is of limited usefulness as the credit facility offered is much lower than that which Crisroe Ltd is asked to provide. The second credit reference, from Wilder's customer, who may be a relative, is worthless.

The request should not be dismissed out of hand, but more investigation is needed before Crisroe grants credit. The reference is unlikely to fulfil Crisroe's credit control guidelines.

Answer 9.3

Credit rating agencies, of which Dun and Bradstreet is perhaps one of the best known, can provide:

(a) A same day analysis, if required, perhaps by an on-line computer link to a VDU in the credit controller's office

(b) Ratio analysis of the business of the customer being assessed

(c) Comment on the customer's credit position

Individual customers (especially non-corporate customers) can be asked to provide the names of **referees** who can be approached for references. One referee will usually be the customer's **bank**. Another might be the customer's **accountant**. The initial procedure is for the referee to be asked if in his opinion the individual is reliable up to certain levels of credit. Usually, this is a low amount to start with, but as confidence develops, so the amount may well be increased.

Answer 9.4

Stock turnover

$$\frac{30,000}{180,000} \times 12 = 2 \text{ months}$$

Debt collection period

$$\frac{75,000}{360,000} \times 12 = 2\frac{1}{2} \text{ months}$$

Credit taken from suppliers

$$\frac{45,000}{180,000} \times 12 = 3 \text{ months}$$

The cash cycle is:

	Months
Stock turnover period	2.0
Credit taken from suppliers	(3.0)
Debt collection period	2.5
Operating cycle	1.5

In this example, Curtis Ltd pays its suppliers one month after the stocks have been sold, since the stock turnover is two months but credit taken is three months.

Answer 9.5

(a) The information should be analysed in as many ways as possible, and you should not omit any important items. For example, the current and quick ratios appear fine, however, these only tell part of the story, as the dramatic change in turnover periods indicate. The relevant calculations would seem to be as follows.

(i)

	20X2	20X3
	£	£
Sales	573,000	643,000
Cost of goods sold	(420,000)	(460,000)
Gross profit	153,000	183,000
Gross profit percentage	26.7%	28.5%

(ii) Size of **working capital and liquidity ratios** (in 20X3, the bank overdraft has been added to creditors):

	£	£
Cash	5,000	(10,000)
Debtors	97,100	121,500
Stocks	121,400	189,300
	223,500	300,800
Creditors	(23,900)	(32,500)
Working capital	199,600	268,300

Current ratio $\quad\dfrac{£223{,}500}{£23{,}900}=9.4{:}1 \quad\quad \dfrac{£310{,}800}{£42{,}500}=7.3{:}1$

Quick ratio $\quad\dfrac{£102{,}100}{£23{,}900}=4.3{:}1 \quad\quad \dfrac{£121{,}500}{£42{,}500}=2.9{:}1$

(iii) Turnover periods

	20X2		20X3	
		days		days
Stock	$\dfrac{121{,}400}{420{,}000}\times 365 =$	106	$\dfrac{189{,}300}{460{,}000}\times 365 =$	150
Debtors' collection period	$\dfrac{97{,}100}{573{,}000}\times 365 =$	62	$\dfrac{121{,}500}{643{,}000}\times 365 =$	69
Creditors' payment period	$\dfrac{23{,}900}{420{,}000}\times 365 =$	(21)	$\dfrac{32{,}500}{460{,}000}\times 365 =$	(26)
Operating cycle		147		193

(b) **Increase in working capital**

Sales were about 12% higher in 20X3 than in 20X2 and the cost of sales was about 10% higher. The investments in stocks and debtors minus creditors (ie working capital ignoring cash) rose from £194,600 to £278,300, ie by £83,700 or 43%. This is completely out of proportion to the volume of increase in trade, which indicates that working capital turnover periods are not being properly controlled.

The **increase in working capital** by £83,700 means that the **net cash receipts from profits** in 20X3 were £83,700 less than they would have been if there had been no increase at all in stocks and debtors (less creditors) during 20X3. The company's overdraft of £10,000 is therefore unnecessary. Furthermore, the **current ratio** is arguably **excessive**. Although the current and quick ratios appear healthy as they stand, the trend is worrying, with the quick ratio declining rapidly. This would not be necessary, if the company controlled debtors and stock better.

Reasons for increase

The causes of the increase in working capital in 20X3 are:

(i) The increase in sales, but mainly
(ii) The increased length of turnover periods

Debtors, already allowed 62 days to pay in 20X2, were allowed 69 days in 20X3 and this would seem to be an excessive length of time. The most serious change, however, is the increase in the **finished goods stock turnover** period from 106 days to 150 days. It is difficult to see an obvious reason why this should have occurred, although there may have been a temporary build-up at the end of 20X3 in preparation for a big sales drive.

Financing of increase

Part of the increase in stocks and debtors has been **financed** by an **increase in the creditors** payment period, from 21 to 26 days. This doesn't seem too bad, but in practice it might be worse. Cost of goods sold includes more than just raw materials, and if we knew the level of raw materials purchases, say, the position might appear worse. For the credit controller there are two worries:

ANSWERS TO ACTIVITIES

(i) The **increase** in the **creditors' payment period**

(ii) The **overall change in working capital** out of all proportion to the growth of business activities, suggesting growing problems in liquidity, even though the current and quick ratios are healthy in themselves at the moment

Answer 9.6

Tutorial note. More than six ratios can be calculated from the information given; we have given all of the most obvious ratios.

			A	B
1	Gross profit margin =	$\dfrac{\text{Gross profit}}{\text{Sales}}$	$\dfrac{1{,}000-400}{1{,}000}=60\%$	$\dfrac{3{,}000-2{,}000}{3{,}000}=33\%$
2	Net profit margin =	$\dfrac{\text{Net profit}}{\text{Sales}}$	$\dfrac{30}{1{,}000}=3\%$	$\dfrac{100}{3{,}000}=3.3\%$
3	Asset turnover =	$\dfrac{\text{Sales}}{\text{Capital employed}}$	$\dfrac{1{,}000}{200}=5$ times	$\dfrac{3{,}000}{650}=4.6$ times
4	Return on capital employed (ROCE) =	$\dfrac{\text{Net profit before interest}}{\text{Total long term capital}}$	$\dfrac{30+(10\%\times 100)}{200}=20\%$	$\dfrac{100+(10\%\times 130)}{650}=17.4\%$
5	Gearing =	$\dfrac{\text{Debt}}{\text{Equity}}$	$\dfrac{100}{100}=100\%$	$\dfrac{130}{(160+360)}=25\%$
	or	$\dfrac{\text{Debt}}{\text{Total capital}}$	$\dfrac{100}{200}=50\%$	$\dfrac{130}{650}=20\%$
6	Current ratio =	$\dfrac{\text{Current assets}}{\text{Current liabilities}}$	$\dfrac{180}{160}=1.125$	$\dfrac{200}{120}=1.667$
7	Quick ratio =	$\dfrac{\text{Current assets - stock}}{\text{Current liabilities}}$	$\dfrac{100}{160}=0.625$	$\dfrac{100}{120}=0.833$
8	Debtors turnover period =	$\dfrac{\text{Debtors}\times 365}{\text{Sales}}$	$\dfrac{100\times 365}{1{,}000}=36\tfrac{1}{2}$ days	$\dfrac{90\times 365}{3{,}000}=11$ days
9	Stock turnover period =	$\dfrac{\text{Stock}\times 365}{\text{Cost of sales}}$	$\dfrac{80\times 365}{400}=73$ days	$\dfrac{100\times 365}{2{,}000}=18$ days
10	Creditors turnover period =	$\dfrac{\text{Creditors}}{\text{Cost of sales}}$	$\dfrac{110\times 365}{400}=100$ days	$\dfrac{120\times 365}{2{,}000}=22$ days

Answer 9.7

Profit margin

Although A and B have similar **net profit margins**, B has a lower **gross profit margin**. A must therefore have a much higher percentage of overheads than B. A's turnover is, however, much lower than B's and so its net profit is also much lower in absolute terms.

ROCE

A also has a **higher ROCE**. This is because it makes more efficient use of its assets, as shown by its high asset turnover. However, B's asset turnover is reduced by the revaluation of its land.

Gearing

A is considerably **more highly geared** than B because its long-term debt is currently as high as its proprietors' equity, whereas B's capital is nearly four times higher than its debt. Thus, A is a higher risk for a potential investor or lender.

Working capital

B appears to **manage its working capital** much **more efficiently** than A. A turns its stock over five times a year but B is about four times as efficient. It may be as a result of this difference in working capital management that B does *not* have an overdraft while A's is quite high. B's liquidity is very much better.

Industry

However, we are not told in which **industry** A and B operate. If, for instance, they are both retailers, it may be that A is an antiques shop while B is selling food or clothes, which turn over much faster but at a lower margin. We are also ignorant of the ownership of each business. If the owners of one business work in it, then part of their drawings are effectively wages and so their profits should be adjusted to be comparable with the other firm.

Financing

Another proviso is that A's **bank overdraft** may **effectively be part of its long-term debt,** in which case ROCE and gearing should all be adjusted accordingly. This leads on to the problem that one balance sheet on its own is not necessarily representative. Ideally, a series should be examined, so that trends can be identified and conclusions can be considered better founded.

Accounts

A further difficulty in looking at the accounts of unincorporated businesses is that they are **not required to give a true and fair view** and so are not governed by SSAPs and FRSs. The accounting policies applied may therefore be quite different in each case.

Finally, we have no idea whether or not **A's assets** could also be **revalued** upwards. If so, its ROCE is almost certainly overstated, and its asset turnover deceptively high.

A tentative conclusion, in spite of the above reservations, would be that **A is a more profitable** but **less solvent** firm than B. This makes it a riskier proposition for lending or investing, especially as it has a much smaller capital base.

ANSWERS TO ACTIVITIES

Answer 9.8

For **new customers** about whom nothing is known, the credit controller can go to Companies House to obtain financial statements on a corporate customer (ie copies of past annual reports and accounts of the customer which have been filed at Companies House). These accounts can then be analysed to assess the financial position of the customer, and changes in this position over time.

Items that might be **studied** and ratios that might be calculated are:

(a) The **amount of annual profit**

(b) The **net assets** of the customer's business

(c) The **return on capital employed** achieved by the customer

(d) The **profit/sales** ratio

(e) **Asset turnover ratios**, in particular

    (i) The current ratio (current assets: current liabilities);

    (ii) The acid test ratio (current assets excluding stock: current liabilities)

    (iii) Debtors' payment period;

    (iv) Credit period taken from creditors (estimated as $\frac{\text{creditors}}{\text{cost of sales}} \times 365 \text{ days}$)

    (v) Stock turnover period

(f) **Gearing ratio** (the ratio of 'prior charge capital' to equity capital)

(g) **Debt ratio** (the ratio of current and long term debts to total assets)

(h) The **percentage increase in annual sales turnover**

The **weaknesses** of this approach to credit risk assessment are that:

(a) The reports and accounts filed at Companies House show an **out-of-date situation** (The customer's financial position might now be completely different.)

(b) Not all customers are corporate customers, and so information about them will **not be held at Companies House**.

Answer 9.9

References

Your refusal would probably not give the customer much hope if they had an **adverse bank reference**; certainly in those circumstances you would need a **positive bank reference ideally from the same bank** before granting credit, and it would take the customer time to build up a good relationship with the bank. Similarly you would probably want to obtain a **positive credit reference,** although you might be able to obtain positive evidence from other sources.

With **suppliers' references**, positive references from more than one supplier might counterbalance a negative reference, so it may be possible to give some hope there.

County court

With a **county court judgement**, you might wait for a certain length of time to see if the customer suffered any more judgements and you would probably look for evidence from other sources.

Press comment

If the customer had suffered adverse **press comment**, this might be outweighed quite easily with subsequent evidence from other sources such as good references or **reasonable figures in the accounts.**

Accounts

With **accounts**, a further year's figures may show a **more positive picture**, so you could hold out the possibility that credit might be granted.

Answer 9.10

(a) A **simple system** for **categorising debtor risk** would be to establish four categories of debtor:

    (i) Strong
    (ii) Average
    (iii) Marginal
    (iv) Weak/poor

Different credit terms might then be offered to a customer according to how that customer is categorised, with strong customers being allowed most credit and weak customers not being allowed any credit at all (ie cash sales only).

(b) Procedures should be in place for **assessing any individual customer's risk categorisation**. Since circumstances change over time, the risk category of existing customers should be reviewed from time to time. All new customers should be put into one of the credit controller's categories.

(c) Procedures should exist for **checking** that **goods** and an **invoice** have been **sent to the customer**, and when customers pay any invoice so that:

    (i) The credit control section is kept up-to-date about the current debt position for every customer
    (ii) The debt collection staff can be notified when debts become overdue.

ANSWERS TO ACTIVITIES

Chapter 10

Answer 10.1

Name	Code	Total owing	0-30 days	30-60 days	60-90 days	>90 days
		£	£	£	£	£
Collyers Ltd	C041	8,000	8,000 Inv 6455			
Hurst and Sons	H036	12,000	7,000 Inv 6667	3,000 Inv 6012		2,000 Inv 4253
WM Mercers	M018	8,000		5,000 Inv 6123	3,000 Inv 5691	
St Leonards & Co	S008	8,000			2,000 Inv 5757	4,000 Inv 5098 2,000 Inv 4554
Total		36,000	15,000	8,000	5,000	8,000
Percentage Nearest whole %		100%	42%	22%	14%	22%

Answer 10.2

When issuing an invoice, sales ledger staff should check the following.

- The **customer's name and address**: are they correct and current?
- Is the **invoice being sent** to the **right place**? Many companies have a central purchasing area and central purchases ledger area
- Is the **invoice recognisable** and how is it to be sent? An invoice sent with the goods that is not immediately recognisable might never get to the staff responsible for paying the invoice.
- Does the invoice have the **customer's authorisation reference** on it? If it is to be matched with a purchase order, then it must quote the purchase order number.
- Are the **details on the invoice correct** as to quantities, descriptions and details, and arithmetic total? The customer will reject the invoice if the details are not correct.
- Having delivered the goods, the invoice should be **submitted** to the customer promptly.

Answer 10.3

£1,700 × 80% = £1,360.

Crisroe gave more credit than was underwritten by the insurance company.

Answer 10.4

The decision to factor the debts should only be taken once a wide ranging assessment of the costs and benefits of so doing has been carried out. This will involve the following steps.

(a) Find out which organisations provide **debt factoring services**. These may include the firm's own bankers, but there might be specialist agencies available who could also do the job.

(b) Some assessment of the services provided should also be made. Factors take on the responsibility of collecting the client firm's debts. There is a variety of factoring services.

   (i) **With recourse factoring.** This is the most basic service, where the factor undertakes to collect the debts and offer an advance, perhaps 80% thereon. The remainder is paid over once the cash has been received from customers. If the debt cannot be collected, the factor can claim back the advance from the client firm.

   (ii) **Without recourse factoring.** The bank undertakes to pay the debts, but cannot claim the advance back from the client if the debt does not prove collectable.

   (iii) Some factors are willing to **purchase a number of invoices**, at a substantial discount. The factor would not be taking responsibility for the client's overall credit administration. In a way, this is like receiving an advance from a debt collector.

(c) The **costs** of the factoring service can then be assessed. The cost is often calculated as a **percentage of the book value** of the debts factored, so that if the factor took over £1,000,000 of debt at a factoring cost of 1.5%, then the client would pay a fee of £15,000. Interest might also be charged on the advance, in some cases, before the debt was recovered.

(d) This can then be compared with the **costs of doing nothing**. If the choice is between either employing a factor or leaving things as they are, then the costs included in the decision include administration, salaries, interest costs on the overdraft, and other cash flow problems (eg delayed expenditure on purchases owing to bad debts, might mean that the company cannot take advantage of settlement discounts offered).

(e) However, before any final decision is taken, the organisation can try to **ensure** that **factoring is still better value** than other choices. These can include:

   (i) The introduction of **settlement discounts** as an inducement to pay early might improve the collection period, and hence reduce the outstanding debt

   (ii) The **use of credit insurance** in some cases

   (iii) A stronger **credit control policy**

   (iv) Perhaps **appointing more credit control staff** might in the long run be cheaper than factoring if the collection rate increases

There may well be operational or management solutions to this problem. These should be investigated first as customers might not like dealing with a third party.

Answer 10.5

Sarhall Ltd
Gemmill House
Black Street
London E23 4AR

Mr Trapnel
20 Camel Street
London N1 4PR

21 August 20X8

Dear Mr Trapnel

Re: Outstanding amount £750
       Due 30 June 20X4

We regret to note that you have not replied to our reminder letter of 14 July requesting immediate payment of the above overdue amount, which represents Elbow Grease supplied on 1 June, invoice ref X123.

Our terms require payment within 30 days of invoice, and you did accede to them.

We would advise you that should the debt remain unpaid within seven days, we will immediately place your account with the County Court. Full payment by return will avoid the need for this unfortunate action.

Yours sincerely

Answer 10.6

(a) At this stage, a **quick phone call** to the accounts department might identify any problems, as the customer is normally reliable.

(b) A more senior official, such as the finance director should **write** to someone of equivalent rank in the debtor company. The creditor's sales director might also bring up the issue with the debtor's purchasing manager.

Chapter 11

Answer 11.1

Here are some examples.

(a) Divorce: joint financial arrangements are unwound; both parties suffer hardship
(b) Long-term illness, resulting in a fall in the customer's income
(c) Redundancy, leading to a reliance on state benefits
(d) The income of a self-employed person might in poor economic conditions greatly diminish
(e) Bankruptcy
(f) Death (obviously)
(g) Redundancy of one partner can adversely affect the income of the entire family unit
(h) Fines or imprisonment imposed by the court, or substantial civil damages
(i) Other factors (eg a rise in interest rates and hence mortgage payments)

Answer 11.2

Here are some examples.

(a) Some customers always being **'slow payers'**: we have identified elsewhere that this is harmful to the business (However, a previously good customer can become slower.)

(b) Other suppliers reporting **similar payment difficulties**

(c) The supplier's sales representatives **acquiring information** 'on the grapevine'

(d) A sense of **impending doom**, poor morale etc, at the customer's place of business, combined perhaps with evident management complacency, indicates problems

(e) **Newspaper articles** highlighting closures, reorganisation, declining profitability

(f) **County court judgements**

(g) **Adverse comments** from credit vetting agencies

(h) **Cheques that 'bounce'**, indicating liquidity problems

(i) **Accounts lodged late** at Companies House

(j) **Auditors' report qualifications** on the accounts

(k) Ratio analysis revealing **declining performance**

Answer 11.3

Before contacting the customer and accusing the customer of default, it is best to eliminate other explanations for the discrepancy.

(a) Is there **any unallocated cash**? In other words, have payments been received which, for whatever reason, have not been matched with the invoice? (In some computer systems an error of 1p prevents matching.)

(b) Have **invoices been posted correctly**? In other words, does the discrepancy arise out of a clerical error? Payment might inadvertently have been posted to the wrong account.

(c) Are there **matters in dispute**? Review of the file should indicate existing correspondence on any items.

(d) Did the customer **return the goods** and send a debit note, which has not reached the system?

Once you are sure of the case, assemble all the relevant information and contact the customer. This customer is generally reliable, so it is best to act to preserve the commercial relationship.

Answer 11.4

A debt collection agency provides a variety of services, but these have their costs.

(a) **What commission** is charged by the agency? Debts which are harder to collect might require a higher price.

(b) The **mere involvement of a third party** might encourage some debtors to pay.

(c) The **cost of a solicitor** should be compared with the cost of the debt collector if legal action has to be taken.

(d) The **collection agency** should keep the client informed about progress.

Answer 11.5

If there is no dispute, then the money is yours anyway. If the debtor is insolvent, you are likely to be overtaken by events.

Answer 11.6

(a) A **petition** is presented to the court, usually by a creditor or the debtor.
A **bankruptcy order** is made by the court.
A trustee in bankruptcy is appointed.

Once the administration is complete the **bankrupt** will be **discharged**.

(b) It is likely that the bank is a secured creditor; in other words the bank debt will be paid off before trade creditors get a look in. There would appear to be little hope of recovery.

Answer 11.7

Debts that should be provided against include:

(a) Invoices over a **certain age** (for example six months)
(b) Invoices which have only been **partly settled**
(c) **Disputed invoices**
(d) Invoices where the customer has made claims on a **warranty**

Answer 11.8

Administration order

An **administration order** provides an alternative to suing for his debt in the courts and/or petitioning for winding up.

The company, its directors or any creditor may apply to the court for an order. Immediately on application, there is a stop on the collection of debts from the company or the seizure of assets. In addition, a winding-up order may not be made. The company must be shown to be unable to pay its debts.

The object of this procedure is that the administrator can **prepare proposals** by which he may achieve the purpose of his appointment, most frequently to ensure the company's survival.

Voluntary arrangements

The other alternative to liquidation as formulated by the Insolvency Act 1986 is the **voluntary arrangement**.

Once the scheme has been agreed, it becomes binding on all concerned. The advantage of such a scheme is that the business may actually **survive it**, and creditors may receive a higher settlement.

Answer 11.9

(a) *Initial working: provision for doubtful debts*

31 December	£	£
20X7 Provision required = £44,000 × 3%	1,320	
20X8 Provision required = £55,000 × 3%	1,650	
Increase in provision – charge to P & L		330
20X9 Provision required = £47,000 × 3%	1,410	
Decrease in provision – credit to P & L		(240)

Profit and loss account charge
Year ended 31 December

	20X7 £	20X8 £	20X9 £
Bad debts	7,000	10,000	8,000
Provision for doubtful debts	1,320	330	(240) credit

ANSWERS TO ACTIVITIES

(b)
Balance sheet extracts as at 31 December

	20X7 £	20X8 £	20X9 £
Debtors	44,000	55,000	47,000
Less provision for doubtful debts	(1,320)	(1,650)	(1,410)
Balance sheet value	42,680	53,350	45,590

Index

Index

Account payee	103	Campari	113
Accruals	13	Cash	12
Acid test ratio	198	Cash budget	31, 32
Additive model	66	Cash cycle	5
Administration	252	Cash flow based forecasts	29
Administrative receiver	251	Cash flow control reports	46
Aged debtors listing	214	Cash forecasting	28
Amortising	121	Cash inflows	9
Amount of the loan	114	Cash outflows	8
Arbitration	246	Cash shortages	48
A-scoring	242	Categorised cash flow	10
		Central bank	87
BACS	106	Certificate of deposit (CD)	143
Bad debts	241	Certificates of deposit market	90
Bailor/bailee relationship	99	Cheque guarantee scheme	104
Balance sheet	44	Cheques	102
Balance sheet based forecasts	30	Cleared funds cash forecast	43
Balloon	121	Clearing House Automated Payments System (CHAPS)	106
Bank of England	87	Collection cycle	169
Bank overdrafts	198	Commercial paper	147
Bank references	189	Commercial paper market	90
Bankers' Automated Clearing Services (BACS)	106	Commercial risks	225
Banker's draft	104	Compound annual rate of interest	138
Bankruptcy	248	Compulsory liquidation	250
Banks	29	Compulsory winding up	251
Base period	72	Confidentiality	101
Bill of exchange	144	Consideration	173
Bonds	146	Consumer credit	161
Buffer	133	Consumer Credit Act 1974 (CCA)	175
Building societies	88	Contract	171
Building Societies Act 1986	138	Convertible loan stock	126
Building societies deposits	138	Count-back method	163
Bullet	121	Country risks	226
Business customers	241	County Court	193
Buyer risks	225	Covenants	122
		Credit cards	104
		Credit control	21, 161

Credit control department	168
Credit cycle	169
Credit in the economy	91
Credit insurance	224
Credit ratings	190, 206
Credit reference agency	192
Credit reporting agencies (credit bureaux)	192
Credit risk	186, 241
Credit taken ratio	206
Credit terms	175
Credit utilisation report	167
Creditors turnover period	196
Crossings on cheques	103
Cum div	140
Current assets	5
Current liabilities	5
Current ratio	197
Customer payment systems	221
Customer record card	229
Cyclical variations	61

Data Protection Act 1998	208
Days sales outstanding	164
Dealing guidelines	151
Debenture stocks	147
Debentures	125
Debit cards	104
Debt collection agencies	244
Debt collection period	196
Debt ratio	200
Debtor/creditor relationship	98
Debtors' turnover	163
Debtors turnover period	196
Default insurance	224
Direct debits	105
Discounting bills	146
Discounts	177
Discretionary cash flows	9
Dividends	133
Domestic credit insurance	224
Doubtful debts	240
Duties of banks	100
Duties of care	189

E-mail	233
Equities	126
Eurocurrency markets	90
Ex div	140
Excess of loss	225
Ex-dividend	142
Export Credits Guarantee Department (ECGD)	226
Export insurance	225
Extel	193

Factoring	226
Fax transmission	233
Fiduciary duty	100
Final demands	229
Finance leases	123
Financial cash flows	9
Financial futures market	90
Financial intermediary	84
Financial intermediation	85
Financial modelling package	75
Fiscal policy	91
Float	42
Forecasting	68

Gearing	199
General crossing	103
Gilts	140
Going concern	17
Government securities	140
Granting credit	203
Guarantees	116

High interest cheque accounts	137
High street bank deposits	137

Income and expenses of a bank	87
Index-linked stocks	141
Inflation	71
In-house credit ratings	206
Insurance against the possibility of non-payment	115
Inter-bank market	89
Inter-company market	90
Interest	138

Interest cover	200
Interest rate policy	92
Interest yield	139
Internet	85
Invoice discounting	227

Key account customers 223

Leading and lagging	49
Leasing	123
Letters	229
LIBOR	89
Liquidation	251
Liquidator	251
Liquidity	20, 134, 144
Loan covenants	122
Loan interest	122
Loan stocks	125
Loans	120
Local authority markets	89
Local authority stocks	143
London International Financial Futures Exchange (LIFFE)	90
Long-term money markets	90

Margin	34
Mark up	34
Mark up and margins	34
Market risks	226
Merchant banks	87
Methods of payment	177
Misrepresentation	173
Mistake	173
Monetary policy	91
Money markets	88
Monitoring credit	205
Monitoring of cash flows	11
Mortgagor/mortgagee relationship	99
Moving average	61
Moving averages of an even number of results	63
Multiplicative model	66

NCM Credit Insurance Ltd	226
Net asset turnover	195
Net cash flow	10

On account payments	224
One-off or occasional cash flows	32
Open offers	248
Operating cycle	5
Operating leases	123
Operational cash flows	9
Opportunity cost	178
Overdraft facility	133
Overdraft facility for day to day trading	118
Overdrafts	117
Overtrading	10, 51, 119

Partial month method	163
Past consideration	173
Payment terms	175
Permanent Interest Bearing Shares (PIBS)	147
Personal customers	241
Personal guarantee	116
Political risks	226
Portfolio	149
Precautionary motive	133
Price index	71
Primary money market	89
Principal/agent relationship	99
Priority cash flows	9
Profit margin	194
Profitability	19, 135
Profits and cash flows	12
Proportional model	66
Provision for bad and doubtful debts	253
PSDR (public sector debt repayment)	93
Public board loans	143
Public sector	137
Public Sector Borrowing Requirement (PSBR)	93
Pull to maturity	139

Quantity index	72
Queries	224
Quick ratio	198

INDEX

Ratio analysis	194
Receipts and payments forecasts	29
Receiver	251
Redemption yield	140
References	189
Refusing credit	203
Regular trading cash flows	32
Reminder notices	223
Repayment terms	115
Reserve requirements	92
Residual	70
Retail banking	85
Retailing business	7
Retention of title	246
Return on capital employed	195
Rights of bank	99
Risk	21, 147
Rolling forecasts	31
Safe custody	152
Safe deposit service	99
Safety	135
Sale and leaseback	124
Sale of Goods Acts	246
Sale of Goods Acts 1893 and 1979	174
Seasonal variations	60
Security	20, 147
Security for a loan	115
Sensitivity analysis	75
Settlement discounts	175, 177
Sight bill	144
Slow payers	228
Solicitors	244
Special crossing	103
Special dividend payment	133
Specific account policies	225
Specific guarantees	226
Speculative motive	133
Spreadsheet model	75
Standing orders	105
Statement	221
Stock turnover	196
Telephone	232
Term bill	144
Time series	
additive model	66
finding the seasonal variations	64
finding the trend	61
residuals	70
Time series	59
Total credit	162
Trade creditors	126
Trade credits	160
Trade references	190
Transactions motive.	133
Treasury management	22
Trend	59
Uncertainty analysis	58
Unsecured loan stock	126
Visits	202, 234
Volatility of cash flows	58
Voluntary arrangements	252
Voluntary liquidation	251
Whole turnover policies	225
Wholesale banking	87
Without prejudice offer	247
Working capital	5, 195
Working capital cycle	5
Yearlings	143
Z-scoring	242

See overleaf for information on other
BPP products and how to order

AAT Order

To BPP Professional Education, Aldine Place, London W12 8AW
Tel: 020 8740 2211. Fax: 020 8740 1184
E-mail: Publishing@bpp.com Web: www.bpp.com

Mr/Mrs/Ms (Full name) _____
Daytime delivery address _____
Postcode _____
Daytime Tel _____
E-mail _____

	5/04 Texts	5/04 Kits	Special offer	8/04 Passcards	Success CDs
FOUNDATION (£14.95 except as indicated)				Foundation	
Units 1 & 2 Receipts and Payments	☐	☐		☐ £6.95	☐ £14.95
Unit 3 Ledger Balances and Initial Trial Balance	☐ (Combined Text & Kit)		Foundation Sage Bookkeeping and Excel Spreadsheets CD-ROM free if ordering all Foundation Text and Kits, including Units 21 and 22/23 ☐		
Unit 4 Supplying Information for Mgmt Control	☐ (Combined Text & Kit)				
Unit 21 Working with Computers (£9.95)	☐				
Unit 22/23 Healthy Workplace/Personal Effectiveness (£9.95)	☐				
Sage and Excel for Foundation (Workbook with CD-ROM £9.95)	☐				
INTERMEDIATE (£9.95 except as indicated)					
Unit 5 Financial Records and Accounts	☐	☐		☐ £5.95	☐ £14.95
Unit 6/7 Costs and Reports (Combined Text £14.95)	☐			☐ £5.95	
Unit 6 Costs and Revenues		☐			☐ £14.95
Unit 7 Reports and Returns		☐			
TECHNICIAN (£9.95 except as indicated)					
Unit 8/9 Core Managing Performance and Controlling Resources	☐	☐		☐ £5.95	☐ £14.95
Spreadsheets for Technician (Workbook with CD-ROM)	☐		Spreadsheets for Technicians CD-ROM free if take Unit 8/9 Text and Kit ☐		
Unit 10 Core Managing Systems and People (£14.95)	☐ (Combined Text & Kit)			☐ £5.95	☐ £14.95
Unit 11 Option Financial Statements (A/c Practice)	☐	☐		☐ £5.95	
Unit 12 Option Financial Statements (Central Govnmt)	☐	☐		☐ £5.95	
Unit 15 Option Cash Management and Credit Control	☐	☐		☐ £5.95	
Unit 17 Option Implementing Audit Procedures	☐	☐		☐ £5.95	
Unit 18 Option Business Tax FA04 (8/04) (£14.95)	☐ (Combined Text & Kit)			☐ £5.95	
Unit 19 Option Personal Tax FA04 (8/04) (£14.95)	☐ (Combined Text & Kit)			☐ £5.95	
TECHNICIAN 2003 (£9.95)					
Unit 18 Option Business Tax FA03 (8/03 Text & Kit)	☐				
Unit 19 Option Personal Tax FA03 (8/03 Text & Kit)	☐				
SUBTOTAL	£	£	£	£	£

TOTAL FOR PRODUCTS £ _____

POSTAGE & PACKING

Texts/Kits	First	Each extra
UK	£3.00	£3.00
Europe*	£6.00	£4.00
Rest of world	£20.00	£10.00
Passcards		
UK	£2.00	£1.00
Europe*	£3.00	£2.00
Rest of world	£8.00	£8.00
Success CDs		
UK	£2.00	£1.00
Europe*	£3.00	£2.00
Rest of world	£8.00	£8.00

TOTAL FOR POSTAGE & PACKING £ _____
(Max £12 Texts/Kits/Passcards - deliveries in UK)

Grand Total (Cheques to *BPP Professional Education*)
I enclose a cheque for (incl. Postage) £ _____
Or charge to Access/Visa/Switch
Card Number ☐☐☐☐ ☐☐☐☐ ☐☐☐☐ ☐☐☐☐   CV2 No ☐☐☐ last 3 digits on signature strip

Expiry date ☐☐☐☐   Start Date ☐☐☐☐

Issue Number (Switch Only) ☐☐

Signature _____

We aim to deliver to all UK addresses inside 5 working days; a signature will be required. Orders to all EU addresses should be delivered within 6 working days. All other orders to overseas addresses should be delivered within 8 working days. * Europe includes the Republic of Ireland and the Channel Islands.

See overleaf for information on other
BPP products and how to order

AAT Order

To BPP Professional Education, Aldine Place, London W12 8AW
Tel: 020 8740 2211. Fax: 020 8740 1184
E-mail: Publishing@bpp.com Web:www.bpp.com

Mr/Mrs/Ms (Full name) _____
Daytime delivery address _____
Postcode _____
Daytime Tel _____ E-mail _____

OTHER MATERIAL FOR AAT STUDENTS	8/04 Texts	3/03 Text	3/04 Text
FOUNDATION (£5.95)			
Basic Maths and English	☐		
INTERMEDIATE (£5.95)			
Basic Bookkeeping (for students exempt from Foundation)	☐		
FOR ALL STUDENTS (£5.95)			
Building Your Portfolio (old standards)		☐	
Building Your Portfolio (new standards)	☐		
Basic Costing			☐

AAT PAYROLL

	Finance Act 2004 8/04 December 2004 and June 2005 assessments	Finance Act 2003 9/03 June 2004 exams only
	☐	☐
	Special offer Take Text and Kit together £44.95 ☐	**Special offer** Take Text and Kit together £44.95 ☐
	For assessments in 2005 ☐	For assessments in 2004 ☐
	£44.95 ☐	£44.95 ☐
LEVEL 2 Text (£29.95)	£ _____	
LEVEL 2 Kit (£19.95)	£ _____	
LEVEL 3 Text (£29.95)	£ _____	
LEVEL 3 Kit (£19.95)		
SUBTOTAL	£ _____	

TOTAL FOR PRODUCTS £ _____

POSTAGE & PACKING

Texts/Kits	First	Each extra
UK	£3.00	£3.00
Europe*	£6.00 £ ___	£4.00 £ ___
Rest of world	£20.00 £ ___	£10.00 £ ___
Passcards		
UK	£2.00 £ ___	£1.00 £ ___
Europe*	£3.00 £ ___	£2.00 £ ___
Rest of world	£8.00 £ ___	£8.00 £ ___
Tapes		
UK	£2.00 £ ___	£1.00 £ ___
Europe*	£3.00 £ ___	£2.00 £ ___
Rest of world	£8.00 £ ___	£8.00 £ ___

TOTAL FOR POSTAGE & PACKING £ _____
(Max £12 Texts/Kits/Passcards - deliveries in UK)

Grand Total (Cheques to *BPP Professional Education*) £ _____
I enclose a cheque for (incl. Postage)
Or charge to Access/Visa/Switch

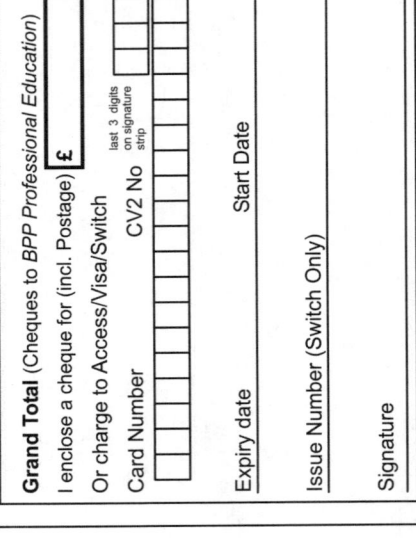

Card Number ☐☐☐☐ ☐☐☐☐ ☐☐☐☐ ☐☐☐☐ CV2 No ☐☐☐ last 3 digits on signature strip

Expiry date ☐☐☐☐   Start Date ☐☐☐☐

Issue Number (Switch Only) ☐☐

Signature _____

We aim to deliver to all UK addresses inside 5 working days; a signature will be required. Orders to all EU addresses should be delivered within 6 working days. All other orders to overseas addresses should be delivered within 8 working days. * Europe includes the Republic of Ireland and the Channel Islands.

Review Form & Free Prize Draw – Unit 15 Cash management and credit control (5/04)

All original review forms from the entire BPP range, completed with genuine comments, will be entered into one of two draws on 31 January 2005 and 31 July 2005. The names on the first four forms picked out on each occasion will be sent a cheque for £50.

Name: _____ Address: _____

How have you used this Interactive Text?
(Tick one box only)
- ☐ Home study (book only)
- ☐ On a course: college _____
- ☐ With 'correspondence' package
- ☐ Other _____

Why did you decide to purchase this Interactive Text? *(Tick one box only)*
- ☐ Have used BPP Texts in the past
- ☐ Recommendation by friend/colleague
- ☐ Recommendation by a lecturer at college
- ☐ Saw advertising
- ☐ Other _____

During the past six months do you recall seeing/receiving any of the following?
(Tick as many boxes as are relevant)
- ☐ Our advertisement in *Accounting Technician* magazine
- ☐ Our advertisement in *Pass*
- ☐ Our brochure with a letter through the post

Which (if any) aspects of our advertising do you find useful?
(Tick as many boxes as are relevant)
- ☐ Prices and publication dates of new editions
- ☐ Information on Interactive Text content
- ☐ Facility to order books off-the-page
- ☐ None of the above

Have you used the companion Assessment Kit for this subject?   ☐ Yes   ☐ No

Your ratings, comments and suggestions would be appreciated on the following areas

	Very useful	Useful	Not useful
Introduction	☐	☐	☐
Chapter contents lists	☐	☐	☐
Examples	☐	☐	☐
Activities and answers	☐	☐	☐
Key learning points	☐	☐	☐
Quick quizzes and answers	☐	☐	☐
Activity checklist	☐	☐	☐

	Excellent	Good	Adequate	Poor
Overall opinion of this Text	☐	☐	☐	☐

Do you intend to continue using BPP Interactive Texts/Assessment Kits?   ☐ Yes   ☐ No

Please note any further comments and suggestions/errors on the reverse of this page.

The BPP author of this edition can be e-mailed at: nickweller@bpp.com

Please return this form to: Janice Ross, BPP Professional Education, FREEPOST, London, W12 8BR

Review Form & Free Prize Draw (continued)

Please note any further comments and suggestions/errors below

Free Prize Draw Rules

1. Closing date for 31 January 2005 draw is 31 December 2004. Closing date for 31 July 2005 draw is 30 June 2005.
2. Restricted to entries with UK and Eire addresses only. BPP employees, their families and business associates are excluded.
3. No purchase necessary. Entry forms are available upon request from BPP Professional Education. No more than one entry per title, per person. Draw restricted to persons aged 16 and over.
4. Winners will be notified by post and receive their cheques not later than 6 weeks after the relevant draw date.
5. The decision of the promoter in all matters is final and binding. No correspondence will be entered into.